T0383195

# FINANCIAL SUCCESS

## IN THE

# YEAR 2000

### AND BEYOND

◆

## *13* EXPERTS SHOW THE WAY

# FINANCIAL SUCCESS

# IN THE

# YEAR 2000

## AND BEYOND

◆

## *13* EXPERTS SHOW THE WAY

Michael P. Eischen, Dennis R. Fletcher,
Joseph D. Longo, William J. Nelson, Tom Nohr,
Lance A. Pelky, Larry Rosenthal,
David W. Shepherd, Floyd L. Shilanski,
Robert Lyndon Taylor, Terry A. Vrieze,
David S. White, Mark Young

EDITED BY

## LARRY CHAMBERS

S$^t$L

St. Lucie Press
Boca Raton   London   New York   Washington, D.C.

**Library of Congress Cataloging-in-Publication Data**

Chambers, Larry.
    Financial success in the year 2000 and beyond : 13 experts show the way / edited by
Larry Chambers
        p.   cm.
    Includes bibliographical references and index.
    ISBN 1-57444-258-9 (alk. paper)
    1. Investments.   2. Finance, Personal.   3. Success in business.   I. Title.
HG4521.C45127   1999
332.024—dc21

99-046798

# Preface

The investment world can be a complex and confusing arena. It is exciting, but also a little frightening to those without a clear understanding of how it functions. Knowledge about how the markets work is progressing rapidly and becoming more refined every year. To invest successfully, you must be able to separate the information that is actually useful from the over-abundance of investment-oriented noise that we all encounter every day.

Success requires being willing to do what the majority of people *don't* do — that is, to take a contrarian approach to the mainstream financial methodologies. Over two years ago, a group comprised of 13 top investment advisors from all over the nation agreed to come together to discuss advanced financial planning techniques. Bill Nelson, one of the foremost financial planners using net planning techniques, moderated these discussions. It soon became evident to us that we were outside the mainstream when it came to our approach to financial planning.

During our meetings, we recognized three prominent issues:

1. The majority of investment advice concentrates on the accumulation phase, with little attention paid to how to handle the assets.
2. With media headlines such as *Buy gold online and make fast profits!* or *Sell your stock now!*, it is difficult for the individual investor to curb emotional responses and determine what is good investment information.
3. What most people want is simply the "Kwan" (a term made popular in the movie, *Jerry Maguire*, Kwan is actually the oldest surviving paper money from the Ming Dynasty) — enough so they can do what they want, when they want, without worrying about their financial future.

Most people invest based on their emotions and plan for retirement based on limited conventional methods. Our group as a whole agreed it takes unconventional behavior to retire in comfort. With some coaxing, I convinced everyone to put into writing those truths that would dispel some of the common myths and empower our readers.

The information contained in this book may be contrary to what you read anywhere else; however, if you do not feel confident that your existing methods are going to achieve your goals and secure your financial future, this book will prove invaluable. We invite you to read on, leaving your preconceptions behind, to discover new financial territory where peace of mind reigns!

*Tom J. Nohr*

# The Contributors

**Larry Chambers, Editor**
P.O. Box 1810
Ojai, CA 93024
Phone: 805-640-0888

Larry is a freelance writer and financial editor based in Ojai, CA. He has written or edited over 600 financial articles and 20 books for major publishing houses, including CRC Press, McGraw-Hill, Random House, Times Mirror, Dow Jones, and John Wiley & Sons. His business background has given him a unique advantage as a financial writer. While a stockbroker with E.F. Hutton & Co. in the 1970s, Larry achieved an outstanding track record and was named one of the top 20 brokers out of more than 5000 and received numerous awards, in addition to being named to the Blue Chip Club.

**Michael P. Eischen, RFC, ChFC, CLU, CFS**
454 E. Main Street, Suite 100
Columbus, OH 43215
Phone: 614-221-2211; Fax: 614-221-9011

Michael teaches personal finance courses at Columbus State Community College that focus on the achievement of lifelong financial security. His most popular courses include Financial Strategies for Successful Retirement and money management seminars. Michael is a financial advisor with 15 years' experience in the financial planning industry. A graduate of Ohio State University, he has completed extensive postgraduate studies in the fields of financial and retirement planning and has instructed thousands of individuals through his personal finance courses. Michael is a Registered Investment Advisor Affiliate of Nelson Financial Group, Inc., and is a Registered Representative of Washington Square Securities, Inc., member NASD and SIPC, which is located at 30 Washington Avenue South, Minneapolis, MN 55401 (612-372-5507). He holds the Registered and Chartered Financial Consultant, Chartered Life Underwriter, and Certified Fund Specialist professional designations.

**Dennis R. Fletcher, CLU, ChFC**
Fletcher Financial Network, Inc.
P.O. Box 915
Oshkosh, WI 54902-0915,
Phone: 920-231-4646; 920-231-4346

Dennis, a Chartered Life Underwriter, Chartered Financial Consultant, and Investment Advisor, has been an advisor in the areas of investments, securities, and insurance planning for individuals and businesses since 1973. Dennis received his Bachelor of Business Administration degree from the University of Wisconsin, Oshkosh. He received his financial credentials from The American College in Bryn Mawr, PA. FFN Educational Seminars is a division of Fletcher Financial Network, Inc., which Dennis founded in 1987. Dennis and his firm teach retirement planning and personal finance courses at six different area colleges and provide financial courses to many large corporations. Each year, over 2000 adults enroll in these courses to prepare for a more comfortable retirement. Dennis is a founding member of the Winnebagoland Estate Planning Council. He is a past president of the Southwest Rotary of Oshkosh and has participated in many fundraising activities, in addition to coaching softball and baseball teams. A resident of Oshkosh for the past 32 years, Dennis and his wife Diane have three children, Tara, Cassandra, and Justin.

**Joseph D. Longo, CLU, CFP, LUTCF, LIC**
Financial Seminars of Michigan, Inc.
2301 W. Big Beaver, Suite 235
Troy, MI 48084-3300
Phone 800-270-7667; Fax: 248-649-6280

Joe is a graduate of Wayne State University in Detroit, MI, and is a Licensed Insurance Counselor, Chartered Life Underwriter, Certified Financial Planner, and Registered Financial Consultant, in addition to having a Life Underwriters Training Council Fellow (LUTCF) designation. He entered the insurance and investment industry in 1967 and is a member of many associations, including the IAFP, ICFP, NALU, ACLU, NAIILBA, GDALU, Financial and Estate Planning Council of Detroit, and the Michigan Life Leaders Club. Joe has taught both the Life Underwriters Training Council and Certified Financial Planner courses as an adjunct faculty member of Wayne State University. Financial Seminars of Michigan, Inc., is a money management educational provider with qualified instructors who teach at various colleges, universities, corporations, and associations. The company also provides a biblical perspective on charitable and tithe-giving to various churches in the Detroit metropolitan area. Joe and his wife Linda have two daughters, Gina and Joleen.

**William J. Nelson**
Nelson Financial Group, Inc. (An SEC Registered Investment Advisor)
2385 Lakeview Drive
Cayton, OH 45431-3696
Phone: 937-426-7032
Fax: 937-426-4220

Bill, Chief Executive Officer of Nelson Financial Group, Inc., has been involved in the financial services industry since 1970. He centers his business on advanced financial, estate, and retirement planning from a net perspective. Throughout his 28 years, Bill has served as a national consultant and in executive management positions to companies and individuals. He is listed in *Who's Who in Executives and Professionals* and has received numerous honors and awards. Bill has received the National Quality Award and is a member of the Registered Financial Consultants' International Board and the Million Dollar Round Table's Top of the Table, their highest level. He also works at the international, community, and local levels with United Marriage Encounter. Bill and his wife Phyllis have two children, Carrie and Jonathan.

**Tom Nohr, CFP, RFC**
Tom Nohr & Associates
20632 Redwood Road, Suite E
Castro Valley, CA 94546
Phone: 510-888-7171
Fax: 510-888-7177

Tom is president and principal of Successful Financial Education Workshops and Tom Nohr & Associates and has been in the financial industry since 1985. He teaches financial and estate planning through the continuing education department at California State University, Hayward. He has been a LUTC moderator to teach insurance professionals about financial planning and is listed in the *Who's Who in Finance and Industry*. Tom, a member of the International Association of Financial Planners, received his CFP designation in 1990 and his RFC designation in 1998. He has contributed articles for the *Daily Review*, *Oakland Tribune*, *Fremont Argus*, and *Tri-Valley Herald*. Tom and his wife Chris have two children, Max and Samantha.

**Lance A. Pelky**
Lance Pelky & Associates, Inc.
9171 Towne Centre Drive, Suite 435
San Diego, CA 92122
Phone: 858-623-9670, 800-746-1100; Fax: 858-623-9572
e-mail: www.teampelky.com

Lance founded his company to assist individuals and businesses in short- and long-term planning. He is a frequent invited speaker both locally as well as nationally. Prior to founding his own firm, Lance held the position of Director of Retirement Seminars for one of the oldest and most respected financial planning firms in America. He also gained valuable experience in the areas of securities and insurance while working for a major insurance carrier. Earlier in his career, he was with one of the largest bond brokers on the west coast, where he conducted research and supervised public education seminars. An active participant in various organizations related to the financial industry, Lance is a member of the Institute of Certified Financial Planners, the Million Dollar Round Table, and the San Diego Association of Life Underwriters. Lance resides in La Jolla with his wife Eileen and their daughters, Mara and Madison.

**Larry Rosenthal, RFC, LUTCF**
Financial Planning Services of Virginia (A Registered Investment Advisory Firm)
9265 Corporate Circle
Manassas, VA 20110
Phone: 703-331-0591; Fax: 703-331-0595
e-mail: larryrose@erols.com

Larry has been in the financial planning business since 1987 and is President of Financial Planning Services of Virginia. He is a frequent speaker at both local and national financial planning meetings. His firm helps clients achieve their financial goals by serving them in the areas of investments, estate planning, mortgages, insurance, and personal and business planning. Larry teaches financial planning classes at various adult education locations around the northern Virginia area, in addition to major employers in the area. His firm also provides financial planning classes from a biblical perspective to numerous churches in the Washington, D.C. metropolitan area. Larry is a member of Northern Virginia Life Underwriters' Million Dollar Round Table and has received the National Quality Award. Larry lives in Manassas, VA, with his wife Holly, daughter Natalie, and Labrador Hayley.

**David W. Shepherd, RHU, ChFC**
Retirement Financial Planning, Inc.
3443 E. Ft. Lowell
Tucson, AZ 85716
Phone: 520-325-1600, 877-325-1600

Dave, a Chartered Financial Consultant and Registered Health Underwriter, is founder and president of Retirement Financial Planning, Inc., a registered investment advisory firm. He has taught numerous financial workshops through Pima Community College in Tucson since 1995 and has contributed articles on retirement planning for *The Arizona Senior World Newspaper* and the *Tucson Citizen*. He received the Excellence in Financial Education award in December 1996 and is a member of IAFP. Dave, his wife Maryann, and their children, David, Michelle, and Matthew, have lived in Tucson since 1982.

**Floyd L. Shilanski**
Shilanski and Associates, Inc.
431 West 7th Avenue, Suite 100
Anchorage, AK 99501
Phone: 907-278-1351
Fax: 907 278 4237

Floyd is president of Shilanski and Associates, Inc., one of the oldest established financial planning firms in Alaska, providing services for clients throughout the state. He was licensed as a life agent in 1980 and became a Registered Investment Advisor in 1981. From 1979 to 1981, he served as president of the Alaska Chapter of the International Association of Financial Planning. Floyd is a life and qualifying member of the Million Dollar Round Table with a Top of the Table qualification. In 1994, Floyd wrote *How To Win at the Money Game*, and he also contributed to *Chicken Soup for the Soul: A Second Helping*. Floyd has served on the board of the Western Alaska Council of the Boy Scouts of America and was actively involved with and served on the board of CRISIS, Inc., as well as being acting president. Floyd and his wife have three children and one grandchild.

**Robert Lyndon Taylor, RFC, LUTCF**
4141 NW Expressway, Suite 370
Oklahoma City, OK 73116
Phone: 405-843-5540

Lyndon is the president and founder of Choice Financial Services in Oklahoma City. Choice was founded in 1994 as an independent office to provide financial planning, financial services, and education to its clients. Lyndon has 14 years' experience in the financial service area. He has spent the last 7 years as a presenter of financial and estate planning workshops. As a lecturer, Lyndon has given presentations at several colleges, including Oklahoma State University, Southwestern Oklahoma State University, Oklahoma University Health and Sciences Center, Oklahoma City Community College, and Francis Tuttle; corporations such as Rockwell, Lucent, AT&T, Delta Faucet, and Blue Cross; and Mercy and Baptist hospitals. He served as the Oklahoma legislative liaison on agriculture policy in 1983 and 1984 and is a past speaker for the Hugh O'Brien Foundation. He earned his B.S. in agriculture economics from Oklahoma State University in 1985. Lyndon is active in youth sports with his four children and wife, Nicole. He is the past president of the Oklahoma City Northwest Kiwanis and serves on the Henry Bennett Society for his *alma mater*, Oklahoma State University.

**Terry A. Vrieze, CLU, ChFC**
Successful Resource Management (A Registered Investment Advisory Firm)
5601 Douglas Avenue, Suite 102, Des Moines, IA 50310
Phone: 515-276-1400 (800-353-7667)
Fax: 515-276-895
e-mail: srm@netins.netsrm

Terry, a Chartered Life Underwriter, Chartered Financial Consultant, and Investment Advisor, is a qualifying member of the Court of the Table and a life member of the Million Dollar Round Table, as well as a member of the National Association of Philanthropic Planners. Terry is sole owner of G.T.&T. Investment Corporation (Successful Resource Management) in Des Moines, IA. Terry specializes in financial planning and long-range strategies for successful retirement and conducts educational seminars on a continuous basis through major Iowa employers, colleges, banks, and national corporations. Terry has more than 30 years of insurance and financial planning experience, is a past president of the Jaycees and Kiwanis organizations, and is a Retired Command Sergeant Major, U.S. Army Reserve.

**David S. White, ChFC**
The Capital Planning Group, Inc.
15200 Weston Parkway, Suite 103
Cary, NC 27513
Phone: 919-547-7220
Fax: 919-547-7221
E-mail: plan@thecpg.com; website: http://www.thecpg.com/cpg

David is principal and vice-president of The Capital Planning Group, Inc., a financial consulting firm in Cary, NC. He has been practicing for 10 years in the areas of investments, risk management, estate planning, and personal financial planning. David serves as an instructor at various adult education programs in central North Carolina and lectures to many corporations and organizations on retirement planning and executive benefits. David is a member of the Wake County Estate Planning Council and volunteers in the Wake County School System as an instructor on finance and investments. He earned his B.A. from North Carolina State University in Raleigh and his Chartered Financial Consultant designation from American College, Bryn Mawr, PA. David lives in Raleigh, NC, with his wife Ann and their son Sloan.

**Mark Young**
1810 Craig Road, Suite 213
St. Louis, MO 63146
Phone: 314-434-0275
Fax: 314-434-6846

Mark, a native of the St. Louis area, graduated from Park College *magna cum laude* in International Affairs. He received his MBA from Washington University in St. Louis, and he has completed additional graduate work in the field of public finance and budgeting at Southern Illinois University at Carbondale. Mark has a strong interest in financial education for individuals and businesses. He is a published author in the field of international trade and export policies and has been a guest speaker for SIU-Carbondale's Business School, Peabody Coal, Olin School of Business, Park College, OASIS, and Lewis and Clark Community College.

# Contents

# Introduction

# 1 Introduction

In the past, investing was simpler, but that was the past. Ten years ago, dramatic changes affected our investment community. The quantity of investment products available to the public increased exponentially, while at the same time the quality diminished significantly. Today, it is difficult for investors to objectively select one investment over another because the services and products offered are often so similar. Because the alternatives appear to be basically alike to the average consumer, the choices are overwhelming.

If you were asked, the probability of your being able to describe even one notable difference of one investment over another is just about zero. There are more than 9000 mutual funds out there and an army of over one million advisors. Not many of those funds are going to do what you want, and most of the advice is wrong for your needs. Successful investing in today's marketplace means you have to combat an entire industry whose central purpose is to get you to buy and sell on a regular basis. Whether it is a stockbroker, online brokerage company, an investment management consultant, financial newsletter, or some other investment "professional", their very existence depends upon getting you to trade often and, they hope, with them.

On Wall Street, trading means market timing and security selection; however, these strategies are costly to implement. They have an extremely low probability of success and, on average, have actually proven ineffective in adding value. In fact, these management strategies contribute less than 6% of a portfolio's profit determination.

The bad news is that gurus who can outperform and beat the market do not exist. The good news is you do not need them. Studies have found that

91% of returns are generated from making appropriate asset allocation decisions. Over the last decade, only a small percentage of mutual fund managers beat the S&P 500 index. By contrast, however, a fully diversified portfolio can be the best defense against market volatility.

## The Purpose of the Book

Most people spend more time planning a two-week vacation than they do planning their future finances. The goal of this book is to help investors learn how to sort through the hype. Investors have ventured blindly with bad advice when they have not understood the elements of investing and without considering the results and future consequences of their actions. This book will show readers how to recognize the advisors' motives or the methodology behind their advice and, thus, the quality of their advice.

Brokers or on-line brokerages know that they can keep you in the buy-and-sell cycle through playing on the emotions of fear, hope, or greed. If they can evoke any of those emotions in you, they can get you to make a transaction. Regardless of their cost, if you make enough transactions you will eat into your profits. The strategy that works over time is to buy and hold, but you will not hear that from Wall Street. Some very successful investors, such as Warren Buffet, maintain the philosophy that if it is a good company, the fundamentals are not likely to change in a day so why would you sell?

Investors who just got into the market three or four years ago have not experienced a negative market, and as a result they are being really aggressive. What they do not know, though, is that they are taking 50% more risk than the market in order to achieve the same returns. The information in this book will prepare the investor to obtain the greatest returns for a reasonable risk.

## Rethink Investment Advice You Have Been Receiving

One well-known study that examined many of these concepts will make readers rethink the investment advice they have been receiving. In 1986, a prestigious pension consulting firm released a startling research report after analyzing the performance variations of 91 large pension funds (see Figure 1.1).[1]

Their conclusions sent shock waves through the traditional investment management community. The report analyzed the three primary investment

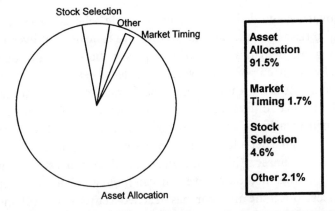

**Figure 1.1. Asset Allocation Graph Showing Total Return Variation.** (Adapted from Brinson, B.G.P., Singer, B.D., and Beebower, G.L., *Financial Analysts Journal,* May/June, 1991.)

strategies that determine variations in portfolio performance: asset allocation, securities selection, and market timing. Here is what should concern you: The two strategies that had the least impact on performance were securities selection and market timing, both of which rely on attempts to predict the future. Most investors spend all their time on what was determined to be least important. On average, these two strategies did not add value; in fact, they contributed to a loss in value. In spite of this, most stockbrokers' recommendations to individual investors are based on these two strategies. Wall Street firms spend billions of dollars each year trying to out-guess their competition in these two areas.

Here is the interesting part: The management strategy that had the most positive impact on portfolio performance is not yet widely recommended for individual investors, even though asset allocation accounted for over 90% of the profit determination. This same powerful concept is the foundation for Modern Portfolio Theory.

## Secrets Revealed

In March 1952, one of the most famous insights in the history of modern investing was published. It appeared in the *Journal of Finance,* and its author was a then-unknown 25-year-old graduate student.[2] For years, Harry Markowitz had been wrestling with a broad investment question: How can you earn attractive returns without accepting undue amounts of risk?

Markowitz was guided by one assumption: He believed that it was possible to minimize risks scientifically and to improve returns in a diversified portfolio. Using mathematics to solve this puzzle, he eventually developed a scientifically balanced portfolio, which he called an efficient portfolio. Based upon his study of historical investment performance, Markowitz created the best combination of different securities. His "mathematically correct" method was designed to achieve maximum returns with the least amount of risk, primarily through asset allocation. This powerful investment strategy works equally well for conservative, moderate, or aggressive investors. Universal in its application, this method of investing can build a portfolio for retirement, protect assets once the investor has reached retirement, and meet other financial goals.

Since Markowitz first published the theoretical foundation for Modern Portfolio Theory over 40 years ago, his ideas have been tested and refined, and the scientific system that Markowitz pioneered has become known as Modern Portfolio Theory. These strategies are now accepted worldwide as an authoritative "blueprint" for prudent institutional investing.

## Why Isn't Everyone Using These Investment Strategies?

If Modern Portfolio Theory is so popular now with institutional investors, why isn't everyone using it — especially as it is now taught in basic finance classes at most of the major universities? We suspect that there is one main reason why the majority of the public does not know about Modern Portfolio Theory: Most major brokerage firms are not in the business of educating the investing public. Their primary concern is their own profit. Many stockbrokers are taught to drive transactions by pushing their clients' emotional hot buttons, as most of them make their money on transaction costs, not performance.

Even among the most senior members of the investment community, the question has been asked, why, given the proven success of Modern Portfolio Theory, has it not met with widespread acceptance?[3] The answer lies in the fact that the organizational politics of major financial services firms have made this acceptance almost impossible.

What about the media? Aren't magazines and television shows in business to help investors make informed decisions? No. They are in business to make money for their owners and advertisers. The media thrive on volatility and uncertainty. If everyone knew how to invest scientifically, there would not be a need for media gurus. Sales of magazines and newsletters would plummet. Profits would suffer. The self-interest of others is one of the main reasons why more individual investors are not using Modern Portfolio Theory.

## A Different Philosophy — Readers Benefit!

Our group has a different philosophy. We think after you read the following chapters you may have a different view of the investment world. We want to communicate these strategies to as many investors as possible. If investors truly understand how everything really works, they will be more inclined to invest. The investment strategies contained in this book can be used to protect principal, generate growing income, or to maximize expected portfolio growth. Our methodologies enable readers to build a scientific portfolio of stocks, bonds, and cash which will allow them to sleep at night while earning the highest returns possible.

We will begin by explaining the myths that all successful investors must overcome. We will clearly show the historical risk/reward relationship between different types of investment strategies and why some strategies have consistently outperformed others. Readers will learn how professionals identify and quantify investment risks and will also discover the professional's secret for taming market volatility.

Our techniques will enable readers to design portfolios with the specific levels of risk that meet their individual comfort level and to counterbalance different investment classes to maximize expected returns. This easy-to-use investment strategy has historically and consistently beaten professional managers as a group.

We will introduce the differences between gross planning and net planning. Gross planning is looking at what your investment returns are, while net planning represents your returns after expenses, taxes, and inflation. Readers will quickly understand why these practical ideas set the standards for prudent investing all over the world.

## Not Like Other Books

At first glance, this book may look like every other book on investing. More than likely, you have even heard these same promises. That's okay — we invite you to be skeptical; in fact, that attitude is the best tool you have for investing. This is not a textbook; it is not written for the academic community. It is written to be a thought-provoking guide for the individual investor. This book will present new information and reinforce useful knowledge and intuitive understanding the reader may have already gained through his or her own experiences and education. We have tried to have fun in communicating this information and have taken some very technical subjects and attempted to make them understandable.

It is not critical that readers understand everything that we have written in this book. In fact, most individuals will still want to work with an investment advisor. That's fine; we provide you with questions to ask when selecting an advisor. You, as an investor, need to know whether or not the advisor understands these concepts and can implement them on your behalf. Many advisors ask their clients to take a leap of faith — to trust that the advisors know what they are doing and are acting in the clients' best interests. Unfortunately, we already know the all-too-frequent end result. We will not ask the reader to take such a leap of faith. Instead, this book will empower you to choose an advisor or make the correct decisions for yourself.

## Why You Should Read This Book

Most investors would like to earn double-digit returns, but it seems they are always following the last hot investment or investment-media guru and end up worse off than when they started. Using our strategies, they will have a higher likelihood of achieving their goals consistently over time with substantially lower risk ... and avoid the tax man as much as possible in the process. There is an intelligent approach that will work for all investors in meeting their personal financial goals. It starts by freeing the mind of all the self-serving investment advice received in the past and learning how investments really work.

## Your Success Road Map

Readers should leave all their thoughts and preconceptions about investing behind and walk with us through this process. This book provides a map for you to customize a course of action and navigate it. The best way to profit from the strategies in this book is to consistently apply them day to day. The book has been written to nurture, encourage, and give readers the confidence to set out on their own paths. Your guides are some of the most successful people in the investment industry. Our clients tell us it has been a freeing and profitable experience. We believe you will also agree!

# References

1. Brinson, G.P., Hood, L.R., and Beebower, G.L., *Financial Analysts Journal*, July/Aug., 39–44, 1986.
2. Markowitz, H., *The Journal of Finance*, 7(1), 77–91, 1952.
3. Michaud, R., *Financial Analysts Journal*, Jan./Feb., 31–42, 1989.

# Part I.
# Myth vs. Reality

# 2 What Worked for Your Parents Does Not Work Today

**W**hat worked for your mom and dad's generation was great for them. Save up a little money, buy a house, put the kids through school — it was a good way of life. Back then, the price of gas was a nickel a gallon, four loaves of bread cost a quarter, and a new car cost less than $500. Many of us can still remember buying an envelope with first-class postage for 4¢. We all know those days are gone.

Our parents worked for 30 years, made a good living, and saved for their retirement — and today many of them are worried about not having enough money to last the duration of their lives. They were taught (and even the great Will Rogers used to say it) that it is not the return *on* your money that is important — it is the return *of* your money. That is true ... and not. What is most important today is what that return on investment can buy.

We can talk about wages and inflation and how things are the same or are not the same, but, to put things in perspective, the reality is that the cost of living doubles about every 10 years. We can blame it on technology or on the information age, but as things continue to get more expensive, our purchasing power erodes.

Today the popular press talks only about the return on your principle. What the media are not writing about is *maintaining* your purchasing power. A silver certificate stated that the dollar was exchangeable for a dollar's worth of silver, and our greenbacks today state *In God We Trust.* Our currency has

1-57444-258-9/00/$0.00+$.50
© 2000 by CRC Press LLC

become simply a medium of exchange because of the condition of our nation's economy. There is nothing wrong with that on the surface, but if there is not enough currency the government prints more. When the Federal Reserve Board puts more money into circulation, that creates an inflationary trend. Where inflation goes, so goes the cost of living. And what inflation does not steal, the tax man does.

That is why the returns on investments need to be measured by the net after taxes and inflation. For instance, what good was a 20% rate of return in 1979 with marginal tax brackets in excess of 50% and inflation running at 21%? Even with huge rates of return, we were going backwards.

The general public needs to be educated, not with conventional wisdom but uncommon wisdom. In a great book by Harry Dent, *The Great Boom Ahead,* and a new one called *The Roaring 2000s,* he writes that everything today is driven by the 'boomers — the economy is driven by sexual activity, with a lag time of nine months. From the 1960s through the mid-70s, the way to build retirement wealth was to own real estate: Live in a house for three years, exchange it for a bigger place, live in that one for three years, and move up again. An ideal retirement plan was to own ten homes and collect rental income or gradually sell them off. That worked while the baby boomers were coming of age, then the demand dropped along with the real estate values and the changes brought about by the 1986 tax laws.

Well, if you couldn't invest in real estate, what could you invest in? The next thing that came on strong was the stock market, of course. And now mutual funds are today's answer. But in the late 1970s, you could not *give* a mutual fund away. Many of us recall when the entire mutual fund list fit on one short sheet of paper. Now mutual funds cover four pages in *The Wall Street Journal.*

Let's talk about the real problem, though — taxes. Taxes are the biggest drain on wealth accumulation. Our great country was built on the dreams of entrepreneurs to create wealth. Now the Rockefeller, Hearst, and Humphrey estates, among others, are national treasures. Why? These super-wealthy families simply could not afford to maintain those estates with after-tax dollars. Wealth accumulation in Europe is a different story; in most countries, they do not tax wealth accumulation. They tax earnings, but not stock or the exchanges of real estate. In the U.S., we have created a society driven to distribute the wealth. As the wealthy become wealthier, we raise the minimum wage laws. The trouble with that is that every time we keep adjusting for inflation the gap widens between the haves and the have-nots.

Each generation tells their youth about the "good old days". For many of our parents, there was no television, just those great old radio shows, and no

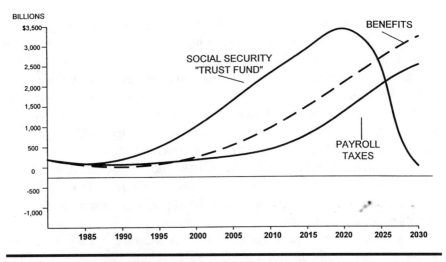

**Figure 2.1. Social Security Trust Fund Goes Broke by 2030.** (From Board of Trustees of the Social Security Administration, Cleveland Federal Reserve, 1997.)

"reach-out-and-touch-someone" long-distance phone calls, just handwritten letters. Our kids will say the "good old days" were e-mail and video-conferencing. They will talk about before and after the Internet the same way our grandparents talked about before and after the car. In changing our mindset, though, we have to move from the familiar, guaranteed "good old days" to an un-guaranteed world.

Why do we have 40-hour work weeks? Why do we have time clocks? The rationale was that as we changed from a society that grew and harvested what we ate, especially when the Great Depression came, we had to create jobs. So we developed a system to generate income — a guaranteed work week, guaranteed hours, guaranteed vacation each year. Work for 20 years and you get a stipend of a pension. Prior to the 1950s and '60s, pensions were non-existent, but life expectancies were only a few years beyond retirement at age 65. It should be noted that Social Security was not designed to provide the fully funded retirements that people talk about now. The original Social Security Act states that Social Security was designed to *augment* personal savings plans. It never was intended to *replace* wages (see Figure 2.1).

John D. Rockefeller said, "It doesn't make sense to pay taxes on the money that your money is making if you're not using that money, if you're not consuming that money." A good way to begin to fight back against taxes is by starting to use your pre-tax dollar to get tax savings so the earnings on those dollars begin to work for you. Then you keep the earnings you would have paid in taxes ... plus the earnings on the tax savings and the earnings on the earnings of the tax savings. Sorry if that sounds like double talk, but what we mean is that you get a triple compounding effect. We have clients who have over $1 million dollars in retirement plans today because of the bullish stock market for the last 16 years and the triple compounding effect. What they do not realize is that the 401(k) plans are really for the IRS. When death occurs, who is waiting out there in the wings to collect on this huge 401(k) or pension plan? Our families? Yes, but that money has to pass through the IRS fists first. There are literally hundreds and hundreds of billions of dollars that at death will be taxed at the income tax level as well as at the estate tax level before the heirs receive a cent — even with the $1million per person exemption that is scheduled for the year 2006.

How do we stop or turn the tides now? It will take some pioneers — people willing to stand up and say, "This isn't working." Our goal in writing this book is to provide our readers with knowledge: forewarned is forearmed. Most of the writers for *The Wall Street Journal* and *Money* magazine are 30 years old, not 50 or 60. They have not had the opportunity of experience and have not learned, as we discussed in Chapter 1, that market timing and stock trading are not effective strategies in the long term.[1]

Do you remember when taxation was 79% back in 1979? The country almost collapsed that year, and the average person did not realize it. An emergency meeting of economists in Washington was quietly called because there was fear of an economic collapse. The events of 1979 led to significant changes. Inflation had to come down, interest rates had to fall, and taxes had to come down. In an attempt to bring about some of these changes, when Ronald Reagan came into office, one of the first issues he addressed was unions. Organized labor at the time had outlived its usefulness and had such a pervasive stranglehold that it was stifling creativity.

In 1981, the Economic Recovery Tax Act reduced taxes from 79% to a flat 50%. What happened to interest rates? They were forced down. Today, inflation and taxation remain our biggest concerns. Inflation currently is running between 2 and 4%. That seems low, but the reality is that inflation will still double our cost of living every ten years. There is a high probability that we will continue to get an above-average rate of return in the stock market for as long as the next ten years, but a big drain will be taxation, whether it is a flat tax at 28% or the current income tax rates.

If a state receives much funding from the federal government and that funding starts to disappear, the state has to find a way to replace what it has lost, which leads to increases in local taxation. It may not be a state income tax, but it may come in the form of a higher property tax or a value-added tax.

There seems no way to hide from the tax man, but do not go away — the story gets worse.

The biggest concern in the investment world is that everyone is going to convert to Roth IRAs and pay their taxes now. But what if in eight to nine years, the government scraps the current taxation system and goes to a value-added tax? Then you will really be double-taxed on your money. Take it out, no income taxes; but if you spend it, you pay a value-added tax.

Readers of this book must put taxation in perspective. That perspective is that there will always be a tax. Here is the point: What we have to do is legally and legitimately use every tax-advantage investment opportunity we have. The invention of new variable insurance products has created a phenomenal opportunity — until Congress closes that loophole.

We need to recognize that, like a lot of things, there is a double-edged sword to taxation. As in real estate, you can depreciate it and that is great while you're doing it — until you want to sell and have to recapture all the depreciation. As a society, we will continue to look for ways to minimize income taxation. Lower tax rates are said to encourage taxable enterprise and produce more revenue. Economics 101 teaches us that a tax dollar circulated in the country goes through the economy two and a half times a year. A private dollar goes through the economy four times because the private dollar goes to pay the taxes but also pays the grocery store, the gas station attendant, and the clothier, and we rotate those dollars. So we want more dollars circulating. If we put more people to work by creating jobs, we create more tax dollars. It does not make a difference if they are at the high end of the tax roll or at the 15% end. They are still tax dollars being redistributed.

*Let's talk about you and the two worlds you live in ...* Going back to our original discussion, there is the familiar world of guarantees and the world of no guarantees. A certain part of our economy is invested in the world of guarantees — the conventional workplace, 40-hour work week, and guaranteed paycheck, benefits, and retirement package. This group is always going to pay income taxes. These are the worker bees. It is in the free world, however — the unconventional world, the no-guarantee world of no guaranteed 40-hour work weeks, no guaranteed paychecks — where wealth is created. Bill Gates does not punch 40 hours a week on a time clock and go home. Rumor has it that he can be seen in the office at 2:00 or 3:00 a.m. No creator of wealth has been a W-2 wage earner. They are people willing to put in the time and energy to create something.

There is a tremendous amount of opportunity today. There are investment vehicles that are not being touted by the popular press because they are unconventional. One of our clients coined the phrase *investment pornography,* which is whatever makes headlines in *The Wall Street Journal, Money* magazine, or CNBC. It is sensationalism based on short-term thinking and hindsight. You have got to train yourself not to listen to that noise and put the time and energy into learning the unconventional. Do not become enmeshed in all of this information overload; instead, seek out solid advice.

A new client wanted to invest but said he had to pay his house off before he did anything else. All of his money was in IRAs, in the bank, and in CDs, and he had a $250,000 in pension plans and guaranteed accounts. He was anxious to appear informed and volunteered, "I'm having another phone line brought into my house so I can have CNBC continually, because I want to be an investor." We said what you are telling us is that you want to be a *trader.* We then went through a discussion about the difference between a trader and an investor. Then we asked, "What happens if the stock market drops 3000 points? The people who do this as their pastime do not realize that it is real money. It's great when the stock market is going up, but when your $40,000 becomes $20,000 overnight, how are you going to feel?" "Not good," the client answered.

The intention of this book is to get our readers to start thinking outside the conventional thinking, the so-called nine dots. Let's be contrarian. When you see a negative article about annuities in *Forbes* magazine, that should probably start you thinking, "I should *buy* annuities." When the press says everyone ought to be investing in banks, you probably ought to go short on the banks because by the time the general media start talking about it, as history has shown, it is too late. Think about Internet stocks right now. If a company has a ".com" attached to its name, you expect a 20% run in one day, but where will the company be in a year or two?

Another one of our clients made a $70,000 profit. At the end of the year, though, he had to pay 28% to the IRS for short-term gains, plus he was penalized for under-contributing to his withholding tax. (By the way, no one ever tells you the end of their investment war stories at a cocktail party; they always seem to leave out the tax consequences.)

We suggest you seek out competent advisors who understand the difference between *gross planning* and *net planning.* Gross planning is looking at what the returns are, while net planning is keeping in mind what will be left after expenses, after taxes, and after inflation.

In the California Gold Rush, the Yukon Gold Rush, the Nome Gold Rush, how many miners struck it rich? Who really made the money in these gold rushes? It was the merchant. The guy who sold the staples and the gold pans. Consider this: Who is going to really make money as the market continues to roll forward? The brokerage firms, the mutual fund companies, the banks, and the insurance companies. Why don't you buy shares in those? With that thought in mind, we recommend three areas on which to concentrate: financial services, health care, and the global market.

You have to know where to put your money, and then you have to find the vehicles to shelter it. On December 31st, you may receive phantom income. Phantom income is when you get a 1099 dividend or interest payment that you have to add on top of your earned income. You never saw it but you spent it by reinvesting and buying more mutual funds. How do you pay that tax bill? You sell off some mutual funds to get the money to pay the tax bill. Guess what? Next year you are faced with double taxation. Again, it is a double-edged sword. At no other time have there been so many investment products and so little advice. You have to seek professional advice, and you have to know how and where to find it.

## One Last Note

Every time your kids get their allowance, take 10% of it and put it in a bank, credit union, or investment portfolio. As they get older and their allowances increase, maintain the 10%. If you do not train them on a dollar basis, when it becomes $100,000 or $1 million, it becomes tougher. The Good Book says that what you give away comes back to you. We are here to tell you we have all reaped far more than we have sown. It does not matter what religion you are, think about giving away 10% to something (not the tax man) somewhere because this great country of ours needs to get off the dole system. We need to put charity back where it belongs — at home, in the Red Cross, and the various agencies — not the government. Families were designed to take care of families, not government agencies.

## Reference

1. Fama, E.F., The behavior of stock prices, *Journal of Business*, January, 34–105, 1965.

# 3 The Investment Myth

There are thousands of people who have built careers and businesses around currently accepted Wall Street investment theories, but the truth is that there is no proven basis for many of the most-touted investment beliefs, including the one that value can be added to an investor's portfolio through individual stock selection and market timing. Many of our most cherished investment beliefs are based on a collection of false assumptions. When the truth is finally sifted from the faulty paradigms, what is left is a lot of experts in the investment community with egg on their faces.

We cannot begin to accept any really new body of knowledge until the chains of our old false beliefs are broken. So let's start breaking those chains and getting our investment-related facts straight. We now have a wealth of data available at our fingertips regarding almost any investment out there. Advances in technology plus the availability of personal computers have made it simple to collect, manipulate, and study mounds of data. Today, it is difficult to believe how little information there was to study 30 years ago. For instance, time-series data were virtually unavailable for most asset categories; even the S&P 500 index time series was hard to find. That has sure changed! Now you can get more information than ever before. What you cannot get is information that is unbiased.

There is a long tradition of an unbiased academic community examining the workings of financial markets. In the early 1900s, a French mathematician named Louis Bachelier set out to study market statistics, specifically the French future markets and French government bonds which traded at the Bourse. He examined a series of future market price changes in an attempt to determine the mathematical properties of these futures. He wanted to find

1-57444-258-9/00/$0.00+$.50
© 2000 by CRC Press LLC

out if there was a way to determine future market movements using past trends — in other words, whether the next event or next time period could be foretold. This is what any investor would love to be able to do. If an investor could accomplish this task, untold riches would await.

What Bachelier found, however, was that no information or statistical pattern was uncovered by any of the time-series information. It was apparent that there was no way to predict mathematically or statistically the future movements of the market. He found that the historical sequence of price changes provided no useable information for predicting the next price change outcome. Bachelier's study was lost to the world for some time and was never looked at in depth again until after World War II. Eventually, however, his work set the stage for the next investigation by academics.

Forty years later, in the 1950s, universities and research institutions had new access to computers and set about using these tools to analyze all types of data; in fact, some of the first computer applications focused on the returns of stock market indices and individual stocks and bonds. The academic community began analyzing this data with no particular theory or outcome in mind, just the desire to learn from whatever might be discovered. It turned out that a number of academics working in different places — Holbrook Working[1] and Harry Roberts[2] at the University of Chicago and Neil Osborne[3] at IBM Research, among others — started noting similar events.

These academics independently found rates of returns and price changes to be serially uncorrelated. Again, the unanimous finding among the researchers was that there was no discernible predictability from historical time-series information in relationship to the next future outcome event. The sequence of rates of returns for weekly outcomes, several years of daily outcomes, or long series of monthly outcomes all appeared random. Studying prior price data uncovered no knowledge of what the subsequent price might be. It was as if the numbers were taken from a table of random numbers; a computer generating a series of random and unrelated numbers could produce the same result. Independent studies, in other words, showed the inability to forecast stock market movements.

Then, in 1959, Harry Roberts, at the University of Chicago Business School, reversed the method of study.[4] He instructed a computer to generate a series of 50 random numbers with a certain mean and standard deviation showing a normal distribution. The result was that famous bell-shaped curve we all love. The resulting 50 numbers corresponded roughly to the typical weekly price change of the typical stock; that is, in fact, why Roberts chose those parameters. Now, remember, there is no predicted value for these numbers; by their very construction, this series of numbers is empty of content. Roberts then arbitrarily started off with a price of $40 and used random patterns to develop graphs that looked like stock returns.

Roberts then made up stock names, assigning a name to each chart, and took these to La Salle Street in Chicago — at that time, the hotbed of technical analysis. He introduced himself and asked for advice from the leading technicians of the day as to how to play the stock market based on the random data assembled in these charts. Every one of the technicians had a very strong opinion about what Roberts ought to do with each of these securities. The patterns that the analysts were observing and speculating about were generated by a computer and were simply the combining of a random series of numbers. There was, by construction, *no* actual pattern, *no* useful information. When random numbers are accumulated, patterns can seem to emerge, but these patterns are in the mind of the viewer, not in the data.

Roberts published his now-famous study, "Stock Market Patterns and Financial Analysts", in 1959.[5] The technical "experts" were not amused, and even today, as you flip through the financial channels on television, you will still see technical experts predicting what the market is going to do next based on the shape and pattern of a chart. They obviously still have not gotten Roberts' message.

## Modern Portfolio Theory

Harry Markowitz is credited with the developing the investment concept known today as Modern Portfolio Theory.[6] This revolutionary concept involved a 180-degree change in viewpoint from what was considered *the* way to design and manage a stock and bond portfolio. Before Markowitz's work, investment portfolio design was centered around superior stock selection. Analysts would research the particular industries and companies. They would take balance sheets and internal company analysis, combine these with earnings projections and future expectations, and come up with predictions for the future. Even now, most Wall Street stock brokerage firms and money managers continue to follow this approach, believing they can somehow discover that one nugget of value and opportunity which no one else has uncovered.

In attempting to find a truly valid investment approach, Markowitz and other financial academics in subsequent years hit upon the concept of considering risk first and returns second. In order to do this, Markowitz determined that the entire portfolio's risk or volatility should be the central issue. It was Markowitz who created a concept of blending investments together in a manner that lowered the overall volatility of the total portfolio. Markowitz found that if an investment that went up in value was blended with an investment that went down in value at opposite times — even if these investments were both so-called risky or volatile investments — the overall portfolio's risk or volatility could be reduced.

The impact upon the total portfolio was a canceling out or reduction of the total portfolio's volatility. Again, this valuable information was ignored by the financial professionals of the time. These scientifically proven concepts were dismissed as the musings of out-of-touch academic eggheads who knew little about the "real world" of investing. It was not until 30 years later that Markowitz was awarded the Nobel Prize for his work.

Next, William Sharpe expanded Markowitz's work and designed a method to measure volatility. Sharpe called the concept the Capital Asset Pricing Model (CAPM). In his mathematical formulations, Sharpe assigned a "beta" measurement of 1.0 to the market. If the beta of a particular investment was 1.10, then the expectation was that it would outperform the market by 10% when the markets went up and underperform by 10% when the markets went down.

Sharpe was able to evaluate a specific portfolio against the market itself, which allowed him to determine mathematically whether the portfolio was getting what the market was offering. To investment professionals, this meant they could, for the first time, determine an expectation for future performance based upon the beta measurement of the portfolio. The result of this knowledge is a greater certainty about unknown future expectations, at least in theory.

Like Markowitz's new thinking before him, Sharpe's concept was slow to be accepted, but eventually the CAPM approach became a centerpiece for portfolio design. His work and refinements over the next 20 years spawned a large variety of changes and improvements in the investment field, including valuable measurements of portfolio performance, creation of index-based funds, and applications in the field of corporate finance. These concepts were major theoretical innovations in the study of market behavior and asset valuation.

Throughout the 1960s and early '70s, the focus of most academic work was to determine how efficient markets are. In 1965, Eugene Fama, of the University of Chicago, wrote his authoritative thesis entitled "The Behavior of Stock Market Prices" (published in its entirety in the *Journal of Business*[7]). In his thesis, Fama coined the phrase "efficient markets" and explained how markets appear to be able to fully absorb new information coming in so that all prices of all securities reflect all known information. This theory is based on the simple truth that, due to the rapid assimilation by the market of any new information, expectations of future price changes are revised randomly and are accurately reflected in the value of the stock. If a stock has an initial price of $10, the next change in price has an equal chance of being an increase or a decrease in value. If it goes up to, say, $11, the next change in price still has an equal chance of going up or down. The implication is that stock market prices follow a random walk and that price changes are independent of one another.

In Fama's empirical testing, he established that:[8]

1. Past stock prices are of no value in predicting future prices.
2. Publicly available information cannot be used to earn excess returns consistently.
3. Mutual fund managers, as a group, cannot *beat* the market.

The most popular test of Fama's proposition was the examination of mutual fund performance in a classic study by Michael Jensen.[9] He looked at the performance of mutual fund portfolios from 1945 to 1964. The managers of the funds he studied were the best and the brightest in the investment community. If anyone possessed special insights into the inefficiencies in the market that could be capitalized upon, these experts would. They would also be able to use these insights to advantage before the rest of the population. If, on the other hand, markets are efficient and stocks are basically correctly priced at any point in time, experts would not be able to beat the naive strategy of buying a sampling of all the securities in the market. Of the fund managers who had experienced exceptional performance on the positive side, the percentage of success was much lower than one would expect. Experts were, in effect, trying to figure what a stock price was worth when the market had already efficiently determined the price.

## The Breakthrough

It was not until 1992 that Eugene Fama and Kenneth French, both from the University of Chicago, created the next major breakthrough. Their landmark research was published in an article, "The Cross-Section of Expected Stock Returns," which explained profit determination in investment portfolios and illustrated why it was not necessary to buy a sampling of the entire market or individual securities that had higher risk in an effort to outperform the market as a whole.[10] Fama and French developed new asset classes that segmented the market and allowed for superior performance at the same risk as the market as a whole.

It is ironic that the most competitive industry in the world, the financial services industry, still gives advice based on the erroneous belief that markets do not work. The truth is that no other pricing system in use in the world today appears better able to allocate resources than the free market system. All an investor needs to do to participate in the free market system's creation of wealth is to own a broadly diversified portfolio of equity securities. The individual companies owned will attempt to maximize shareholder value to the investor's benefit.

This is significant to the first-time investor in that it means that nothing is hidden from you. No one out there knows if a stock is undervalued or overvalued. There is no secret information that gives someone else an advantage not available to you. There are no gurus. Every year *The Wall Street Journal* has a special section in which they pick the top financial analysts. One year, they profiled 36 top financial analysts, one for each of the 36 market sectors (e.g., transportation, utilities, financial services). The average age of these analysts was 27 years, and they were making $200,000 to well over $1 million a year. *The Wall Street Journal* ran their pictures in the paper, and their article made 36 sets of parents really proud.

There was a little column in the back of the paper that pointed out that if you did nothing more than just buy all of the stocks, equally weighted, in each of those 36 categories, 33 of the times you would have outperformed these top analysts. From a marketing standpoint, most financial professionals are going to tell you that they are going to show you how to beat the market. We are going to show you that is the wrong goal to have. You do not need to beat the market. All you have to do is to take an efficient risk to get most of what the market returns, avoid the tax man, and follow a systematic method for investing, and we are going to show you how.

# References

1. Working, H., A random difference series for use in the analysis of time series, *Journal of the American Statistical Association*, 29, 11–24, 1934.
2. Roberts, H.V., Stock market patterns and financial analysis: methodological suggestions, *Journal of Finance*, XIV(1), 1–10, 1959.
3. Osborne, M.F.M., Brownian motion in the stock market, *Operational Research*, 7, 145–173, 1959.
4. Roberts, H.V., Stock market patterns and financial analysis: methodological suggestions, *Journal of Finance*, XIV(1), 1–10, 1959.

5. Roberts, H.V., Stock market patterns and financial analysis: methodological suggestions, *Journal of Finance,* XIV(1), 1–10, 1959.

6. Markowitz, H., Portfolio selections, *The Journal of Finance,* March, 77–91, 1952.

7. Fama, E.F., The behavior of stock prices, *Journal of Business,* 37(1), 34–105, 1965.

8. Fama, E.F., The behavior of stock prices, *Journal of Business,* 37(1), 34–105, 1965.

9. Jensen, M.C., The performance of mutual funds in the period 1945–1964, *Financial Analysts Journal,* November, 587–616, 1989.

10. Fama, E.F. and French, K.F., The cross-section of expected stock returns, *Journal of Finance,* June, 427–465, 1992.

# 4 Planning From a Net Perspective

*"Don't tell me how much you earned — tell me how much you kept after you paid your taxes; then we'll know how successful you truly are."*

**M**ost investors want to be able to retire with financial dignity, self-esteem, and peace of mind, without being a burden to their family. Planning from a *net* perspective allows investors to improve their yield and reduce risk. Let's first identify three phases of financial planning. The first phase, *accumulation*, is the period of holding onto the assets we are acquiring. The second phase, *distribution*, is the manner in which we liquidate and use our wealth; this phase is the reason for investing — to provide an income sufficient for our retirement or other goals. We call the last phase the *pass-through* phase, in which we plan the preservation and transfer of our accumulated wealth to our heirs.

We teach a simple formula known as *TIP*, which is an acronym for taxes, inflation, and procrastination. We believe that understanding how these three factors erode the net value of your wealth is key to achieving investment success. The Internal Revenue Service (IRS) is going to become the senior partner in most Americans' retirement years. Inflation will further reduce the power of your remaining dollars. The longer you wait to address these factors in your plan for accumulating wealth, the more harmful their impact.

You would not think of buying a mutual fund that had as much as a 35% expense charge in it, but consider that dividends are fully taxable income and that the federal tax rates on short-term capital gains are at 28% and at 20% for long-term gains. When you also add in state and local taxes, these taxes could easily amount to a 35% bite out of your return.

Let's say you want to cross a lake as quickly as possible. You have a choice of a 300-hp jet boat or a pontoon boat with a 20-hp motor. There is one problem, though; the jet boat has a 3-foot hole in its hull. Which would you choose? Okay, let's say we put a 1000-hp motor on the jet boat. Would that affect your decision? It shouldn't, because no matter how big the motor is, you still have no chance of making it to the other side of the lake. Taxation is the hole in your accumulation boat. Unless you patch the hole, it does not matter what rate of return you get because you are not going to keep it.

One of the myths promoted to retail investors is that you are instantly in a lower tax bracket when you retire, so you do not need as high a gross income as you had in your peak earning years. What is not figured into the equation is that after retirement you will continue to buy goods and services and those are going to cost more in the future than they do today. That means you need *more* income. And, if you produce this additional income, how can you be in a lower tax bracket? Our current highest tax bracket is probably the lowest we have seen in our lifetime, but the U.S. government is currently running close to a $5 trillion deficit, so it would be reasonable to anticipate an increase in our tax rates.

Depression-era economics taught us to protect our dollars from risk; what we have not been taught is to protect our purchasing power. The typical person who retired from the 1930s to the 1950s lived only an average of six to eight years following retirement. They experienced less than a 2% inflationary cycle from their retirement until death. For the last 20 years, though, inflation has been consistently running between 4 and 5% per year. Inflation may rise and fall, but it will almost certainly continue. What will our dollars be worth when we retire? American consumers are paying more for an automobile today than they used to pay for their first house. An average car today costs around $25,000 compared to $3500 around 17 years ago — almost a seven-to-one increase! At that rate, in 18 years, an average automobile could easily cost $100,000.

The typical investment advisor is taught how to grow money, and the typical tax accountant is taught how to reduce your taxes each year. There are very few people who are astute in coordinating both activities. Only through the coordination of tax and inflation planning and asset allocation on long-term investments can you achieve net planning. The first step in net planning is quality accumulation. Unless you save money, you cannot retain it. The sooner you begin to save, the longer your savings will be able to grow. Okay, we know you know this, but you have got to create an automatic savings system that becomes a way of life.

Next, you have to learn how to avoid paying taxes on your investment. There is a major difference between tax *avoidance* and tax *evasion*. The best definition came from a U.S. Supreme Court Justice: "If you cross a toll bridge in New York City and do not pay your toll, that is evasion. If you elect to go four blocks north and go across the public bridge where there is no toll, that is avoidance."

Probably one of the greatest tax avoidance vehicles available today is the Roth IRA. Investments in a Roth IRA are not pre-taxed and are tax deferred. Of course, there are limitations such as a maximum investment of $2000 annually and an annual gross income of less than $110,000 (for a single individual), and investing only $2000 a year will not accumulate a large amount of wealth.

Another popular tax avoidance vehicle is a municipal bond, but this, too, has some major problems. Are you better off with good growth equities or bonds? Many advisors would say you are better off investing in a good mutual fund and paying taxes than investing in a municipal bond that has no taxes, as there is no growth in a bond.

A promising tax avoidance vehicle is called (maximum funded/NON-MEC) variable universal life insurance. You can invest any amount of money you want without IRS restrictions, and any remaining benefit after your death will be income-tax free to your beneficiaries.

In 1986, the tax laws changed for mutual funds. You used to be able to reinvest your dividends and capital gains in a tax-deferred manner. With the tax law changes, you lost that advantage. That left the variable annuity as the only product still offering tax-deferred accumulation. This does not mean tax-free income, as you still pay taxes on the distributions, but, because you get the combination of tax deferral and diversification, you come out ahead.

You can get as many as five, six, seven, or eight different fund companies under one umbrella. This is good diversification. Many variable annuities have as many as 28 and 40 sub-accounts (a sub-account is that portion of the variable annuity's separate account that invests in shares of a mutual fund's portfolios). A variable annuity is the only product that will give you one check per month and is part of a net planning strategy.

Would your spouse like to rely on a reduction of risk in a down market if you died? Variable annuities can offer a reduction of risk in case of death. They also offer diversification. In many variable annuities, there is constant asset reallocation. Every year the sub-account manager, in a manner similar to a mutual fund manager, rebalances at no additional cost to you. This feature is built into your variable annuity. We all like those benefits; we need equity growth and we want to reduce some of our risk component.

What about your home? Most Americans are not in the equity market-place because the largest asset in America is home equity, but what rate of return does your home equity offer you? Zero. This is why it is not listed as part of an asset in a financial plan. It totally throws your asset allocation mixture out of whack.

A real problem today is the way most Americans invest in the stock market. The typical investor does not make much on his or her investments. If you do make any money in the stock market, the tax man is there to take it away. We believe you need an advisor to help you avoid the tax man and to endure the roller coaster of investing. Anybody can be happy when the market is up, but the market goes in cycles. We tell our clients that three out of ten years they will experience a down market. We cannot predict when these down times are going to occur, so that is why you should use a dollar cost averaging system of investing. Such a system, however, is not generally taught by investment people or the news media, and, without a good financial education, the American consumer has no chance for success.

The trick is to have your money exceed your purchasing power so you can still have the same goods and services in the future that you have today. Only equities (stocks) can do that, but there are two hurdles. The first is procrastination. The reason people procrastinate is not because they want to; rather, fear of making a bad decision stops most of us in our tracks. Because you do not want to look ignorant in front of your friends and you do not want to be laughed at, you end up making no decisions. The second hurdle is the money paid to taxes. If you have $1000 and you make 10% interest, you have made a hundred bucks. If you are in a federal/state local tax bracket of 35%, you have given away $35 to the IRS. What if you could have invested that $35? The opportunity you have lost cost twice as much as the tax and is what we call the lost opportunity cost.

For example, say you paid $67,000 in taxes. If you could have made 12% on that money, and could have invested it over ten years, it would have been worth $208,000. If we could reduce those taxes from $67,000 to $40,000, you could have saved $27,000. That money, invested tax-free, would have become an additional $83,000. It is the opportunity of investing the taxes that you are giving up. This is why we need to look at every investment from a net planning prospective. We will continue to investigate "net techniques" throughout this book.

# Part II.
# Accumulation Strategies

# 5 Give Yourself a Raise: Investing Ins and Outs

**B**asically, there are four ways to invest money into the marketplace: (1) dollar cost averaging, (2) buy-and-hold, (3) market timing, or (4) individual stock picking. Dollar cost averaging is putting the same amount of money into the same investment on the same day every month (or every interval), regardless of the price of the investment. The buy-and-hold or buy-and-forget approach is when someone puts a lump sum of money in an investment and never moves it around or changes it over a period of time. Market timing involves correctly predicting the movements of the stock market in advance. This is the most difficult and time-consuming approach and requires the best luck in the world and all the possible research facilities available. From an academic standpoint, it simply does not work, as it is virtually impossible to guess the correct day each month that the market is going to be at its lowest. The last method, and most difficult, is stock picking. Stock picking involves trying to identify securities that are undervalued and will deliver market-beating returns. Stock picking attempts to select the best individual stocks through research and analysis. Studies show that the last two methods actually reduce performance rather than improve it,[1] while buy-and-hold and dollar cost averaging perform the best.

Many investors look to the stock market for capital growth, investing in individual stocks or mutual funds. Historically, the stock market has charted a long-term upward trend. In the short run, however, daily fluctuations in market prices can make it difficult to decide when to buy. Dollar cost averaging does not guarantee the best results, but it does provide the greatest opportunity to have the best price on securities over the long run, and it is the safest way to enter the market. Dollar cost averaging is the most functional way to accumulate wealth regardless of whatever type of investment goals you have — college funding, retirement planning, a ski vacation condo in Vermont, whatever. With dollar cost averaging, you put the same amount of money into the same investment (say, monthly) on the same day — regardless of the price of the investment. So if the market drops 500 points, for example, you end up getting more shares. When the market is high, you are buying fewer shares. Because nobody knows what day of each month is the actual best day to buy a security, dollar cost averaging places an investor in the best possible position to obtain the average price of the investment over the life of investing. Dollar cost averaging eliminates reliance on market timing and superior stock selection.

We recommend using dollar cost averaging except when very large sums are involved. And each investor should always take into account his or her individual situation. For example, for the regular investor, in times when the market has pulled back and everything is very attractively priced, we would recommend putting the money in lump sums. For a young or middle-aged person, with an investment time horizon of ten years or longer and a large lump sum to invest, we again recommend putting the entire lump sum in at once, and the money should be invested in different asset classes.

There is nothing wrong with starting off with a lump sum and then dollar cost averaging to add to it. For example, see Figure 5.1, where we assume that a person invests $100 per month for 12 months in XYZ mutual fund. The investment community makes it very easy to invest your dollars these days; you can do an automatic withdrawal from your checking or savings account or have your paycheck deposited directly. That way you can automatically take advantage of dollar cost averaging.

The days of market timing are gone. Anybody who is trying to use a market timing investment strategy is, in our opinion, fooling themselves. In huge downturns, market timers may do well if they are in the exact right place at the right time. The problem is that no one knows when that is. Anybody can take a look at the marketplace right now and, based on the projections of downward spirals, start selling short or buying puts and doing day-trading and timing. But in environments such as these, everybody who wants to become an immediate expert crawls out of the woodwork. As soon as the market returns to the norm, which is growth of about 10 to 12% a year, and there are no frills, no huge gains or losses, but normal growth, all those people on the sidelines will be crying the blues, saying, "Boy, I wish it would drop

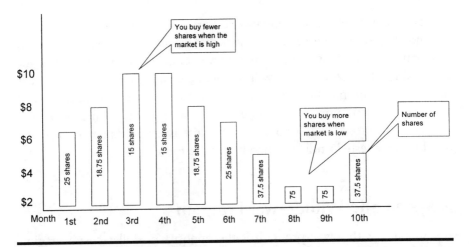

**Figure 5.1. Dollar Cost Averaging.** Total amount invested is $1500 ($150/month); average price of these ten purchases is $6.00; total number of shares is 342.50; average cost per share is $4.38. Average cost per share = $150/month × 10 months = $1500; $1500/342.50 = $4.38 average cost.

down again." The last major spike down for any period of time was in 1994, and before that in 1987. So market timing people have been sitting on the sidelines for a period of many years.

In investment classes, we describe it as "chasing the wave that's already crashed on the shore." What is a surfer's goal? To be ahead of the wave, so the wave lifts him up and places him on shore to meet his destiny. But when you chase the wave, you are always chasing returns. You are in the deepest water up to your neck, and you are swimming harder. The guy who is already in place gets to ride the wave. Dollar cost averaging will put you in the right place for advantageous investing.

You may have seen one of the television investment shows on CNBC recently, where they were observing the inflow of funds and the outflow of funds in 401(k) plans across the nation. When the market went down, at the end of the business day a lot of money moved out of the equities and into the fixed accounts. The next day, when the market came back up, the majority of the money moved out of the fixed accounts and back into the market. So essentially people sold low and they bought high. That's chasing the wave. Doing something like that completely wipes out the benefit of all the dollar cost averaging the investor has done in the past.

Often we hear investors saying, "Let's just put the money in the S&P 500 index or in dividend reinvestment programs." There are 11 different asset classes from which to choose and three different tax systems in which to grow our money. Successful investing requires that we place our money in as many different asset classes as necessary to achieve our goals. Within each class, you can position for aggressive growth, moderate growth, conservative growth, income, or a combination of these. Basically, the closer you are in time to distributing your money, the more conservatively you should have your money positioned. The bottom line is to select assets, to dollar cost average, and to stay invested until it is time to use the money.

## A Systematic Withdrawal Program

A systematic withdrawal program is the opposite of dollar cost averaging. Systematic withdrawal programs are the most effective and efficient way to withdraw dollars during retirement. A systematic withdrawal program enables you to receive the income you need during retirement and still have your remaining principal grow large enough to help outpace taxes and inflation over time. Figure 5.2 shows an investor starting with $100,000 in life savings. The money should be put into a good variable annuity or mutual fund, or a combination of both, or several funds primarily designed for growth and income.

In this example, the investor has $100,000 and wishes to receive $8000 a year. The investor puts in the $100,000, it grows for a year, and then the investor pulls out the desired $8000. The remaining money in the account is still earning dividends that are being reinvested and still earning capital gains that are being reinvested, and the value of the shares on paper is still continuing to grow. On the right-hand side of the chart, you see that the year-end market value fluctuates somewhat. Some years it goes up, and some years it goes down. The investor is still withdrawing the same amount of money each year.

There are people who, in their retirement years, take their equities and move them into fixed accounts because of a change in the marketplace, and 99.9% of the time they are doing it after the correction has already happened. If you are not in the market on the downturn, you will not be there on the upturn.

You can change how much income you receive each month if you want to, because you are not actually annuitizing this. A systematic withdrawal program is not a product; it is a strategy. If you have a growth mutual fund, for example, the primary objective is growth, and dividend income is secondary. With a bond mutual fund, however, the primary objective is income, and

| Initial Investment $100,000 | Investment | Earnings | Withdrawals | Balance |
|---|---|---|---|---|
| 12/87 | $100,000 | $ 0 | $ 0 | $100,000 |
| 12/88 | 0 | 10,546 | 8,000 | $102,546 |
| 12/89 | 0 | 19,006 | 8,000 | $113,552 |
| 12/90 | 0 | 324 | 8,000 | $105,876 |
| 12/91 | 0 | 25,636 | 8,000 | $123,512 |
| 12/92 | 0 | 8,553 | 8,000 | $124,064 |
| 12/93 | 0 | 13,979 | 8,000 | $130,043 |
| 12/94 | 0 | -2,293 | 8,000 | $119,750 |
| 12/95 | 0 | 27,927 | 8,000 | $139,677 |
| 12/96 | 0 | 17,304 | 8,000 | $148,981 |
| 12/97 | 0 | 28,548 | 8,000 | $169,529 |
| Total | $100,000 | $148,529 | $80,000 | $169,529 |

**Figure 5.2. Hypothetical Systematic Withdrawal Plan**

growth is secondary. So, you would look for a growth and income fund, one that might be buying large-dividend-paying stocks and a combination of high-yield bonds. Or, you could look for corporate bonds that are paying out a good dividend, while at the same time the dollars are still growing.

You can do a systematic withdrawal from a 401(k) plan, an IRA, a variable annuity, a mutual fund, or a combination of mutual funds — whatever it is that you want to do it from — as long as you make sure your dollars are in a position to give you a combination of growth and income at the same time. A combined growth and income fund is an appropriate environment for your dollars during retirement because (1) it will give you the income you need, and (2) it will also help you outpace taxes and inflation down the road.

# Reference

1. Brinson, G.P., Hood, L.R., and Beebower, G.L., *Financial Analysis Journal,* July/Aug., 39–44, 1986.

# 6 Managing Expectations and Emotions

**M**ost investors let their emotions drive their investment decisions. When people start investment programs, they have their own expectations as to how their programs are going to perform. When their expectations are not met, most react by making an emotional decision — often the worst thing an investor can do.

If you do not manage your expectations, the financial world will. If your expectations are based on emotions such as fear, the media and salespeople will be right there to help you, even if their suggestions are not necessarily logical or realistic. Wall Street would have you believe there is a black box and that somebody is actually in control. As you will soon discover, however, there are no secrets. Nobody on Wall Street knows what earnings are going to push a stock up or which stocks are worth more or less than the prices show. When you listen to the nightly news, sit back and ask yourself, "What does this really have to do with me?" Worrying about the daily moves of the stock market is like watching a police chase on the 6:00 news. It plays on the viewers' emotions.

Meet Larry. Larry was the typical baby boomer investor back in the early 1980s. He had read how pre-1964 silver coins were going to be the next hot investment. He was mildly excited, but, being cautious, he held back until the next issue of his financial journal hit the stands. He flipped through the pages to read how silver coins were doing and became convinced silver was moving up. His hopes turned to real excitement. It made him feel like he had made a private discovery. Greed hit hard. He called his brokers and purchased two bags of pre-1964 dimes. You can guess what happened next. As soon as he had his hands on the bags, the price of silver started to drop.

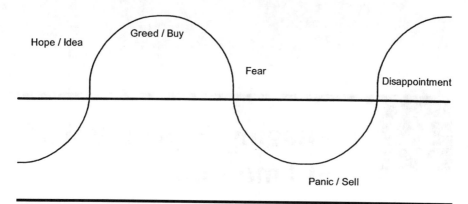

**Figure 6.1. The Emotional Roller Coaster**

Greed was replaced by embarrassment. Larry started hoping his invest-ment-grade coins would go back up. He would have been happy if they just went up to where he bought them. He would break even and would not have to tell his spouse anything about his stupidity. Instead, though, the entire silver market collapsed.

Embarrassment was replaced by panic. Larry tried to sell, but no one wanted to buy back the coins. He drove to a coin dealer in Las Vegas who gave him near the face amount on the silver dimes. That was half what he had paid for them. Still, he was relieved ... until the next week when silver hit an all-time high. Get the picture? We call this the emotional roller coaster ride of investing (Figure 6.1).

Another example is the investor expecting to earn a 20% return in mutual funds for the rest of his life without risk. Making investment decisions based on this expectation is unrealistic. In fact, an article in *Forbes* magazine noted that, "According to a recent survey by the Jersey City, NJ-based Institute of Psychology and Markets, the average investor expects an annual 18.6% rate of return on stock and stock fund portfolios." The article also stated that an expectation like that would put the DOW at 45,000 in 10 years and 210,000 in 20 years! If that happened, a $100,000 investment today would turn into $3 billion in 2068!

When people do not have realistic goals or try to play catch-up at an older age, they attempt to time the market and thus take unnecessary risks. When they experience a downturn, they wonder why they ever went into the fickle stock market. Well, the market is no more fickle than it ever has been. The problem is, when these investors read the newspapers, it sounded as if the market was going gangbusters, so they hopped on the express train. Then they

**TOP 20 MUTUAL FUNDS, 1995 TO 1996**
**ONE YEAR RANK VS. THE NEXT YEAR (1996)**

| 1st Year | Next Year | 1st year | Next Year |
|----------|-----------|----------|-----------|
| 1 | 2898 | 11 | 7261 |
| 2 | 7268 | 12 | 7297 |
| 3 | 45 | 13 | 1705 |
| 4 | 7283 | 14 | 6 |
| 5 | 262 | 15 | 2497 |
| 6 | 6290 | 16 | 2719 |
| 7 | 7233 | 17 | 7050 |
| 8 | 3473 | 18 | 3256 |
| 9 | 7256 | 19 | 5383 |
| 10 | 7061 | 20 | 7351 |

**Average run of top 20 in subsequent year = 4388**
**Average number of funds = 7857**

**Figure 6.2. Mutual Fund Selection.** (From RWB Advisory Services, Inc.; San Jose, CA. With permission.)

hopped off when things corrected. Most people are relying on seriously out-of-date information. By the time they find out that the XYZ fund or stock was the number one performer last year, it is virtually guaranteed it will not be number one again, but they jump on it anyway. In fact, look at Figure 6.2 and notice how many of the leading funds for one 5-year period ended up at the bottom for the next 5-year period. Sometimes, even the opposite was true; some of the bottom performers surfaced near the top.

On the other end of the scale, you have the people who settle for minuscule returns on cash investments because they are so intimidated by the whole process. How do you know what is realistic? You can do some research, read academic books on investing, or find an advisor who can help. It is unrealistic for investors to think they can succeed with no cost or very little at all. Also, things that appear to be free usually have a hidden cost. Investors tend to forget the historical risks and rewards of stocks and have a distorted expectation that this time it will be different (see Figure 6.3). It is interesting to note that nearly 80% of investors do not expect a one-year stock market decline of 20% within the next 10 years, and, according to most psychologists, investment decisions are 80% based on emotions.

Most people not only have unrealistic expectations about performance, but also about the price of performance. Especially in this decade, when the

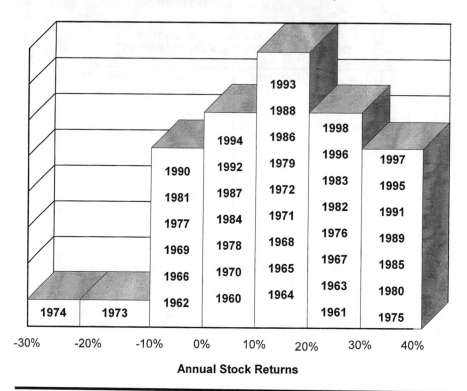

**Figure 6.3.** Uncertainty and Investment Risk

market has been up, there is a false sense of reality about how inexpensive it is to start investing and to do well. The Internet has really played to the do-it-yourselfers. The argument one hears is why pay somebody a commission when you can read a magazine and learn how to make 25 to 30% a year? This is an overly simplified view of things and can get investors in trouble.

Investors who simply have a goal of getting rich will usually fail because when the road gets bumpy, they will exit and look for a smoother road. However, those who love their professions and are committed and connected to their work can hardly avoid success. Why? Because they weather the storms and persevere. We think you should manage your money as if it is a business. Successful business owners are successful at setting goals, believing in them, and staying committed to their course of action.

Take a realistic approach by asking yourself the following questions. How did these funds perform during the down time? How volatile were they? Historically speaking, is my portfolio diversified and allocated properly? Remember that a well-diversified and allocated portfolio can reduce your risk

**Table 6.1. A $100,000 Investment: The Mathematics of Loss**

| | Year 1 | Year 2 | Year 3 | Year 4 | 4-Year Total | 4-Year Average |
|---|---|---|---|---|---|---|
| Mutual fund A | 20% | 20% | 20% | −15% | $146,880 | 10.1% |
| Mutual fund B | 12% | 12% | 12% | 5% | $147,517 | 10.2% |
| Mutual fund C | 15% | 15% | 15% | −15% | $129,274 | 6.63% |

*Note:* The Year-5 return necessary to average a 15% return for 5 years is 56%.

exposure over the long term and potentially enhance your overall return. Table 6.1 illustrates how detrimental wide swings in performance can be. Imagine what your expectations and emotions would be if you endured these wide swings of performance, compared to the smoother ride that is also illustrated.

Another example is what happened to real estate in the late 1970s. Anybody could make money in real estate — and everybody was — and then everybody lost it. Why? Because they had the false expectation that real estate would continue to keep doubling, which was ridiculous optimism driven by emotions.

John Marks Templeton said, "Bull markets are born on pessimism, grow on skepticism, mature on optimism, and die on euphoria." If you choose to invest in the stock market, you are going to have to get comfortable with being an optimist. Optimism is lucrative and realistic, and if you want to achieve financial success, you need to adopt an attitude of responsible optimism.

We want to stress the importance of using a personal investment advisor to help you learn to manage your investment expectations. A personal investment advisor can provide expert guidance in setting your goals, and because your goals dictate your expectations, you will be way ahead of the game. Find an advisor who has the courage to explain the cost of investment success and also the courage to deal with the fears and emotions most people have about investing. Any investor can benefit from this type of help, particularly in the area of proper asset allocation.

## Volatility

Volatility is nothing more than the ups and downs of the stock market. It is the price we pay for any investment gains that we enjoy. In other words, volatility is part of the process. It is the nature of the market to be volatile, and

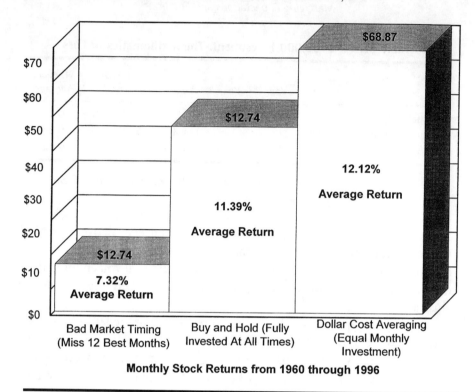

$70
$60
$50
$40
$30
$20
$10
$0

$68.87

$12.74

$12.74

12.12%

**Average Return**

11.39%

**Average Return**

7.32%

**Average Return**

Bad Market Timing
(Miss 12 Best Months)

Buy and Hold (Fully
Invested At All Times)

Dollar Cost Averaging
(Equal Monthly
Investment)

**Monthly Stock Returns from 1960 through 1996**

**Figure 6.4. Risk of Poor Market Timing**

investors must weather the storms in order to enjoy the sunshine. If you try to avoid the volatility, you will avoid the reward. So, we have to embrace volatility and understand it in order to participate and benefit from the market (see Figure 6.4).

While we are talking about stock market volatility, it is interesting to note that American consumers buy everything on sale, except stocks. Most investors do not think about stocks being on sale; they are too dependent on the hype they hear and read about in the media. Unfortunately, by the time the average investor hears about the market being up, it is already too late to cash in on it. But what do they do? They buy stock just when the market is ready to come back down. We could all benefit from listening to Warren Buffet, who said his favorite holding period for stocks is *forever.*

To forge a winning investment strategy, go back to the basics — learn to manage your emotions and your expectations:

1.   Set goals.
2.   Set realistic performance expectations.

3. Use proper asset allocation.
4. Track your plan every year to make sure you are still on course.
5. Prepare yourself mentally and financially in the event of a market decline.

In this next chapter, you will learn how to survive excessive volatility.

# 7  Asset Allocation

The essence of asset allocation is dividing assets among different areas of the market, which could include stocks, bonds, cash, and tangibles such as real estate. The purpose of asset allocation is to create an insulating effect around your entire principal so it does not move up or down as fast or as harshly — which, in turn, will give you a more consistent return over any long time period (5-, 10-, 15-, or 20-year time frame). Asset allocation can level the peaks and valleys of the effects of volatility on the value of your portfolio. There was more volatility throughout 1998 than during the previous 20 years. We really had not experienced anything similar since 1973/74. When you invest in a single area of the market, you can experience this volatility to excess.

If this describes you, then you are riding one horse, and that horse does not always place first every time, or even second or third. If you are too heavy in one sector or one stock, volatility will decrease returns over any given time period in history. If you try to own just one type of asset class, you will have in excess of a 40% deviation in any given year. Owning more and more different types of asset classes reduces your deviation. Twelve to 16 has been found to be the optimal number of asset classes. Holding more than that will give you a further decrease in deviation, but you reach a point of diminishing return. In reality, if you own 60 or 70 stocks, you have created your own mutual fund, anyway.

As you build your portfolio, it is helpful to take the approach that you are "employing" the mutual funds or stocks or bonds or real estate, much as you would employ somebody to build your home. You employ different stocks or

1-57444-258-9/00/$0.00+$.50
© 2000 by CRC Press LLC

mutual funds for a time period to help build your portfolio. If your assets are allocated properly (you own different types of stocks that have a history of moving at different levels of velocity during market changes), then you are going to be able to build a much more solid portfolio as you move on into the retirement years and even beyond.

This raises the questions of how many assets to invest in, and how often should you rebalance?[1] The answer is different for each individual, depending on age and the types of goals established. If you are younger, you can afford to let the growth stocks run a little longer before you rebalance them, but if you are three to five years away from retirement, or already in retirement, then you may need to review your allocation every six months.

As we get closer to retirement, we need to be invested in more stable asset classes, such as bonds of short- and intermediate-term duration and high and medium quality. Low-quality bonds can be used early on, but they should be de-emphasized the closer we get to retirement because of their volatility and the possibility of their price movement.

When we retire, we still have to maintain a position in stocks or equities to keep pace with or stay ahead of inflation. The ultimate goal or strategy of asset allocation is to give you the opportunity to earn a positive 2% after tax, after inflation. You can go back to the period from 1982 to 1995 and track the best performing sector, and then match it against the worst performing sector in each year. In 1982, foreign stocks were the worst performing sector, but in 1983 they were the best. The worst performing sector in 1983 was government bonds, but then bonds were back in 1984 as the top category. Your neighbor or co-worker may advise, "My fund did 36% last year — you really ought to buy it," but that is exactly the fund you do *not* want to buy because you are buying it at its peak and not its valley.

If you had been 100% invested in stocks over that time frame, you would have averaged 11.2% and you would have had seven down years. If you had been 100% in bonds, you would have averaged 8.7% and you would have had six down years. If you had invested 60 and 40% in stocks and bonds, respectively, you would have averaged 10.5%, with three down years. If you had been divided equally among stocks, bonds, and cash, you would have averaged 9.6%, with two down years. And, finally, if you had invested 20% each in stocks, bonds, real estate, foreign stocks, and cash, you would have averaged 11.2%, with three down years.

If you were trying to achieve an average rate of return of 10%, then you would have needed a 60/40 mix of stocks and bonds, but you would have to have been willing to accept 14% negative as your worst year and 34% positive as your best. Sometimes, you have to accept 12% or 14% as your rate of return in order to accomplish your goals, but with that comes added risk or volatil-ity. If somebody says, "I think I could earn 12% forever," they had better be prepared for a roller coaster ride, because their worst possible year is going to be a negative 23% and their best is going to be 48%.

The last three years have driven most people into complacency, thinking that they can earn 20% a year without risk. It is the first time in history we have had a three-year repeat (20%-20%-20%) with the S&P. We cannot afford to get complacent with this return, however, because history has proven it will turn around. After the market corrections of 1998, we started to hear about people deciding to delay their retirement because they lost 15% on their portfolio.

Investors need to understand that if they are going to try to achieve a 10% rate of return, there is going to be some volatility; however, if you properly allocate and have investments that do not carry a history of traveling at the same velocity of growth as stocks, these investments are going to create some balance on the backside of the portfolio and offer you a life jacket or buoyancy.

Investors also do not always have to accept loanership money as the rate of return. There are two kinds of money. *Loanership* money is what you are willing to give someone in return for some structure — a CD or a bond, for example. You are willing to accept a 4 or 5% rate of return on your money in exchange for structure and a sense of security with no risk. That classification applies all the way to the point where you are getting into the higher yielding type of corporate bonds. Once you exceed 8 to 9%, though, you have moved into *ownership* money. This is when you have assumed the position of own-ership and accept that the ownership of any business includes risk. That risk also carries with it the opportunity for reward over time.

The ultimate goal is to make your money work for you at the best level possible, with the least amount of risk or volatility. People usually invest based on one of two emotions: greed or fear. The problem is that fear is stronger than greed, which causes investors to sell out early, and with that comes the eventual loss of money. At this point, we should address two obvious questions: Which assets should I invest in, and what percentage should I invest in each asset? The answers lie in understanding effective diversification.

## Diversification

The term *diversification* is used so often by so many people that it has lost its meaning. Diversification is not asset allocation. In the financial world, diver-sification means not having all your money in any one type of investment.

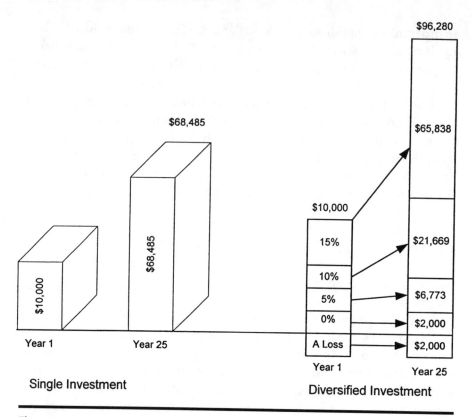

**Figure 7.1. Diversification.** These graphs illustrate the compounding growth on two $10,000 investments over a 25-year period. The $10,000 on the left assumes a single investment at an 8% return. The graph on the right assumes diversification of the $10,000 into five $2000 investments at different returns. While three of the five investments on the right were at a lower return than the single investment on the left, the total for the diversified side was substantially higher.

Mutual funds, by design, are diversified. Investing in mutual funds is the first step you can take to reduce your investment risk. Your overall investment performance should be less volatile with a broad variety of investments rather than in a single type. Figure 7.1 illustrates the importance of diversification by depicting a single investment of $10,000 at an 8% return over 25 years. It also illustrates the various returns produced by diversifying the same $10,000 investment into five separate $2000 accounts. Three of the five investments showed a lower return than the single investment, but the total for the diversified side was substantially higher. While it is true you would have been further ahead by being invested in just the "hot" fund, that is a matter of luck and not likely to be predicted beforehand.

Each asset responds differently to changes in the economy and investment marketplace. When interest rates drop, stocks take off. If you look back at the 1970s and '80s, the market was down while interest rates and real estate soared. The trick is to own a variety of assets, because a short-term decline in one can be balanced by others that are stable or going up in value.

The stock markets may go up one year and down the next, while other investments such as CDs might remain unchanged. Investors who own a combination of shares of a stock fund and bond funds are usually better off in such a situation than those who limit themselves to stocks only. The higher volatility of stocks and bonds means higher risk.

A diversified portfolio provides both liquidity and comparative stability. Suppose all your money is invested in stocks and you need to sell some of your holdings to meet an emergency. If the stocks in your mutual funds are depressed when you need to sell, you could be forced to take a loss on your investment (forget the tax deferral for now, as it is only one part of the equation). Owning other investments would give you flexibility to raise needed cash while allowing you to hold your stocks until those prices improved.

Over the long run, owning a wide variety of investments has been the best strategy. Money market funds or cash can provide a foundation of stability and liquidity that is ideal for a cash reserve. Bonds are good for steady high income, and stocks have the greatest potential for superior long-term returns.

The true measure of diversification is not how many different investments you have; rather, it is how negatively correlated they are to each other, so that when one is rising in value, the other is declining or holding a stable position. Investments, even if different, that move in the same direction will tend to increase risk and reduce predictability. The efficient frontier curve (Figure 7.2) is produced by plotting on the axis of the model what the probability of your return is in relationship to the risk of your portfolio. When your portfolio gets too heavy in a certain class or sector of the marketplace, your risk tends to increase, reducing your probability of return.

A portfolio of over 100 securities that are not properly allocated may carry a greater systematic risk than a portfolio of only 20 securities that are spread properly across industry and asset class lines. Having many investments that possess the same characteristics will not improve your portfolio's performance.

## Effective and Ineffective Diversification

Diversification is a prudent method for managing certain types of investment risk. For example, unsystematic risks, those risks associated with individual

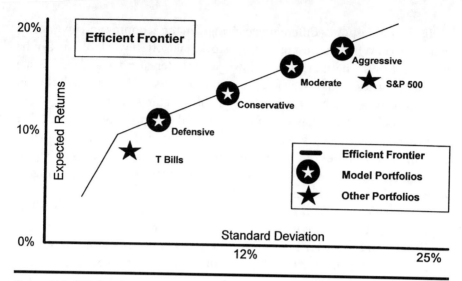

**Figure 7.2. Efficient Frontier Curve.** The efficient frontier is the point at which an investor's appetite for reward and stomach for risk intersect. For asset-class investors, there are strategies that use research to build standardized risk/reward profiles. Investors can often find appropriate portfolios within the above choices: global defensive, global conservative, global moderate, global aggressive, and global equity. Their equity allocations are 25%, 50%, 70%, 85%, and 98%, respectively. Once you determine your risk tolerance, you can select the model portfolio that suits you. Do not be swayed by the names of the portfolios. Each investor has his or her own risk tolerance. What is right for you may not be right for someone else.

securities, can be reduced through diversification. However, it is ineffective work to invest all your assets in the same market segment or in segments that tend to move in tandem. The risk is that all your investments could decrease in value at the same time. For instance, investing in both the S&P 500 and the Dow Jones Industrial Average would be ineffective diversification, as both tend to move in the same direction at the same time. Both are indexes composed of large, capitalized companies in the U.S.

Effective diversification (Figure 7.3) is having a portfolio of investments that tend to move dissimilarly. This is the premise of Harry Markowitz's Nobel Prize-winning theory (see Chapters 1 and 3). He showed that, to the extent that securities in a portfolio do not move in concert with each other, their individual risks can be effectively diversified away. The overall risk of a portfolio is *not* the average risk of each of the investments. In fact, you can have a low-risk portfolio that is actually made up of high-risk assets. When investments are combined in this way, you have achieved effective diversification. Many investment professionals now recognize that effective diversification reduces portfolio price

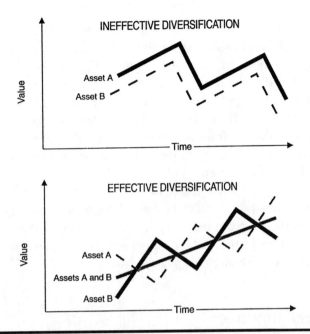

**Figure 7.3. Ineffective/Effective Diversification: The Concept.** *(Top)* Suppose you owned a representative equivalent of the S&P 500 Stock Index and the Dow Jones Industrial Average. Because both tend to move in the same direction at the same time, this would not be effective diversification. *(Bottom)* While all diversification is good, certain types of diversification are better. This was the premise of the theory developed by Markowitz, who showed that, to the extent that securities in a portfolio do not move in concert with each other, their individual risks can be effectively diversified away. Effective diversification reduces extreme price fluctuations and smooths out returns. Over the long-term, owning a wide variety of investments is the best strategy for the investor trying to achieve investment success.

changes in mutual funds and smoothes out returns when coupled with investments such as bank CDs and fixed-income types of investments.

## Combining Dissimilar Investments

Combining dissimilar investments can significantly enhance returns. If you have two investment portfolios with the same average or arithmetic return, the portfolio with less volatility will have a greater compound or geometric rate of return. For example, assume that you are considering two mutual funds. Each of them has an average annual expected return of 10%. How would you determine which fund is better? If one fund is more volatile than the other, their compound return and ending values will be different. It is a mathematical fact that the one with less volatility will have a greater compound return.

What do we mean by "low correlation"? Technically, correlation is a statistical measure of the degree to which the movement of two variables is related. (There is a simplified explanation in Burton Malkiel's book, *A Random Walk Down Wall Street*.[2]) If portfolios of volatile stocks are put together in a similar way, the portfolio as a whole will actually be less risky than any one of the individual stocks in it. It is this *negative covariance* that plays the critical role in successful management of stock portfolios.

Covariance measures the degree to which two risky assets move in tandem. A *positive* covariance indicates that asset returns move together, while a *negative* covariance means they vary inversely. As long as there is some lack of parallelism in the fortunes of individual companies in an economy, diversification will always reduce risk.

## The Secret Ingredient

Investment success is time *in*, not timing. Selection should not be based on hot issues. You have to look at the long-term percentile performance among peer groups. Given enough time, investments that might otherwise seem unattractive may become highly desirable (Figure 7.4). The longer the time period over which investments are held, the closer the actual returns in a portfolio will come to the expected average. This means short-term market fluctuations will smooth out.

The real challenge is to commit to a discipline of long-term investing and avoid compelling investment distractions. Commit to the strategy. With a long-term view, you can better choose investments that have the best chances for success. By adding the essential ingredient of time to your investment plans, you can almost be assured of success. Beware of conventional approaches that measure rates of returns over one-year periods. While this is the widely used approach, a 12-month time frame simply is not the best length of measure.

Do not listen to the news media, because they also use an extremely short time frame — often limited to that particular day! The media play to the public's belief that experts exist who can accurately predict when the market will turn up or down, and that a knowledgeable person can pick the *right* individual security or mutual fund. But, every year, about half or more of the mutual funds do not outperform their benchmarks, and those in the upper half one year have only about a 50% chance of repeating in any other year.

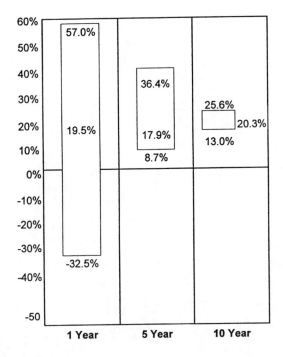

**ROLLING PERIODS**

**Figure 7.4. Risk Over Time.** Global equity portfolio returns from January 1972 to December 1997 (compound annual rates of return).

Uninformed investors believe that by regularly reading a financial publication, such as *The Wall Street Journal* or similar magazines, they become insiders to information that gives them some necessary advantage. When you look at long-term common stock investments, however, the ups and downs tend to straighten out. Wars and threats of wars merely become blips on the chart. Economic events are put in their proper long-term perspective. Analysis shows that over and over again, the trade-off between risk and reward is driven by one key factor — *time*.

## References

1. Rebalancing is a process by which funds are shifted within asset classes and between asset class to ensure maintenance of the efficient frontier.
2. Malkiel, B.G., *A Random Walk Down Wall Street,* Norton & Company, New York, 1973.

# 8 Taxable Investing

There are three different ways you can invest money: taxable, tax-deferred, or tax-free. In this chapter, we will talk about taxable dollars. For example, suppose you buy a mutual fund with money you have paid income tax on, and you pay tax every year on the dividends and/or interest. Then, when you ultimately liquidate that investment, you pay tax on the capital appreciation portion. So, eventually, the government is going to end up with 35 to 50% (depending on your tax bracket) of all the money that you put away. In the long run, the primary recipient of the results of the growth of that mutual fund — the dividends, the capital gain — is the tax man.

Another factor is that if you continually generate more and more income, that income goes right to the very top of your taxable income. Consider Bob and Helen Jones, who have a combined income of $170,000. They have been living frugally for years. She is 54, and he is 49. They have about $1 million, maybe a little more, in mutual funds. It is just hanging out there and generating about another $80,000 a year in dividends and capital gains. So that puts the couple in the 39.6% tax bracket (in addition to their state taxes) and they lose all their deductions.

This also typically happens with people who are doing day-trading — they are probably giving away 40% of everything they make. Day-trading gets a lot of exciting press, but such investors fail to factor in the tax man. It is the investor who is taking all the risk; they are risking capital they have already paid taxes on. The tax man has no risk. Next year, these investors could lose

1-57444-258-9/00/$0.00+$.50
© 2000 by CRC Press LLC

50% and actually go backwards. What they need to do, obviously, is either shelter that money for the future or do a tax shift (see Chapter 13). What we are saying is that the better way to invest your money is to do it systematically over a long period of time and to do it in a tax-efficient manner.

When you are dealing with stockbrokers, the only thing they look at are the gross returns. Many of you may have seen a *mountain* chart in a stockbroker's office that shows the history of the stock market over the last 25 years. They show you how if you had put a dollar in the market back then, this is what you would have now. They do not show you what happened to that dollar after taxes and inflation. Let's say that one dollar grew to $1000; after taxes, you might be left with $100 or $150. Factoring in inflation, that amount might be worth about $30.

There are several ways in which you keep your investment dollars exposed to taxes. Number one, you can put them in the bank at 5%, but inflation eats away at it at a rate of 3%. Then the government takes 40% of your 5%, and the end result is you are going backwards. Even though your account has more money in it, you have actually lost purchasing power. Your money is pretty safe because it is backed by the Federal Deposit Insurance Corporation (FDIC), but the FDIC is only an agency of the federal government. They get their support from the federal government. Why not just put your money in government bonds? The U.S. government is really safer than anybody because they have some awesome powers: They can tax and they can print money, and they can change the interest rate to cause inflation or deflation.

Municipal bonds are tax free, and that is a great thing, but the income from them could put you in another tax bracket. Plus, if interest rates go down, you could conceivably have capital appreciation on your bonds because the drop in interest rates would create a long-term capital gain.

Another thing you could do is put your money in corporate bonds, but those are semi-lazy dollars. They might get 6, 7, or even 8%, but you are paying tax as you go which lowers the actual return that you get on your money. And, there is the risk that the bond is only as good as the good faith and economic value of the corporation.

Yet another alternative would be to put your dollars into a fixed annuity. You might only get 4 or 5% but you will not pay any current taxes. The government is just waiting for you to take the money out at some point, and then you are going to pay tax. So, it is like a savings bond. You put in $50, take out $100, and pay tax on the ordinary income. That is probably a better idea than leaving everything exposed.

But, what if you did exactly the same thing and did not pay the tax? For example, if one person invests $1000 a month at 12% for 20 years, he will accumulate about $560,000. If another investor does exactly the same thing at the same rate of return, but shelters his money and delays paying taxes, he will accumulate over $800,000. The second investor did not take any more risk than the first, but was investing the dollars that the first investor was paying in taxes.

Let's break it down further. If you assume only a 10% return from each of those scenarios, in one case, you will get $56,500 a year; in the other, $82,000 a year. Then, if you are in the 40% tax bracket, you are going to net 60% of either of those amounts to spend. You will have a bigger net income as a result of your investment in either circumstance, but the end result is 30% greater if you defer your tax rather than pay it on an ongoing basis. You have not taken any more risk; you have just invested a little more tax efficiently. And this is what the average investor is *not* doing. The key to successful planning is not to rely on any one strategy to accomplish your goals. While it is true that you will need to have some investments taxed currently, they need to be at the proper levels and not be too much.

# 9 How Do You Climb Out from Behind the Eight Ball?

## Getting Out of Debt

**W**e live in one of the most prosperous countries in the world, yet we have one of the highest personal financial failure rates in the industrial world. Last year, 1.7 million Americans filed for personal bankruptcy, an increase of more than 360% since 1980. As a result of these bankruptcies, at least $44 million worth of debt was not paid last year.

Federal Reserve Board research shows that the proportion of consumer debt to income currently runs at about 21 to 22%. The U.S. Census Department released a study showing that 30.3% of the population lived below the poverty level for at least two months during the two-year period 1993 to 1995.

We searched the Internet and came up with the following ways to get out of debt, each focusing on a different aspect of the problem: (1) highest debt, (2) lowest debt, (3) highest monthly payments, (4) lowest monthly payments, (5) highest percent, (6) lowest percent, (7) fastest payoff, or (8) longest payoff. If you put all those side by side, there is not that much difference between any of them. The one that made the most sense and was the easiest to understand came from the Financial Independence Network, Ltd. (FINL).

1-57444-258-9/00/$0.00+$.50
© 2000 by CRC Press LLC

John Camood, president, has written a little program called *Debt Free and Prosperous Living*, in which he discusses a great way to get out of debt by targeting 10% of your income to reduce debt.

Most people work like neon lights — they are trying to hit everything. We need to change from the broad beam of a neon light to the focus of a laser. If all we are doing is throwing money at every debt out there, we will never make a dent in them, will we? Instead, we need to become absolutely focused on destroying debt.

What is the best way to do this? Take the account balance of each debt and divide it by your minimum monthly payment. That becomes a number and helps prioritize the debt. For example, suppose you have a credit card debt of $3000 with minimum monthly payments of $20, a car loan balance of $15,000 and minimum monthly payments of $235, and another credit card with $2000 remaining and minimum monthly payments of $15. On the first credit card, the number obtained with our formula would be 150 (3000 divided by 20), the car loan number would be 63, and the other credit card would be 133. For the payoff order, we start with the lowest number. So, the first one we are going to focus on is the $15,000 car loan. Now, assume you have been saving $200 each month; rather than continuing to do so, you are going to add that amount to your car payment and pay $435 each month.

If you look at how much faster the debt is paid off, the interest rate being charged does not matter. Instead of the 63 months it would have taken to pay off the car at $235 a month, it will now take us 34 months. Then, we will take that $435 and roll it over to the $2000 credit card with 100 months remaining. We will have it paid in about 3 months. Then, we take the $450 now available and add it to the $20 payment on the remaining $3000 credit card debt, which will be paid off in 5 months. When the debt is paid off, you have $470 a month extra in your budget to apply to savings. How much faster will you get ahead, saving $470 a month as opposed to saving $200?

This is the fastest and easiest way of getting out from behind the eight ball, but then you have to do a little "plastic surgery" — cut up the credit cards. Keep only one credit card, preferably one such as American Express, which you have to pay off every month.

Should we eliminate all debt, though? Banks leverage their capital and corporations operate most profitably with a certain percentage of debt. True, the interest on credit card debt can quickly offset any savings growth, but what about your home mortgage? The interest you pay is a tax shelter. More importantly, the capital you would have tied up in a fully paid home would earn far more invested than the market value on the home.

# What Can You Do?

The following are easy steps anyone can follow:

1.  Build a saving program and start saving money now.
2.  Turn your debt into equity.
3.  Evaluate future needs.
4.  Have a strategy.
5.  Maintain investing focus and discipline.
6.  Seek professional help when appropriate.
7.  Teach children about investing.

Let's examine these steps more closely:

## *Build a Core Savings Program*

The first step to creating a sound financial future is to develop a positive savings mentality. This might require changing your internal conversation about money. Many of us feel we do not have enough money to set aside a portion of it in savings. We complain that it is too late to begin, or we postpone getting started until some future event comes to pass. And, if we do have some savings, we do not want to risk them by investing.

Begin to identify good personal motivators for changing your own internal conversation, and practice making statements to yourself that reflect a positive, empowered attitude. Overcome the hurdle of getting started. Start small, but be consistent. Put money into a savings vehicle where you virtually cannot spend it. You will be encouraged by how quickly your weekly or monthly contributions add up. Challenge yourself to increase the amount frequently. From time to time, add a lump sum to your savings as if you are paying yourself a bonus or a reward.

Saving that is automatic is a far more successful method than just hoping to have some money left over at the end of every month. Set up a plan with your bank or employer for an amount to be deducted from your account monthly and sent to your savings account automatically. Consider this as paying yourself first. You will soon forget that it is even being deducted. Would giving up 5% of your monthly income really cramp your lifestyle? Whether you want to save for higher education for a child, a new home, or a comfortable retirement, *paying yourself first* is a prudent layaway plan for your future.

Utilize liquid or short-term interest/dividend-producing savings vehicles, such as savings accounts, money market funds, and CDs. Even after you have begun investing, retain a core savings vehicle for emergency funds. A core savings vehicle will be the base upon which you build overall financial security. The point is to first establish a safe place to start saving, then to build outward. Think of this core vehicle as the mother ship as you explore the infinite space of investing. It is your energy source.

*Saving is not the same as investing.* A *saver* is someone who saves money regularly but who does not assume the risks of ownership. An *investor* is someone who is rewarded for assuming the risks of ownership and who has an expectation of return through appreciation in the capital value of the securities owned. I see over and over people using investment products with a saving mentality who end up disappointed when returns are not regular or do not match advertised performance, and savers who end up disappointed because they never get ahead. The secret is to build your resources in a core saving vehicle and then to move into investing from this base.

## Turn Consumer Debt into Equity

Use the same muscles you have been using for years. You have regularly made payments on a car and/or credit cards and still survived. As you pay off consumer items, take the previous outgoing monthly amount and send that same amount to a mutual fund company or an investment fund. We have all built up this muscle, and we do not want to lose it.

Too much debt creates fear, and a decision made from fear is too often a wrong decision. But, there is an easy formula to follow to reduce your debt: Prioritize your monthly debts based on how long it would take to pay each of them off just paying the minimum payment due each month. Beginning with the debt with the shortest payoff time, add some nominal amount, perhaps $200, to each monthly payment. You will be amazed at how much faster that one debt will disappear. Now, take the amount you had been paying and add it to the monthly payment of the next shortest-term debt on your list. Continue with each debt until you are free and clear! Imagine how quickly that total sum of monthly payments will now build a savings account with no interruption of your lifestyle.

## Evaluate Future Financial Needs

Why are you saving anyway? Do you have a clear vision of what you want to achieve and how much money you will need to achieve it or are you shooting in the dark? Charles Greenwald, past General Motors chairman of the board, estimated that every hour of planning returns three hours of execution. What are your chances of accumulating a million dollars? This is the conceptual point of no return where most people feel so overwhelmed or defeated that they lose the motivation to even begin. But, if you saw that you could realistically have that much accumulated at a certain future date — and the math when double-checked actually added up — would you not then be highly motivated to begin saving?

This is where the difference between saving and investing begins to make sense. You can *invest* your savings at a return rate that will accelerate accumulation and put your financial goal within your reach — without risking your base savings. The methodologies in this book will show you how. Once you see that you can reach your goal, you can start on that road by comparing what you have now with what you need to accumulate to achieve that goal. This difference is called a *short-fall,* which is the amount of money necessary to fill the chasm between the reality and the fantasy of reaching your goal. Then you can begin to make your dream a reality. What better motivation is there in life than that?

### Establish a Core Investment Strategy

The problem is most investment strategies are full of two-dollar words that most people do not understand and are as unfathomable as an algebraic equation to the uninitiated. Investment people have their own compete language, as do lawyers, doctors, and other specialists. I am going to simplify investing language into concepts that make sense and that you can apply.

- Find a simple strategy that builds on what you already know.
- Find a strategy that organizes your resources — money and time — in order to achieve a specific result consistently. A good approach that builds confidence is to start small and watch to see if a certain result is repeated. The brain craves certainty and is always trying to distill the predictable from the uncertain.
- If you can benefit from reading a book that took somebody ten years to research and write, then you should do that.

The first action in this sequence is establishing a place for your money that you feel confident about and where your money will grow without you having to check up on it constantly. When you watch your money grow, your confidence grows with it. Start by making small investments ($100, $200, or

$1000) and watch the results. An index mutual fund or a favorite growth mutual fund is your best bet at this point. These funds can reduce investment risk through diversification and offer professional money management. According to Lipper Analytical, 94% of managed mutual funds underperformed the average performance of the S&P 500 index over the past five years.[1]

The point is not to get a 1% higher rate than in your savings account, nor to find the mutual fund with the highest return. The idea is to start to use an investment vehicle that you understand and that builds your confidence. You can expand that vehicle in stages. If you cannot sleep at night, back off.

Get started *now* in order to give your investment program as much time as you possibly can. Every year that you put off investing, accomplishment of future financial goals becomes more difficult. For every year you wait, you will need to increase both your monthly investing amount and the risk you take to achieve the same result. Go step by step, noting all the details. When you establish systems that work, a high degree of trust will accrue. Constantly make improvements.

## Develop Your Investment Focus and Discipline

Put time into developing your own personalized investment policy statement. This document should reflect your return objectives and constraints, such as time horizon, liquidity needs, and available funds. This will serve as the blueprint by which to measure the effectiveness of your investments. Look past all the hype and maintain realistic expectations. Upgrade your knowledge about investing. Education is the key to simplifying all the investment advice and products available and knowing how to apply proven principles to your own situation. Do not let someone tell you that he or she can achieve a 100% return for you without offering proof — lots of proof. Set investment boundaries. If something does not fit your plan, do not do it. Your personal investment policy statement can be a gauge to keep you from making emotional decisions about your investments that are inappropriate.

## Find a Financial Coach

Most people need some help with their investment decisions. Most of us are busy making the money to invest and do not have the time or expertise to research every vehicle. Even top athletes have a coach. True, you can get started investing on your own, but you will reach a point where a knowledgeable financial coach is your best guide to achieving the next level.

## Teach Your Family About Investing

Providing for your family is at the heart of everyone's financial concerns, but who said it was up to you alone? Do not operate in a vacuum, leaving those you care about in the dark. There is no better way to provide for the future of your loved ones than to teach them to help themselves. Not only does this empower them as participants, it also gives them a better appreciation of your efforts. Once you know your savings/investment strategy, and you can do it again and again, you are ready to teach it to your family.

# Reference

1. *Dalbar Mutual Fund Market News,* May 11, 1998, p. 10.

# 10 Basic Financial Blunders To Avoid

Aside from your partnership with the tax man, nothing can stop you from meeting your future financial objectives more than making dumb investment errors. The common mistakes provided below are not limited to inexperienced investors or those with moderate incomes. In fact, they have been provided by seasoned, sophisticated investors with years of hands-on experience. It is important for you to recognize these errors so you can avoid them.

## Being Embarrassed To Invest Your Small Savings

Small amounts add up. Begin saving something each month.

## Listening to Investment Noise

It is very difficult to stay on track with the tremendous amount of noise present. Develop a strategic, long-term plan and turn a deaf ear to the noise.

## Lack of Follow-Through on Long-Range Goals

Concentrate on those instruments designed to fulfill your financial plan instead of a hodgepodge of investments bought on tips, hearsay advice, or

1-57444-258-9/00/$0.00+$.50
© 2000 by CRC Press LLC

casual comments from friends. Customize your portfolio to reflect your objectives and your ability to assume risk. If you are a stock investor who likes to invest exclusively in one industry or sector, you may wish to consider abandoning this practice and instead diversify into several sectors. This can help reduce vulnerability to certain cross-cutting variables, such as government policies or consumer preferences, and can eliminate emotion-based actions.

## Riding the Emotional Roller Coaster

To take the emotion out of purchasing stocks, you could use a mechanical means such as dollar cost averaging that demands a specified contribution on a regular basis, regardless of market conditions.

## Lack of Detailed Records for Investments, Loans, and Taxes

Many investors fail to maintain accurate financial records. Make the effort; it can help you monitor the performance of your investments as well as aid your heirs after you are gone.

## Going Against All the Odds

Find out what is realistic and set your personal investment expectations to match reality. Start looking at stocks the way you look at life. Use guidelines to keep you from reacting to market fluctuations. The fact is, nobody knows what the market is going to do.

## Confusing Income with Appreciation

Do not confuse saving with investing. Do not expect index funds to pay high dividends or income. Understand your investments. Some stocks that have a high percent of earnings and dividends may be a poor investment in terms of growth, but a lot of people believe that as stock dividends increase, so does the worth of their holdings.

## Procrastinating

Becoming an investor is going to require some of your attention and time. How much time? Set time deadlines and take small, easy investment steps, one at a time, but do not put off starting.

## Not Having an Emergency Fund

Investments that lack liquidity either prevent you from getting your money quickly or force you to sell at discount prices. We have always heard you should have the equivalent of about six months' living expenses in liquid assets, or cash. Make a game out of saving to cover living expense and keep extending the time periods out further.

## Failing To Use Professional Advisors

Unless you have broad experience and plenty of spare time, you may be able to save more in the long run by obtaining professional help. Advisers such as financial planners, accountants, and tax attorneys can help you build and implement a comprehensive financial plan.

The real message here is to control everything you *can* control. Take actions that are consistent with your financial goals, and be guided by sound advice.

# Part III.
# Tax-Deferred
# Investing Plan

# 11 Annuities

With the creation of the Roth IRA there has been much discussion among financial planners whether annuities are still a viable asset to have as a part of your portfolio. The answer depends on a number of factors. What is right for one person may not be for another.

A *fixed annuity* is one in which the principal is put with an insurance company who guarantees a rate of return. In the early 1980s, this was great because you had double-digit returns without much risk; however, a reduction in interest rates led to mutual fund investing and to reinvesting the dividends. That all changed in 1986 when reinvested dividends were no longer tax deferred, so every major mutual fund company married themselves to an insurance company to offer variable annuities. A *variable annuity* is a mutual fund (called sub-account) with a tax wrapper around it, administered by an insurance company. The difference between a variable and fixed annuity is that money invested in a variable annuity does not stay with the insurance company. The investor decides which professional mutual fund money managers will handle the funds. Most variable annuities are flexible investment vehicles that allow you to continue to add money to them. A hybrid of the two is the *indexed annuity*, which takes part of the deposit(s) and buys S&P 500 index futures. The advantage with this one is that it has a floor and guarantees with upside potential, but for this discussion we will concentrate on variable annuities.

Another difference between fixed and variable annuities is that the variable annuity is considered to be a security under federal law and therefore is subject to a greater degree of regulation. Anyone selling the variable annuity

1-57444-258-9/00/$0.00+$.50
© 2000 by CRC Press LLC

must have acquired securities licenses. Any potential buyer of a variable annuity must be provided with a prospectus — a detailed document which provides information on the variable annuity and the investment options.

Working with a variable annuity you can develop an investment portfolio that is very similar to your qualified retirement plan. It offers you the potential for a much better long-term rate of return than a fixed-income investment, offsets the effects of inflation, and allows you to modify your investment decisions as the investment climate changes. Proper asset allocation theory would have you rebalance a portfolio from time to time. People who are paying a lot of taxes resist doing so because selling assets in their portfolio would trigger capital gain taxes; therefore, they tend to leave their portfolios unbalanced. This puts a portfolio at higher or lower risk which might not be as productive as a perfectly balanced portfolio. The variable annuity solves this dilemma because the rebalance does not trigger a tax.

The real power of tax-deferred annuities is not the deferral of the current tax, but the larger income stream they produce during the retirement years when you take the money out. For example, a single investment of $25,000 over a 30-year period, put into a taxable investment (assuming only a 28% federal tax bracket), would have a remaining value at the end of 30 years of $107,318. If the same amount were invested over 30 years in an annuity with full tax-deferral, it would have a value of $201,253.

At some point you will want to start taking income out, and let's assume it is at the end of the 30-year period of time. Which one of those lump sums is going to give you the greatest stream of income, the $107,318 or the $201,253, assuming the exact same rate of return on both? Let's say we wanted a 10% stream of income. The first investment, with a value of $107,318, at 10% will generate $10,731.80 of fully taxable income. The annuity, with a value of $201,253, at 10% will generate $20,125.30 worth of *partially* taxable income due to the exclusion ratio, which considers part of your withdrawal under various annuity settlement options as being a return of your already-taxed cost basis (original investment). It is easy to see that you are going to end up with a significantly larger amount of net dollars (see Figures 11.1 and 11.2).

Most high-quality variable annuity plans offer anywhere from three to ten different families of mutual funds, which means that in a single account you can have anywhere from 10 to 50 different investment choices. You can select the best choices from among several fund families and receive only one check during the payout phase, a feature which many retirees value.

Use of an advisor can help you establish your personal asset allocation for your portfolio. It is important to find a qualified advisor who can help you

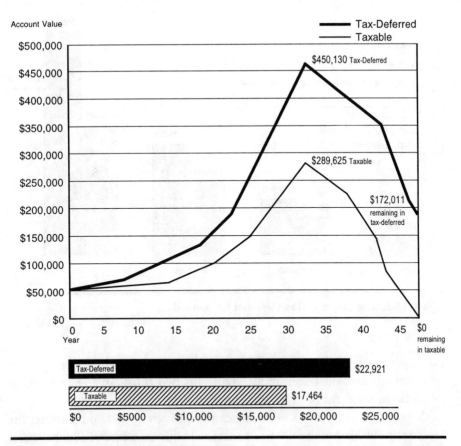

Account Value

Tax-Deferred
Taxable

$500,000
$450,000
$400,000
$350,000
$300,000
$250,000
$200,000
$150,000
$100,000
$50,000
$0

$450,130 Tax-Deferred

$289,625 Taxable

$172,011 remaining in tax-deferred

0  5  10  15  20  25  30  35  40  45  $0 remaining in taxable
Year

Tax-Deferred          $22,921

Taxable          $17,464

$0  $5000  $10,000  $15,000  $20,000  $25,000

**Figure 11.1. The Power of Tax Deferral.** *(Top)* Fixed payments for a specified period of time; the tax-deferred investment, assuming a $30,000 after-tax annual withdrawal, retains the accumulated value of the investment at a much higher level and for a much longer period than the taxable investment. *(Bottom)* Withdrawal of earnings only; if annual earnings alone are used to augment income, the tax-deferred investment also generates more income every year. The result: 31% greater net earnings from the tax-deferred plan. The longer the values are allowed to grow tax-deferred, the greater the earnings differential will be.

determine your own personal objectives and the best way to meet them. The first thing you and your advisor should do is look at the time horizon for the various investment sources you have. If, for example, you have money in short-term investments such as CDs or Treasuries that is earmarked for retirement, you are giving up, on average, one third of your return every year because you are only earning 5 to 6% on that money. Additionally, you are giving up all the future investments on that extra one third. Over a 20-year period, if you have also paid out one third of your investment portfolio in

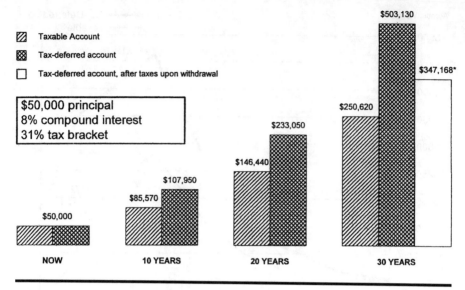

Figure 11.2. The Power of Tax-Deferred Compounding

taxes, your loss has now doubled. Ask yourself this question, "Twenty years from now, how will I feel about giving up two thirds of my investment portfolio in the form of taxes and lost earnings?"

Magazine articles and advertising campaigns advise that you consider the fees for annuities. Some folks are concerned with the perceived higher costs involved with a variable annuity, but a study done by Lipper for Fidelity Investments found that the additional cost, on average, for a variable annuity was only about .6% higher than traditional mutual funds when all their costs were included. This is the average, so you can find higher costs on both sides of the equation. One reason this can happen is that the fund managers for variable annuities deal with large volumes of money through insurance companies. They benefit from economies of scale, and their operating expenses are usually lower than those of traditional mutual funds. The insurance companies market the product, so the providers of the funds do not have the expense of buying television and print advertisements to promote the funds or staffing extra toll-free lines.

Most variable annuities have a deferred investment charge, which means that you are not paying a front-end investment fee which would lower your principal amount, but you will have a surrender charge for a few years. On the other hand, all the money works for you without a deduction for a sales charge.

# Restrictions

Like qualified retirement plans, variable annuities are long-term investment vehicles, and they have certain restrictions you need to be aware of. The most important restrictions are those imposed by the federal government. Like an IRA or retirement plan, because the government does not tax the earnings presently, you are required to leave the money invested until you are age 59-1/2. Early withdrawal will subject you to a penalty of 10%; however, there are ways to obtain the money earlier, without a penalty. In cases of permanent disability or death, the penalty is waived by the IRS. And you can also have the penalty waived by withdrawing the money in equal installments based on your life expectancy. If you opt for this early withdrawal plan, you must continue it for 10 years or until age 59-1/2, whichever is longer (per IRS code 72q). A worst-case scenario would be your needing the money immediately because of unforeseen circumstances such as a financial crisis. If that should happen, you will pay a 10% nondeductible penalty on any of the money you take out, and the earnings will be taxable to you as ordinary income.

You also need to be aware of possible deferred contingent investment charges. For example, if you were to start an annuity at age 45 and decide three years later that you want your money back, you would most likely pay a deferred investment charge to the annuity company, in addition to the IRS penalties.

# The Investment Benefit Guarantee

Another valuable feature of the variable annuity is the investment benefit guarantee, which is the only way that you can invest in mutual funds or growth-type investments and have your family or estate guaranteed a full return of principal (less any investments or withdrawals you have taken out) if you die or if the value of the fund goes down. How does the investment benefit guarantee work?

Let's say you invest $50,000 in a variable annuity today, and six months from now, due to a market correction, your investment is only worth $44,000. If you were to die before the market turned around and you were able to recover your earnings, your spouse or estate or beneficiary would receive the full $50,000.

Let's assume you invest $50,000, and three years later it has grown to $60,000. At that point, your new investment basis guarantee steps up to $60,000. (On average, this step-up occurs anywhere from once every three years to once every seven years.) In year four, the market corrects, and the value of your investment drops to $56,000; however, if you were to die, your family would receive the full $60,000. Because the investment basis guarantee provides a way to lock in gains periodically, it allows the investor to be a little bit more growth oriented in investments without having to worry about dying at a time when the market is down. Basically, you are buying a mortality policy, and you are not going to see that type of feature in a conventional mutual fund. The cost of this guarantee ("mortality and expense charges") is typically anywhere from 1/4 to 1/2% per year, but it is built into the overall variable annuity fee, so when you look at everything combined, you are not going to see much difference compared to the mutual funds.

## Investment Guarantees

Most people are not concerned with getting the greatest return; they are more concerned with the safety of their principal — and these guarantees let them sleep at night. Some variable annuities have a minimum interest rate guarantee. We think of it as a safety net you cannot get anyplace else.

## Estate Friendly

Annuities, whether variable or fixed, are also estate friendly. As a legal contract issued by an insurance company, the annuity is paid to a named beneficiary at death and can avoid creditors' claims and being tied up in probate. Another valuable feature of non-qualified annuities is the fact that you are not forced to start taking income or distributions out at age 70-1/2, as you are in retirement plans. Many people who look to these sorts of investments end up being more successful in their investment returns than they ever thought they would. There comes a point when the IRS requires mandatory distributions out of your qualified retirement plans. When that point comes, it would be nice to know that you do not have to take distributions out of your variable or fixed annuity on a non-qualified basis. While you are being forced to take distributions out of your retirement plan, you are still able to let the money in your annuity grow, and you continue to defer the taxes.

Please note that we are not really for or against any particular investment. What we *are* for is using the right tool for the right job, and annuities can be a very good tool. If you want to read more about annuities, please see Appendix D.

# 12 Is Your Retirement Plan an IRA for the IRS?

W hen IRAs were first made available in 1981, it made sense for you to put your money into one. Back then, you could have found yourself in a tax bracket as high as 70%, and if you put $2000 in an IRA, you got a big deduction. Your money grew, tax-deferred. The idea was, when you retired, you retired in a lower bracket. But the tax codes have changed many times since then. In recent years, we have seen the highest tax bracket climb from 28% to its current 39.6%. You cannot forget state and/or local taxes, which could be another 3 to 18% Now when people retire, they remain in the same bracket, if not a higher tax bracket. The typical modern-day retiree does not use the IRA money because of its tax liability. That is why, upon death of the last spouse, Uncle Sam winds up with much of the IRA.

Everyone tends to focuses on the rules of accumulation (i.e., you can only put so much into a 401(k) or an IRA), but overlooks the rules of distribution and transfer. The distribution phase is the best part — spending the money. People forget that they take "net" money to the grocery store. The amount of money that you have in qualified retirement plans is "gross" money. When you take a distribution from a qualified retirement plan, you must take out the government's portion of the withdrawal, as well. For example, suppose that 25 years from now you need to buy $1000 in groceries. You would have to make a withdrawal from your qualified plan of $1540 (assuming taxes are not higher than 35%) in order to net the $1000 you need to buy groceries. If, however, you had an account that distributed *net* dollars, you would only be

1-57444-258-9/00/$0.00+$.50
© 2000 by CRC Press LLC

required to withdraw $1000 for $1000 worth of groceries. If you had such a net account and it was the same value as your qualified retirement plan, it would last longer buying the same goods and services, and buying goods and services in the future was the reason you put money away in the first place. Also, if there is anything left over after your spending, you want to transfer it to the people you love instead of to the IRS and the probate courts.

There are basically two forms of assets: government and private. Government assets include Social Security, 401(k) plans, IRAs, 403(b) plans, pension plans, SEP-IRAs, Keoghs, etc. The government controls how the money goes in and how the money comes out. Private assets are yours to decide if you want to subject them to more government control or not. What if you could grow the private assets tax-deferred and then distribute that money tax free? That would be truly painless money!

When they retire, most individuals generally have some money coming in from somewhere — such as a pension, teacher's retirement, or part-time work. It is usually enough income for them to exist on. But, they also have their 401(k)s, which are now part of their IRA statements. Why haven't they started taking that money out as soon as they turned retirement age? Because of the income taxes, both federal and state, and the possible hefty penalties and additional taxes.

## The Too-Early/Too-Late Tax

The too-early tax is a 10% penalty for pulling your money out of your retirement plan before age 59-1/2, while the too-late tax is imposed when you fail to take the minimum required distribution by April 1 following the year you turn age 70-1/2. If this happens, the government imposes a 50% penalty on the amount you were supposed to take out. If you were supposed to take out $6000 as your minimum distribution, for example, and did not, you will face a $3000 penalty, plus the income tax on the $6000. That is an 85% loss! It is especially difficult for people who have investments spread out in various banks, credit unions, and brokerage accounts.

Suppose you retire at age 60 and have $200,000 in your retirement plan. If you used the rule of 72 and you had a 7% return, your $200,000 at age 60 would be worth $400,000 by age 70. Your minimum required distribution usually turns out to be somewhere in the neighborhood of 4% of the account. If the account is growing at a 7% return, you actually have a net growth of 3%. That is why we say that many people are unknowingly creating an IRA for the IRS!

# The Transfer Problem

A frequent scenario looks like this: A husband worked full-time and his wife was in and out of the workforce while they raised two or three kids. Assume the husband retires at age 60, when his wife is 58 years old. They do not take any money out of their IRAs if they can avoid it because that is their security. It is worth about $400,000 when the husband turns 70, and the couple take the required minimum distribution. The husband lives to the ripe old age of 85, and now the IRA is probably worth about $500,000. When the husband passes away, the IRA goes to the beneficiary, who is the wife. She can elect to continue the distributions from the plan, but because this is all the money she has left in this world, is she going to do that? No way. Her husband of 50 years is dead and she is all alone in this world. So, she keeps the money in the IRA and passes away a couple of years later. The couple had two children, but by then, one of them had already passed away. The surviving heir receives the $500,000 but will have to pay federal income tax and probably state tax, as well, so the money goes through the meat grinder.

Now suppose our couple also had a home worth about $300,000 and a $100,000 CD at the bank. If you include the $500,000 IRA, that brings the total value up to about $900,000. The amount over $650,000 (indexed) is also subject to estate tax, which is about 50%. That means about another $150,000 in taxes to pay, in addition to the federal and state taxes and probate fees.

Net planners have a saying: When you get a deduction as a business person, it is what we call a "good" deduction because Uncle Sam wants nothing back in return. A mortgage interest expense on a home is a good deduction, too, because Uncle Sam wants nothing in return. But, when you get a deduction by putting money in IRAs and 401(k) plans, there is a price to pay. A delay in taking money out of IRAs and 401(k) plans only creates a bigger tax problem later.

Our grandparents did not have IRAs and 401(k) plans, so our parents did not go through this transfer problem. It is starting to happen now for the first time. Uncle Sam is just waiting in the shadows to gobble up the money. What can we do to fix this picture?

# The Retirement Spend-Down Plan

Here is our suggestion. Use a *retirement spend-down plan.* It is less expensive to take money out of your IRAs and pay the taxes now while you are alive than to die with the money still in your IRA, but you have no idea how long you are going to live beyond age 59-1/2. Private asset money grows tax deferred and comes out tax free. Upon death, it also transfers income-tax free to the heirs. Because it comes out tax free, it is what we call "painless" money. When we retire, if we do own some of these assets, we are tempted to use them up first — because it is painless; however, by *not* spending the private assets down and keeping them for later years, the money continues to grow tax deferred and leaves a lot more tax-free cash for the back end. On the other hand, if there is a dime left in the IRAs, it is taxable.

## The Alternatives

Everyone should have a variety of income sources subject to different tax treatments at retirement because nobody knows what taxation will be in the future. This way you will be in more flexible in regard to your tax liabilities at retirement, as opposed to having only qualified plan distributions and Social Security.

## Another Consideration

Conventional wisdom told us to maximize our 401(k) plans and pay off our mortgages. Having done so, when you retire you may find yourself filling out an EZ form for your taxes. The same goes for business owners who have sold their businesses and do not have a complicated tax situation anymore, so they, too, are filling out the EZ form.

Rather than paying off your mortgage and maximizing an IRA or 401(k), it might be wise to invest in some private assets. If your employer matches the money you put into the 401(k), you should only contribute up to the match because your employer is helping you pay the tax on the way out. For any amount you can invest above the match, consider using alternative saving techniques.

## The Baby Boomer Story

After World War II, the folks who were fortunate enough to return from the war came back to an economy that was doing pretty well, so a lot of babies were born (see Figure 12.1), and these babies required a lot of goods and services. And, of course, houses had to be built for all these people to live in.

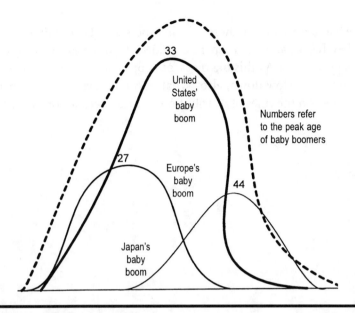

**Figure 12.1. Global Baby Booms**

Besides such essentials, the hula hoop was designed for baby boomers, as was the Ford Mustang.

A baby boomer born in 1946 was 30 years old in 1976. No wonder we had a massive real estate housing boom in the 1970s. When these baby boomers bought houses, they filled them full of stuff. Then they had a couple of kids and, after about five years or so, moved into a larger house, which led to another real estate boom in the mid-1980s.

Today the biggest crop of baby boomers are in their late 40s and early 50s. They are putting their money into 401(k) plans and retirement plans, and that money has driven the market up. Even if they buy CDs, 60% of the CD money in banks is invested in bonds, so their investments continue to drive the market up. Consider, too, the technology explosion. Prior to 1914, less than 10% of all U.S. households had a car. By the end of the 1920s, over 90% had cars — and it did not stop at cars. After Henry Ford perfected the assembly line, you had telephones, radios, talking movies, and so on. Technology was used to manufacture all kinds of things, and the technology explosion continues today. When computers and then microcomputers were born, the latest information became instantly available to anyone. Computer companies today are like the car companies of the 1920s, and it makes for one of the best times in history to be in the stock market.

But what happens when these baby boomers have been retired for a while? When they have pared their spending down to basic expenses and are no longer big spenders? As this big block of people slows down on consuming, the economy will slow down, also. What do we do when that happens? The key is to focus on the rules of distribution and transfer, not on accumulation.

# 13 Tax-Free Income

We can be fairly certain that the tax rate will increase, not decrease. When the government gets into a cash-flow problem, it finds ways to tax where the money is. Currently, most of the money is in 401(k)s, IRAs, TSAs, pension plans, and profit-sharing plans — qualified money, money on which nobody has ever paid any taxes. Qualified money represents the biggest bucket of money in the free world today, and the government is now eyeing that money, so the focus in this chapter is on ways to increase our net income at retirement.

In addition to the normal taxes on qualified retirement plans, the government imposed an additional 15% tax on excessive distributions. No one was taking the money out of qualified plans, because they did not want to pay this tax. People were taking minimum distributions at age 70-1/2, which the government did not like. So, they repealed the 15% surtax for three years, and then on August 5, 1997, Congress permanently eliminated it. This, of course, assumes that members of the next Congress understand the meaning of the word "permanent" (don't be surprised if the tax returns). The government has to go wherever the money is, so eventually all of the money people invest is vulnerable to the tax man.

The government also uses inflation as a tool for paying off its debts. The government tries to control inflation, which it does by either adjusting interest rates or by taxation. If the chairman of the Federal Reserve decides he wants to drop interest rates, the market responds. If the government wants to have more money, they have the options of taking away a benefit, increasing

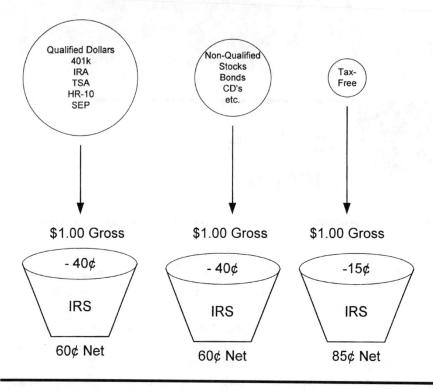

**Figure 13.1. The Three Buckets of Distribution.** Your objectives are to grow your money tax-deferred and keep it productive, keep your money for tax-free income, and pass the money on to your heirs tax-free through the use of estate-planning controls.

taxes, or printing more money. They make the rules, and the only thing you can do is play by the current rules.

There are three major buckets of money (see Figure 13.1). First, there is the 401(k), which represents qualified dollars. It is usually the biggest bucket, representing as much as 80% of all the income-producing property. Next is a very small bucket that we call the non-qualified bucket. These are dollars on which people have paid taxes. They are now investing the money and will realize tax-deferred income or long-term capital gains, but the money has been invested after the taxes were paid.

The last bucket is the tax-free bucket, but very few people have any money at all in this bucket. Basically, you have four items in the tax-free bucket:

1.  *Municipal bonds.* The problem with municipal bonds is that they are lazy dollars. They do not produce much income. Sure they are tax free, but they do not earn enough to keep up with inflation.

2. *Tax credits and investment tax credits.* These, too, are tax free, but the problem is that it takes money to earn a tax credit, and people believe they are giving up liquidity. This may be far from the truth, but how much liquidity do you still have in taxes you have paid?

3. *Roth IRA.* The problem with the Roth IRA is that you are severely limited so that you cannot put enough money into it; however, this should not stop you from putting some money into a Roth if you are eligible. In general, the people who should do it, can't, and the people who can do it, can't afford to.

4. *Variable universal life.* Here is an area where you can add as much money as you want so long as you comply with the 1986 rules and do not create a modified endowment contract. You set it up in such a manner that you can get your money out tax free.

We believe variable universal life could be one of the best vehicles that has ever been created to retain money while you are alive. That's a strong statement, so let us explain. Insurance contracts have always offered great tax benefits, but they have been terrible accumulation vehicles. But, because of changes in the tax laws for mutual fund companies, nearly every major insurance company now has sub-account money managers who have the same type of investment expertise as mutual fund managers.

Our suggestion is that you start thinking about taking your dollars and doing what we call a *tax shift*. If you are putting too much money into your 401(k), and you have already put the maximum in that is matched, maybe the excess dollars should go into a tax-free area. If you have dollars in non-qualified money that you want to start shifting, you may want to build up your tax-free bucket so you at least have some dollars that will provide tax-free income, thereby increasing your net income.

Important considerations at this point include figuring out what your tax bracket will be when you retire and how you can avoid paying more taxes than necessary. If you do go ahead and put all your money in tax-free strategies, is it not true that the government could one day change the rules? Yes, it could, but look at it this way. It is going to take a long time for the government to take a really close look at these options as viable sources of tax dollars; it is so much easier for them to go where the greatest amount of money is invested. In addition, Congress has generally grandfathered old contracts.

Probably the least desirable option is to pay your tax as you go and then pay the capital gains on the appreciated capital when you retire. You will accumulate less money, and it is very conceivable that you will elevate yourself to a higher tax bracket in the accumulation process. Not only will you lose money to taxes but you will also lose any gain to the taxes paid.

Another investment strategy is to buy mutual funds inside of a variable annuity, which defers your tax. So you invest your money, and you do not pay any tax currently, letting your taxes accrue as an investment, which offers you a way to control your tax. When you take money out of your variable annuity, you will pay tax, but you will accumulate more money in the variable annuity than you would if you just bought mutual funds that are exposed to taxation on an ongoing basis. When you take your money out of the variable annuity, it is all taxed not as a capital gain, but as ordinary income, which right now is a more favorable rate. You will have more money to use to pay your taxes due to the accrued value, and there is no guarantee that the capital gain rate will not change by the time you start taking distributions.

If you put $1000 a month into a variable annuity contract with 12% interest and you do that for 20 years, you will accumulate about $800,000. During retirement, taking out a 10% return gives you $80,000 to live on. Why take out 10%, when it has been accumulating at 12%? Remember that inflation is not going to stop just because you have retired, so you might want to leave a couple of percent in your account to continue to grow. If you are in the 40% tax bracket 20 years from now, you will be able to spend $48,000 of the $80,000 after tax.

If you are a 45-year-old investor and put $1000 into variable universal life insurance, at the end of a 20-year period, you will have accumulated about $585,000. A 10% distribution would amount to $58,500 per year, tax free (see Figure 13.2). In these examples, with the annuity you accumulated $800,000. With the life insurance, you only accumulate about $585,000, but your distribution is "net" because it is not subject to taxes.

When you invest money before taxes in a 401(k), IRA, TSA, HR10, pension, or profit-sharing plan, you get a tax deduction, but these investments become vulnerable to the tax man. One goal is to put your money away after taxes but get the distribution tax free. Sometimes it is better to pay taxes on the seeds rather than the whole crop.

Take a look at Figure 13.3, which shows how various items are taxed: Social Security, your pension plan, your profit-sharing plan, your 401(k), your regular assets, and your life insurance asset. The life insurance asset is the last asset that you want to liquidate in your life. You want it to become a death benefit if you can, because then the entire amount becomes income-tax free to your heirs. If you put your money into an irrevocable insurance trust, it is income-tax free and estate-tax free, but then you have lost the income from it, thus defeating the purpose.

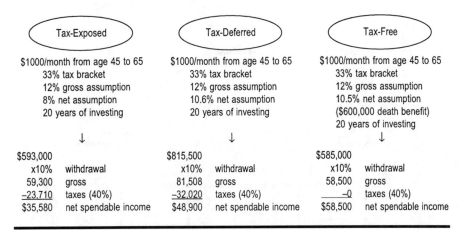

Figure 13.2. Distribution vs. Accumulation in the After-Tax Accumulation Market

Let's say you have a net worth of $1 million, you have $100,000 a year coming out of your 401(k), and you want to have enough income from your insurance contract to get another $100,000. In the first 10 years of your retirement, from 65 to 75, you would be better off using up your 401(k), then during the second 10 years of your retirement, you should start using the tax-free dollars. That makes sense, because chances are you will use a diminishing amount of money during the course of your retirement anyway, plus the value of tax-free accumulation tends to grow greater with time.

Let's look at the distribution in retirement if you or your spouse gets sick. We will assume you are a person who accumulated everything in a 401(k) because you worked for a company that had a good match, and at retirement you had $1 million in your 401(k), so you felt really good. Now, at 75 years old, you have got $700,000 left, and you or your spouse has to enter a nursing home. Say you need $50,000 to pay the nursing home. You will have to liquidate about $75,000 to $80,000 from your 401(k) and pay the taxes on it to net the $50,000 you need. As you can see, it will not take very long to kill off the qualified dollars. Instead, if you use tax-free insurance dollars to pay the nursing home, then you can preserve the dollars in your 401(k), allowing you to control your tax bracket.

Using your 401(k), you have no control over your tax. Let's say you are making $80,000 a year in retirement, and you are in the 28% tax bracket. If you draw another $70–80,000 from your 401(k) so you can pay the nursing home, all you have done is elevate your tax bracket from 28% to 36%. But, if you have some money in a variable universal life, you can take that money out tax free and will have no change in your tax bracket.

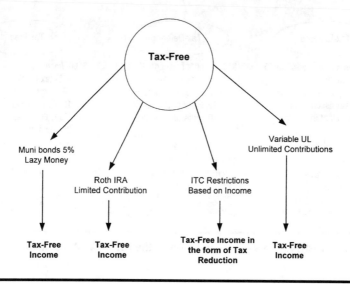

**Figure 13.3. Tax-Free Distribution**

Medical costs can literally destroy whatever a person has accumulated over a lifetime. People work all their lives and save and feel really good about themselves and their future. Then their spouse ends up in a nursing home, the savings evaporate, and then they look to Medicaid, which is usually not anyone's first choice. That is why the government has come up with incentives for us now. A Roth IRA is an incentive for us to try to accumulate some tax-free money so we can pay for our own benefits later on when we encounter all these problems. (It is interesting to note that there are currently at least 56,000 seniors over the age of 100.)

For further information about this product, refer to *The New Life Insurance Investment Advisor* by Ben G. Baldwin (Probus Publishing, 1994). Specifically, read Chapter 7, Understanding Universal Variable Life Insurance; Chapter 8, How To Invest in a Universal Variable; and Chapter 9, Getting Rich Using Universal Variable. This book thoroughly covers all aspects of these tax-avoidance vehicles and is a definitive guide through the maze of investment-oriented life insurance products in the market today. The information in this book is absolutely indispensable for individual investors and their professional advisors. Baldwin provides a comprehensive, insightful, and entertaining treatment of one of the most important tax-deferred investment options available in the 1990s.

*Warning:* Reading this next chapter could be hazardous to your present peace of mind. It is intended to turn upside down everything you ever believed about your home and its mortgage.

# 14 The Mortgage Myth

A s you read this chapter, you will discover ideas and proven techniques that will forever change the way you look at owning your house and having a mortgage on that house. Consider the possibility that what you have always believed about home equity and your mortgage may not be true or, at the very least, may not be the most advantageous method of equity management. As individuals, we need to expand our thinking to include the idea that managed debt might be beneficial, even when you take into consideration the disadvantages of consumer debt.

First, let's define home equity. Home equity is the value of your ownership position in your home (see Figure 14.1). An easy way to quantify your home equity is by subtracting any outstanding mortgages and/or liens from the market value of your home. Outstanding mortgages should represent the total of any mortgages, as well as home-equity lines of credit, liens, or claims against your property. The market value of your home can be approximated by finding out the price of any comparable homes in your neighborhood that have sold recently (or by consulting with a real estate agent).

Next, let's examine the common American notion that financing a home means a 30-year, fixed-rate mortgage. Instead, consider that there are many different types and styles of mortgages, just as are there different types and styles of automobiles. Each one is designed to meet a specific goal or purpose. Maybe the first advice you heard on how to finance your house went something like this: "Get a fixed-rate mortgage; otherwise, the rate will go up and you won't be able to afford the payment anymore. The lender will foreclose

1-57444-258-9/00/$0.00+$.50
© 2000 by CRC Press LLC

**Fair Market Value (FMV) – Mortgage(s) = Home Equity**

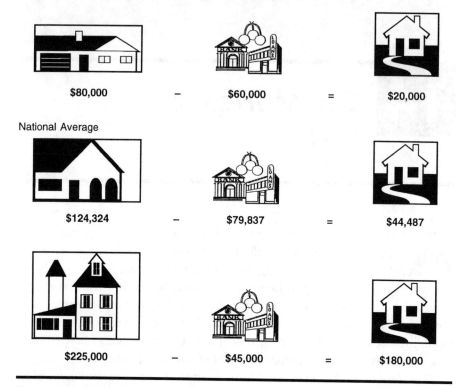

| $80,000 | – | $60,000 | = | $20,000 |

National Average

| $124,324 | – | $79,837 | = | $44,487 |

| $225,000 | – | $45,000 | = | $180,000 |

**Figure 14.1. National Average Numbers from Federal Reserve Board, April 1998**

and take your home away from you." So, you took out a 30-year, fixed-rate mortgage for your house without realizing that there are viable reasons to consider the multitude of variable-rate mortgages. Nor did you understand that a 30-year, fixed-rate mortgage is usually the most costly to the consumer and the most profitable for the lending institution.

Much of how most Americans behave and think about both investing and debt has been passed down from one generation to the next. The typical American has remained true to traditions that were prevalent before the turn of the century. Though successful businesses stay current and on the cutting edge when it comes to money management (more specifically, debt management), when it comes to making important personal decisions regarding debt and money management, most individuals still rely on what their parents and grandparents did, which today is not necessarily correct.

Your home is probably the single biggest investment you will make. As one of your largest assets, it is imperative that you make a wise choice, not only in regard to how to finance it but also, more importantly, in regard to how to manage this asset wisely all throughout your ownership.

The print media are full of articles and advertisements for a wide variety of mortgage strategies. To make the best choice, you need all the facts regarding each strategy, but you also need to know how to assess your individual financial circumstances in order to make the wisest decision. It is hoped that this chapter will give you enough information to make a wise decision.

The following three questions are a good way to measure *any* investment and must be clearly understood in order for you to manage your equity as successful individuals and businesses do.

1. Is your investment safe?
2. Is your investment liquid?
3. Does your investment earn a rate of return?

Asking these same three questions about home equity might help us better understand the wisest place to position our home equity:

1. Is your home equity safe?
2. Is your home equity liquid?
3. Does your home equity earn a rate of return?

## Is Your Home Equity Safe?

Safety is often confused with stability. A CD in a bank is stable; because of the FDIC, you will never lose your money. But a CD is not safe against inflation. A CD is not safe against taxes. A CD is not safe against lost opportunities had it been invested elsewhere. Similarly, your home equity is not safe against the upward and downward movements in the real estate marketplace. Many homeowners in the New England area watched their home equity vanish in the 1980s and 1990s.

Remember the drop in oil prices in the 1980s which had such a severe impact on the economy in Houston, TX? Over 15,000 homes were turned back over to lenders because people lost their jobs and could not make their mortgage payments. Most of these homes were sold in the open marketplace at or below their outstanding mortgage, which meant most consumers lost all their home equity.

A few years back, we had a client who lived just outside of Springfield, OH, who was contemplating downsizing her home in preparation for her retirement years. Her home was valued at $75,000, and she only owed $25,000 on a first mortgage, but then, just two blocks away from her home, a trash landfill was built. What do you think happened to the value of her home equity? Where she spends her retirement years has been determined for her because of the landfill. Her home equity was not safe against external forces over which she had no control.

Consider the family that owned a home in Texas valued at $250,000 in the early 1980s. They had a mortgage of $150,000. Their equity position in their property was $100,000. Unexpectedly, he (like so many other individuals during the oil crisis in Texas) was given a pink slip and had to live off of his inadequate cash reserves, which ran out in only about two months. He went to a local lending institution and said, "I've got a house valued at $250,000; I only owe $150,000, and I have $100,000 of equity. Here are my credentials; you can see all those initials after my name. I've got all these accolades and referrals, and it's just a matter of time before I get a high-class job or return to a position in my career field. Please lend me $25,000 of my $100,000 equity to help me and my family get by until I find another job." What do you think the lender said? He said, "Hey, you're about the fourteen thousandth person to come through my door. *I'm an income lender, not an asset lender.* I don't want to own any more houses; I'm already gonna get stuck owning more than I want to. What ability do you have to pay me back?" His application for an equity loan, like so many others during this time, was denied. He, like so many others, had his home foreclosed and lost all his home equity when the bank was forced to sell it in a very depressed market.

Keep in mind that your home equity is *not* safe.

## Is Your Home Equity Liquid?

By liquid, we mean how easily can we convert it into cash or separate it from the property? A CD, as an example, is very liquid in that we can cash it in any time and typically only be penalized 3 months' interest. A stock or bond, on the other hand, is not considered liquid because the penalty could be severe if market conditions are depressed when we need to cash it in. Let's consider how easily we can convert our home equity into cash. To convert our home equity or separate our home equity from our property we could:

1.  Refinance the original mortgage.
2.  Obtain a new first mortgage.
3.  Obtain a second mortgage or equity line of credit.
4.  Sell or rent the home.

The first three alternatives all require financial underwriting, but financial institutions are income lenders, not asset lenders.

Suppose you are in an automobile accident, and as a result of the accident you are disabled for 18 months. (Note that the number one reason for foreclosures on home mortgages is disability; the number two reason is termination of employment.) You lose your job because your employer is not large enough to keep you on the payroll or hold the job until you are well again. So, you are forced to live off your cash reserves and savings, which hold you for about 3 or 4 months. Now that the money has run out and because you have been the primary breadwinner, the pressure mounts for you to continue to provide for your family. You contact your local lender to get access to some of the equity in your home. Your home is valued at $150,000 and you only owe $50,000 on a first mortgage, thus you have $100,000 equity in your home. Will you qualify for an equity line or second mortgage? No. Again, lenders are income lenders not asset lenders. Lenders want to know what ability you have to pay back the money borrowed.

Even though you are not completely recovered, in 12 months you find a job in an unrelated career field. Now you have income coming in. You again approach the lender. Because you ran up your credit cards and borrowed from the in-laws to get through your time of unemployment, you now want to consolidate these bills with a single lower interest rate loan. Surely the lender will not deny you a loan now. Not true! Because you are no longer in your former career, the lender will now want you to have one to two years' experience in your new position before looking favorably on approving your requested loan.

It should be obvious at this point that your home equity is *not* liquid. For this reason, we counsel many of our clients to apply now for an equity line of credit. That way if the financial need ever arises they are *pre*-approved. When should you apply for a loan, then? When you do not need one, which is when you look the strongest financially.

## Does Your Home Equity Earn a Rate of Return?

This can be best understood by the following illustration. Place a dollar bill inside a can, put a top on the can, and seal it up tightly so no outside elements can get in. Then at 2:00 a.m. one morning when most people are sound asleep, sneak outside and make a map of your backyard. Count out so many paces one way and so many paces another way and just so many paces from that oak tree. Pull the turf back and dig a hole. Then put the can with the dollar bill sealed inside down in the hole. Put topsoil on top and the turf on top of the soil so no one can tell that anything has been buried.

Now, let's apply the three-question test for measuring an investment. Is the dollar *safe* inside the can? Yes, as long as nobody saw it being buried, as long as the map isn't lost, as long as the can remains sealed and no outside elements or bugs can get in to destroy the dollar bill. Is it *liquid?* Yes — anytime you want to, you can dig it up and spend it. How about the last question, though. Does your dollar bill *earn a rate of return?* No.

Now, wait a second. Do you mean to tell me that a week later, if I dig up the can and shake it, I won't hear some change rattling around because it has earned interest while buried in the ground? Of course not. And the same thing happens when you take your dollar bills and put them into windows, doors, mortar, garage doors, or carpeting (i.e., your equity). Your equity in your house does not earn a rate of return.

Let's say there are two identical houses side by side, each constructed by the same construction company, and everything inside the houses is identical, too. One of the houses is purchased by a little old lady who pays $100,000 in cash. Maybe the money was an inheritance or maybe it was her life's savings. The identical house next door is purchased by a veteran. Instead of paying $100,000 cash, the veteran finances 100% of the cost by taking out a GI loan for the full amount. How much equity does the little old lady have? 100%, or $100,000. How much equity does the ex-GI have? None.

Assume now that in one year the houses appreciate by 4%. What, then, is the market value of each house? $104,000, right? How much dollar increase in equity did the little old lady who paid cash for the house receive? $4000. How much dollar increase in equity did the veteran, who started out with no equity, receive? $4000. Do not confuse appreciation of your home with a rate of return on the equity that you have in the home. The equity in your home does *not* earn a rate of return. Now, let's apply our three questions to home equity as an investment again:

1. Is your home equity safe? No.
2. Is your home equity liquid? No.
3. Does your home equity earn a rate of return? No.

What does this tell you? Your home equity is a dead asset. It is not safe, it is not liquid, and, most importantly, it does not earn a rate of return. Let's examine the merits of separating our home equity for investment purposes. If the equity is left in your home, an opportunity cost is incurred because the equity is not working for you and it is not invested in a manner that generates investment earnings.

In order for equity to earn a rate of return, it must be converted to cash. In order to separate your equity from your home, you must obtain a mortgage. A mortgage requires the borrower to pay interest over time. The interest expense is the employment cost of borrowing. Because home equity offers no economic benefit other than reducing mortgage payments, each family should examine the opportunity and employment costs of converting their home equity into investable dollars.

Some people would suggest that you need to find investments that are going to earn a higher after-tax return than the after-tax cost of the mortgage in order to justify separating equity from your home. Not us! It is great if you can earn more on your investment than you pay to borrow, and we know for a fact that there are many investments that will easily beat the cost of a mortgage. However, depending on one's risk tolerance and financial objectives, this will not always be the case, and it does not need to be. Figure 14.2 shows the past performance over 10- and 20-year periods for selected investments and the cost of mortgage financing.

Let's discuss the employment cost of separating your equity from your home. As an example, assume that John Q. Public has a home valued at $150,000. John owns this home free and clear. As illustrated in Figure 14.3, John can take out a $120,000 first mortgage financed over 30 years at 8% interest. His employment cost would be a mortgage payment of $880.52 every month each year for 30 years. At the end of 30 years, he would have paid back his borrowed principal of $120,000 and another $196,983 in interest to the lending institution, for a total of $316,983.

What would be John's true net employment cost each year? Not $10,566.24 ($880.52 monthly payment × 12 months). A majority of that $10,566.24 is interest ($9564), which provides tax relief each year. In an overall 35% tax bracket, that equates to a $3347 tax savings in the first year, or approximately $280 tax savings per month in the initial months of the mortgage. So, John's true net employment cost is about $600 each month in the first year of his mortgage.

Let's discuss John's potential opportunity if he invested the $120,000 (see Figure 14.4). Investing $120,000 at 6% will grow to $689,219. Here is a not too difficult question: Would you be willing to give up $316,000 (employment cost) to make $689,000? There are guaranteed contracts that earn better than 6%! What if you could get 8%? That figure then would grow to $1.2 million. Would you be willing to give up $316,000 to make $1.2 million? And what if you could make 12% on your $120,000 investment? The average balanced mutual fund for the last 10 years has averaged 12.9% (see Figure 14.5). At 12%, your investment grows to over $3.5 million. Would you be willing to give up $316,000 to make $3.5 million?

| | S&P 500 Index[1] | Dow Jones Industrial Average[2] | Fixed-Rate Mortgages[3] | ARMs[3] |
|---|---|---|---|---|
| 1978 | 6.39 | 2.79 | 9.63 | N/A |
| 1979 | 18.2 | 10.55 | 11.19 | N/A |
| 1980 | 32.27 | 22.17 | 13.77 | N/A |
| 1981 | −5.01 | −3.57 | 16.64 | N/A |
| 1982 | 21.44 | 27.11 | 16.09 | N/A |
| 1983 | 22.39 | 25.97 | 13.23 | N/A |
| 1984 | 6.1 | 1.31 | 13.87 | 11.51 |
| 1985 | 31.63 | 33.55 | 12.42 | 10.05 |
| 1986 | 18.56 | 27.1 | 10.18 | 8.42 |
| 1987 | 5.1 | 5.48 | 10.2 | 7.82 |
| **10-yr average** | **18.76** | **19.21** | **18.78** | **6.5 (14-yr)** |
| 1988 | 16.23 | 16.14 | 10.33 | 7.9 |
| 1989 | 31.37 | 32.19 | 10.32 | 8.81 |
| 1990 | −3.27 | −0.56 | 10.13 | 8.36 |
| 1991 | 30.47 | 24.19 | 9.25 | 7.1 |
| 1992 | 7.61 | 7.41 | 8.4 | 5.63 |
| 1993 | 10.02 | 16.94 | 7.33 | 4.59 |
| 1994 | 1.32 | 5.02 | 8.36 | 5.34 |
| 1995 | 37.57 | 36.94 | 7.95 | 6.07 |
| 1996 | 22.96 | 28.91 | 7.81 | 5.67 |
| 1997 | 33.36 | 24.94 | 7.9 | 5.61 |
| **20-yr average** | **17.24** | **17.23** | **10.75** | **7.35 (14-yr)** |

**Figure 14.2. Performance of Investments and Cost of Mortgages Over a 10- and 20-Year Period (ending December 31, 1997).** Past performance is no guarantee of future results. Investment returns and the principal value of common stock will fluctuate. ARM (adjustable rate mortgage) rates are shown for only the 14 years of available data and will also fluctuate. No adjustments have been made for any income tax liabilities or deductions, nor for any mortgage and investment acquisition expenses. [1]From CDA/Wiesenberger, 1998. [2]From Chase Global Data and Research. [3]From Freddie Mac, 1998.

Now consider the case of John and Mary, who are both 55 years of age and whose $150,000 home has been completely paid off for five years now. They would like to retire at age 65, but after meeting with their financial planner, they realize they will have a considerable shortfall in their projected monthly retirement income. Getting started late in life, they have been saving 24% of their gross income. They do not feel as if they could save any more without dramatically reducing their current lifestyle. They do not want to push back their scheduled retirement age of 65 and are seeking advice to make up this shortfall over the next 10 years.

Our recommendation is for John and Mary to take out a $120,000 mortgage and to leave 20% equity in the home so they do not have to pay private

Loan Principal: $120,000.00
Monthly Loan Payment: $880.52

Loan Interest Rate: 8.00%
Loan Term in Years: 30.00

| Yr | Principal Balance | Annual Principal Paid | Annual Interest Paid | Principal Paid to Date | | Interest Paid to Date | | |
|---|---|---|---|---|---|---|---|---|
| 1 | 118,998 | 1,002 | 9,564 | 1,002 | + | 9,564 | = | $10,566 |
| 2 | 117,912 | 1,086 | 9,481 | 2,088 | | 19,044 | | |
| 3 | 116,736 | 1,176 | 9,390 | 3,264 | | 28,435 | | |
| 4 | 115,463 | 1,273 | 9,293 | 4,537 | | 37,728 | | |
| 5 | 114,084 | 1,379 | 9,187 | 5,916 | | 46,915 | | |
| 6 | 112,590 | 1,494 | 9,073 | 7,410 | | 55,988 | | |
| 7 | 110,973 | 1,617 | 8,949 | 9,027 | | 64,936 | | |
| 8 | 109,221 | 1,752 | 8,815 | 10,779 | | 73,751 | | |
| 9 | 107,324 | 1,897 | 8,669 | 12,676 | | 82,420 | | |
| 10 | 105,269 | 2,055 | 8,512 | 14,731 | | 90,932 | | |
| 11 | 103,044 | 2,225 | 8,341 | 16,956 | | 99,273 | | |
| 12 | 100,634 | 2,410 | 8,156 | 19,366 | | 107,429 | | |
| 13 | 98,024 | 2,610 | 7,956 | 21,976 | | 115,386 | | |
| 14 | 95,198 | 2,826 | 7,740 | 24,802 | | 123,125 | | |
| 15 | 92,137 | 3,061 | 7,505 | 27,863 | | 130,631 | | |
| 16 | 88,822 | 3,315 | 7,251 | 31,178 | | 137,882 | | |
| 17 | 85,232 | 3,590 | 6,976 | 34,768 | | 144,858 | | |
| 18 | 81,343 | 3,888 | 6,678 | 38,657 | | 151,536 | | |
| 19 | 77,133 | 4,211 | 6,355 | 42,867 | | 157,891 | | |
| 20 | 72,572 | 4,560 | 6,006 | 47,428 | | 163,897 | | |
| 21 | 67,633 | 4,939 | 5,627 | 52,367 | | 169,524 | | |
| 22 | 62,284 | 5,349 | 5,217 | 57,716 | | 174,742 | | |
| 23 | 56,491 | 5,793 | 4,773 | 63,509 | | 179,515 | | |
| 24 | 50,218 | 6,274 | 4,293 | 69,782 | | 183,807 | | |
| 25 | 43,423 | 6,794 | 3,772 | 76,577 | | 187,579 | | |
| 26 | 36,065 | 7,358 | 3,208 | 83,935 | | 190,787 | | |
| 27 | 28,096 | 7,969 | 2,597 | 91,904 | | 193,385 | | |
| 28 | 19,466 | 8,630 | 1,936 | 100,534 | | 195,320 | | |
| 29 | 10,119 | 9,347 | 1,219 | 109,881 | | 196,540 | | |
| 30 | 0 | 10,119 | 444 | 120,000 | + | 196,983 | = | $316,983 |

**Figure 14.3. Loan Amortization Schedule**

mortgage insurance. They could invest the $120,000 wisely, perhaps in a sound mutual fund. When John and Mary saw the loan amortization schedule (Figure 14.3), Mary exclaimed, "We can't afford that $880 monthly mortgage payment!" We reassured them it will be taken care of. Next, John said, "Wait a second. I'm 55, and this mortgage won't be paid off until I'm 85 years old!" We reassured John that he can pay it off sooner if he so elects and it is in his best interest to do so.

## INVESTMENT ACCUMULATION ANALYSIS

| Yr | Net Outlay | Fund 1 @ 6% End of Yr Value | Fund 2 @ 8% End of Yr Value | Fund 3 @ 10% End of Yr Value | Fund 4 @ 12% End of Yr Value |
|---|---|---|---|---|---|
| 1 | 120,000 | 127,200 | 129,600 | 132,000 | 134,400 |
| 2 | 0 | 134,832 | 139,968 | 145,200 | 150,528 |
| 3 | 0 | 142,922 | 151,165 | 159,720 | 168,591 |
| 4 | 0 | 151,497 | 163,259 | 175,692 | 188,822 |
| 5 | 0 | 160,587 | 176,319 | 193,261 | 211,481 |
| 6 | 0 | 170,222 | 190,425 | 212,587 | 236,859 |
| 7 | 0 | 180,436 | 205,659 | 233,846 | 265,282 |
| 8 | 0 | 191,262 | 222,112 | 257,231 | 297,116 |
| 9 | 0 | 202,737 | 239,881 | 282,954 | 332,769 |
| 10 | 0 | 214,902 | 259,071 | 311,249 | 372,702 |
| 11 | 0 | 227,796 | 279,797 | 342,374 | 417,426 |
| 12 | 0 | 241,464 | 302,180 | 376,611 | 467,517 |
| 13 | 0 | 255,951 | 326,355 | 414,273 | 523,619 |
| 14 | 0 | 271,308 | 352,463 | 455,700 | 586,453 |
| 15 | 0 | 287,587 | 380,660 | 501,270 | 656,828 |
| 16 | 0 | 304,842 | 411,113 | 551,397 | 735,647 |
| 17 | 0 | 323,133 | 444,002 | 606,536 | 823,925 |
| 18 | 0 | 342,521 | 479,522 | 667,190 | 922,796 |
| 19 | 0 | 363,072 | 517,884 | 733,909 | 1,033,531 |
| 20 | 0 | 384,856 | 559,315 | 807,300 | 1,157,555 |
| 21 | 0 | 407,948 | 604,060 | 888,030 | 1,296,462 |
| 22 | 0 | 432,424 | 652,385 | 976,833 | 1,452,037 |
| 23 | 0 | 458,370 | 704,576 | 1,074,516 | 1,626,282 |
| 24 | 0 | 485,872 | 760,942 | 1,181,968 | 1,821,435 |
| 25 | 0 | 515,024 | 821,817 | 1,300,165 | 2,040,008 |
| 26 | 0 | 545,926 | 887,562 | 1,430,181 | 2,284,809 |
| 27 | 0 | 578,682 | 958,567 | 1,573,199 | 2,558,986 |
| 28 | 0 | 613,402 | 1,035,253 | 1,730,519 | 2,866,064 |
| 29 | 0 | 650,207 | 1,118,073 | 1,903,571 | 3,209,992 |
| 30 | 0 | 689,219 | 1,207,519 | 2,093,928 | 3,595,191 |

Figure 14.4. Putting Your Dollars To Work with Compound Interest

Now turn your attention to the hypothetical situation for a sound mutual fund presented in Table 14.1. Because there are no guarantees on any mutual funds and we cannot predict future performance, we took John and Mary through a "what if" scenario. We considered what would have happened if we had implemented this idea in June 1970 by looking at the actual performance of a mutual fund that was average to better than average. When John asked, "Why start in June of 1970?," we replied, "Mainly because '73 and '74 are two of the worst years back to back that you and I have ever lived through. This

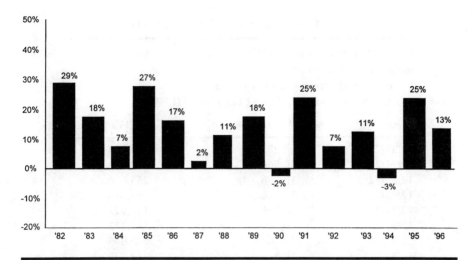

**Figure 14.5. Mutual Fund Returns (Balanced; 1982–1996).** These funds invest in stocks, bonds, and sometimes preferred stocks and convertible securities. Because stocks and bonds are both rarely negative for the same calendar year, balanced funds are normally less volatile than stock funds and sometimes less risky than long-term bond funds. There are over 330 balanced funds.

should provide a worst-case scenario." (*Note:* Keep in mind that past performance is no guarantee of future performance.)

We showed them the $120,000 initial investment in a mutual fund. Starting in Month 1, we withdrew $880 to pay the mortgage payment from this mutual fund and continued each month no matter what the market conditions. In 1973, when most consumers lost 14% in the marketplace, this fund lost 13.5%. In that year, we still took $880 each month.

We continued all through 1974, withdrawing $880 each month, even though most consumers lost 24% in the market in that year (this fund lost 27%). Though our mutual fund shares were only worth $131,227 at the end of Year 5, we lived through two of the worst years (excluding the Great Depression) of our lifetime.

We discussed with John and Mary the tax relief this proposal would provide them — they would be in the 28% federal tax bracket after deductions. In fact, by taking out a $120,000 mortgage, they would generate an additional $9500 interest expense for their IRS Schedule A. This equates to over $2600 less in taxes they would owe in the first year of having their mortgage. That is over $200 additional monies each month they could save to help them accomplish their retirement income goals, besides the additional growth accumulating in the mutual fund.

## Table 14.1. Systematic Withdrawal Plan

Prepared for John Q. Public
Initial investment: $120,000
Dividends and capital gains reinvested
Monthly withdrawals of $880.52 beginning 7/15/70

| Date | Annual Withdrawal | Total After Withdrawal |
|------|-------------------|------------------------|
| 12/31/70 | 5283 | 140,854 |
| 12/31/71 | 10,566 | 180,173 |
| 12/31/72 | 10,566 | 235,096 |
| 12/31/73 | 10,566 | 192,815 |
| 12/31/74 | 10,566 | 131,227 |
| 12/31/75 | 10,566 | 163,117 |
| 12/31/76 | 10,566 | 218,545 |
| 12/31/77 | 10,566 | 218,749 |
| 12/31/78 | 10,566 | 277,461 |
| 12/31/79 | 10,566 | 386,230 |
| 12/31/80 | 10,566 | 503,665 |
| 12/31/81 | 10,566 | 499,908 |
| 12/31/82 | 10,566 | 565,394 |
| 12/31/83 | 10,566 | 663,761 |
| 12/31/84 | 10,566 | 614,737 |
| 12/31/85 | 10,566 | 761,867 |
| 12/31/86 | 10,566 | 881,280 |
| 12/31/87 | 10,566 | 963,514 |
| 12/31/88 | 10,566 | 990,788 |
| 12/31/89 | 10,566 | 1,356,134 |
| 12/31/90 | 10,566 | 1,456,558 |
| 12/31/91 | 10,566 | 1,994,314 |
| 12/31/92 | 10,566 | 2,005,751 |
| 12/31/93 | 10,566 | 2,183,085 |
| 12/31/94 | 10,566 | 2,079,878 |
| 12/31/95 | 10,566 | 2,809,962 |
| 12/31/96 | 10,566 | 3,348,299 |
| 12/31/97 | 10,566 | 4,164,743 |
| 6/30/98 | 5283 | 4,749,154 |
| | | **4,749,154** |

And what if John wants to have his mortgage paid off when he retires at age 65? Many of our retired clients come to us crying, "Help me! The tax man has eaten us alive! We thought we'd be in a lower tax bracket, but we've found ourselves in one of the largest tax brackets. What can we do?" By having their homes paid off in retirement, they have eliminated one of their single biggest write-offs.

We told John that when he turns 65 and has retired, he could cash in his mutual fund, now worth approximately $500,000, and pay off his mortgage of approximately $105,000 (see Figure 14.3). That would leave him with almost $400,000 with which to start retirement. (And who couldn't use an additional $400,000?) Or, what if John could fight off the depression-era mentality of having to have his home paid off in retirement and could wait until the 20th year of the mortgage to consider paying it off? Now he only owes $72,572 and has used the best years (the first 20 years of a 30 year mortgage) for tax relief. We told John to look at the mutual fund value in the 20th year, even after paying the $880 mortgage each month. It is now worth $1.3 million, and would he still prefer to leave his kids and grandkids a debt-free house as opposed to $1.3 million with a house that has a $72,000 mortgage?

Now let's examine three separate cases in which each family could use their home equity to position themselves much stronger financially both today and in the future and not have to spend any more money monthly than they already are spending.

The Smiths, both age 38, are in their prime accumulation years. They have three children and own a $200,000 home, for which they originally financed $150,000 at 8% for 15 years. The mortgage is paid down to $100,000. They have two automobiles on which they owe $9000 and $11,000 and are paying $350 and $450 on each per month. They also have four credit cards with a total outstanding balance of $15,000 between them and are currently able to pay a total of $400 each month towards their balances. They have $3000 in a bank savings account, but have not been able to add to it. They pay $200 each month on two $50,000 life insurance policies for each of them. Each policy presently has $1500 cash value, for a total of $3000 between the two of them. Their total monthly cash outflow for these items is $2933 (see Figures 14.6 and 14.7). (Note that this case has been simplified to avoid confusion. Obviously, this couple has other monthly cash outflow obligations such as food, clothing, insurance, etc.)

Their first goal is to increase their cash reserves for emergencies. Their second goal is to create a college fund for their three children. Their third goal is to increase their life insurance. They realize if either parent died unexpectedly the surviving spouse would only be able to maintain their present lifestyle for about one year due to loss of income. Their fourth goal is to somehow begin saving for retirement even though they do not see how this is possible, as they live from pay check to pay check. Let's look at how this couple can immediately begin accomplishing all four goals and position themselves much better virtually overnight.

*Today's Cash Flow Management*

**The Smiths**

Family income = $90,000

Ages: 38, 38, 7, 5, 3

|  | Value | Debt | Payment |
|---|---|---|---|
| Equity in house | $200,000 | $100,000 | $1433 |
| (Original $150,000 @ 8% for 15 years) | | | |
| Auto 1 | | $9000 | $350 |
| Auto 2 | | $11,000 | $450 |
| Credit Card | | $4000 | $125 |
| Credit Card | | $1000 | $75 |
| Credit Card | | $5000 | $150 |
| Credit Card | | $5000 | $150 |
| Bank Passbook | $3000 | | $0 |
| $50,000 Whole Life | $1500 | | $100 |
| $50,000 Whole Life | $1500 | | $100 |
| **Total Monthly Cash Flow** | | | **$2933** |

**Figure 14.6**

First, we recommend that this couple refinance their first mortgage with a $160,000, 7.5%, 30-year mortgage. They would receive a cash-out at closing of $60,000, which they would use to pay off both autos and all four credit cards. They have just converted non-tax-deductible, high-interest, bad debt for tax-deductible, lower interest, good debt. After paying off all consumer debt, they are left with $25,000 from the refinancing. We recommend that $5000 of this be added to their bank savings account to make a total of $8000 in this account. For the remaining $20,000, we recommend positioning in a few good growth mutual funds, which will be designated as the children's

*Tomorrow's Cash Flow Management*

## The Smiths

Family income = $90,000

Ages: 38, 38, 7, 5, 3

| | Value | Debt | Payment |
|---|---|---|---|
| Equity in house (Refinance @ 7.5% for 30 years) | $200,000 | $160,000 | $1119 |
| Auto 1 | | $0 | $0 |
| Auto 2 | | $0 | $0 |
| Credit Card | | $0 | $0 |
| Credit Card | | $0 | $0 |
| Credit Card | | $0 | $0 |
| Credit Card | | $0 | $0 |
| Mutual Fund | $20,000 | | $814 |
| Bank Passbook | $8000 | | $0 |
| $50,000 Whole Life | $0 | | $0 |
| $50,000 Whole Life | $0 | | $0 |
| $500,000 Variable Universal Life | $1500 | | $500 |
| $500,000 Variable Universal Life | $1500 | | $500 |
| **Total Monthly Cash Flow** | | | **$2933** |

**Figure 14.7**

college fund and not to be tapped until the oldest turns 18 in 11 years. For an itemization of the payoff, see Table 14.2.

Refinancing and paying off the consumer debt have freed up $1714 each month. We recommend that $814 be invested each month in mutual funds designated as being for college for the children. Averaging 12%, the mutual

### Table 14.2. Payoff Itemization
### for the Smiths

| | |
|---|---|
| $160,000 | New first mortgage |
| −100,000 | Old mortgage |
| 60,000 | Balance at closing |
| −9000 | Auto loan 1 paid in full |
| −11,000 | Auto loan 2 paid in full |
| −4000 | Credit card paid in full |
| −1000 | Credit card paid in full |
| −5000 | Credit card paid in full |
| −5000 | Credit card paid in full |
| 25,000 | Subtotal |
| −5000 | To bank passbook savings |
| −20,000 | To mutual funds for college funding |

funds could be worth over $250,000 in 11 years when the oldest child is ready for college.

Because of the cost of the life insurance policies and their poor return on the cash value, we are recommending they cancel these policies only after they both have been approved for new hybrid variable universal life policies. The cost of insurance with the new policies is less, and the cash values are positioned in various mutual funds which grow tax deferred and can be accessed as tax-free income in the future to supplement retirement income. So, with the remaining $1000 available cash each month, we recommend that the Smiths split it between two variable universal life insurance policies with a $500,000 death benefit on each. We would roll the $1500 from old policies to the new ones. If these policies average 12%, they would be worth over $1.3 million at age 65 and could provide over $120,000 annual tax-free income throughout their retirement years.

Let's suppose, in the Smiths' present condition, one of them loses his or her job. They would have to come up with $1433 each month to keep their home. If they do not come up with $350 and $450 each month for the automobiles, those will be repossessed. And, they should pay at least minimum on credit cards or run the risk of ruining their good credit standing. If the Smith's implement our recommendations, however, they would need to come up with only the new $1119 mortgage payment. They are now in a stronger position financially, as they have additional monies in the bank and could, if they really needed to, draw on the mutual funds set aside for college funding to pay the mortgage payment until a new job is found.

*Today's Cash Flow Management*

### The Joneses
Family income = $103,000
Ages: 45, 45

|  | Value | Debt | Payment |
|---|---|---|---|
| Equity in house (7% for 30 years) | $275,000 | $127,000 | $931 |
| Taxes |  |  | $1500 |
| Sailboat | $25,000 | $15,000 | $507 |
| $500,000 Insurance Policy | $22,000 |  | $850 |
| Mutual Funds | $50,000 |  | $500 |
| **Total Monthly Cash Flow** |  |  | **$4288** |

**Figure 14.8**

Now let's look at another couple, the Joneses, who are empty nesters with no kids. They have an income of $103,000 per year. Their home, which they bought seven years ago, is valued at $275,000, and they have the mortgage paid down to $127,000. They started out with a $140,000, 7%, 30-year loan. They have a $25,000 sailboat, on which they still owe $15,000 and are paying $507 each month. They pay Uncle Sam $1500 each month in taxes. Tim Jones has a $500,000 life insurance policy on which he is paying $850 per month. The Joneses have a $50,000 mutual fund portfolio and are presently contributing $500 each month to their mutual funds. Their cash outflow for these items is $4288 (see Figures 14.8 and 14.9).

Their goals are to increase mutual fund contribution for retirement, increase cash reserves for emergencies, pay off the sailboat, reduce taxes, reduce their monthly insurance costs, and protect their present assets against the risk of personal judgment. Why should most of us be concerned about the risk of personal judgment? Nowadays, much litigation goes on at the drop of a hat, and, when we reach our later years of life, we can ill afford to

*Tomorrow's Cash Flow Management*

**The Joneses**

Family income = $103,000

Ages: 45, 45

| | Value | Debt | Payment |
|---|---|---|---|
| Equity in house (8% for 30 years) | $275,000 | $220,000 | $1614 |
| Taxes | | | $1300 |
| Sailboat | $25,000 | $0 | $0 |
| $500,000 Insurance Policy | $100,000 | | $0 |
| Mutual Funds | $50,000 | | $1374 |
| **Total Monthly Cash Flow** | | | **$4288** |

**Figure 14.9**

lose everything due to some frivolous law suit and begin all over at 55 or 65 trying to accumulate for retirement. For that reason, many consumers should have a least a $1 million umbrella liability policy covering their home and autos.

How can this couple, dramatically and immediately, improve their current and future financial position? Though their current mortgage is at a good interest rate of 7%, we recommend that they refinance the first mortgage by obtaining a new first mortgage of $220,000 financed at a current rate of 8% over 30 years. At closing, after paying off the old first mortgage, the Joneses will have $93,000 available. With this $93,000, they can first pay off the $15,000 balance on the sailboat. This leaves $78,000, which we recommend putting toward the $500,000 life insurance policy. The $100,000 cash value of the policy is protected against judgments.

This would also immediately increase their cash reserves, because they would have access to the cash value of the policy any time they want. The

*Today's Cash Flow Management*

**The Johnsons**

Family income = $62,000

Ages: Retired

| | Value | Debt | Payment |
|---|---|---|---|
| Equity in house | $245,000 | $0 | $535˙ |
| ˙ Property taxes, maintenance, insurance | | | |
| Taxes | | | $900 |
| Auto | $29,000 | $21,000 | $513 |
| Motor Home | $90,000 | $25,000 | $728 |
| CD | $200,000 | | –$1000 |
| $25,000 Insurance Policy (2) | $15,000 | | $120 |
| **Total Monthly Cash Outflow** | | | **$1796** |

**Figure 14.10**

money is probably earning at least CD rates and is accumulating at least tax deferred (some of the new hybrid contracts are actually income-tax free). The larger mortgage payment each month, to a large extent, is mostly tax-deductible interest, resulting in a $200 monthly tax savings. This refinancing would free up an additional $874 each month that can then be invested in the Joneses' mutual funds.

A retired couple, the Johnsons are worried about depleting their assets. Because of inflation, they cannot take as many trips as they did when they first retired. They are also concerned about the rising cost of home maintenance. They also are frustrated at how much federal income tax they pay (for more about their financial situation, see Figures 14.10 and 14.11). When we met with the Johnsons and asked them why they still have a big five-bedroom home, they replied that it was primarily to entertain their children when they

*Tomorrow's Cash Flow Management*

### The Johnsons
Family income = $62,000
Ages: Retired

| | Value | Debt | Payment |
|---|---|---|---|
| Equity in house | $120,000 | $96,000 | $965 * |
| * Property taxes, maintenance, insurance | | | |
| Taxes | | | $656 |
| Auto | $29,000 | $0 | $0 |
| Motor Home | $90,000 | $0 | $0 |
| CD | $20,000 | | –$100 |
| $1,000,000 Survivorship Policy | $150,000 | $0 | –$800 |
| $120,000 SPIA + $100,000 SPDA | $220,000 | $0 | –$1500 |
| **Total Monthly Cash Inflow** | | | **–$779** |

**Figure 14.11**

come home for special occasions such as Thanksgiving and Christmas. We told the Johnsons it would be cheaper for them to rent out the wing of a Holiday Inn for their visiting children rather than spending a week after they go home cleaning up after them. Most couples do not picture their retirement years cleaning and maintaining a big house, so we asked the Johnsons if they had ever considered downsizing to a condo or smaller, newer home. They reflected on the idea and actually got excited about building a new retirement home just the way they want it.

We recommended that when they sell their big $245,000 house they not pay cash for the new $120,000 retirement home. Instead, they can make a downpayment of $24,000 and take out a $96,000 mortgage which will cost

### Table 14.3. Pay Off Itemization for the Johnsons

| | |
|---|---|
| $245,000 | Sold property |
| –24,000 | 20% downpayment on condominium |
| 221,000 | Subtotal |
| –21,000 | Auto loan paid in full |
| –25,000 | Motor home loan paid in full |
| 175,000 | Subtotal |
| +180,000 | From CDs |
| 355,000 | Subtotal |
| +15,000 | From cash-value life insurance |
| 370,000 | Subtotal |
| –150,000 | To survivorship policy |
| 220,000 | Subtotal |
| –100,000 | to SPDA |
| –120,000 | to SPIA |

them $965 every month (including new property taxes, maintenance, and insurance). We also recommended that they pay off their car and motor home. The return on the CDs that they held did not warrant the size of the investment in them, so we dropped that amount down to $20,000. We put $150,000 into a new survivorship policy with a last-to-die death benefit of $1 million. This takes care of their estate planning and will also pay them $800 tax-free money each month for the rest of their lives, no matter how long they live. That is the way life insurance policies should work — they should start paying you while you are still living.

With the money left over (see Table 14.3), we put $220,000 into two different types of annuities: a single-premium immediate annuity (SPIA) which immediately starts paying the couple $1500 per month for as long as both of them live, and a single-premium deferred annuity (SPDA) which defers any kind of income to some later point in time. If, five to ten years down the road, their monthly income is not buying what it was buying before, they can start to implement a monthly income from that SPDA.

Here is the bottom line for the Johnsons. They went from an outflow of $1796 to an inflow of $779. Unfortunately, there are many individuals in similar situations who are not enjoying their retirement years because they are caught up in this big piece of brick and mortar and windows. They say they want to pass it on to their children, but in reality when children receive a house from their inheritance, they most often sell it anyway. The objective is to trade down from a large, high-maintenance home to a smaller, low-maintenance home and conserve the estate while increasing disposable income.

At retirement, most Americans' single largest financial asset is their home. Today, there are approximately 21.7 million debt-free homes in the U.S. Unfortunately, there are over 4.5 million retired individuals who have incomes *below* the national poverty level. These senior homeowners have found themselves in a position of being house-rich and cash-poor. Their golden years of retirement have become years of financial frustration, without a way to tap their single largest asset — their home equity. The fact is, most consumers would be financially stronger today and in the future by having a mortgage than not having a mortgage.

# Part IV.
# The Final Insult

# 15 Estate Planning: How To Keep the IRS from Being Your Biggest Beneficiary

I magine working hard all your life and amassing a sizable net worth, but, because you had not taken the time to understand estate planning, your family ended up with only 50¢ cents of each of your hard-earned dollars? You would never have agreed to an outcome like that for any of your other business decisions. When you die, though, if your financial affairs are not in order, more than half of your wealth can go to the IRS and beneficiaries you did not choose. A lifetime of great efforts and good investments can be undone by no or poor pre-death or disability planning.

When Joe Robbie, the owner of the Miami Dolphins, died, his family sold the team, in large part to pay estate taxes to the IRS which are due 9 months after death. In contrast, Malcolm Forbes' family retained his business empire, because he had done the necessary estate planning. This chapter is designed to help you understand estate planning in a new light, so you can enjoy the fruits of your labors and be assured that your appointed beneficiaries will receive what you intended, unburdened by complicated legal hassles and severe tax penalties.

1-57444-258-9/00/$0.00+$.50
© 2000 by CRC Press LLC

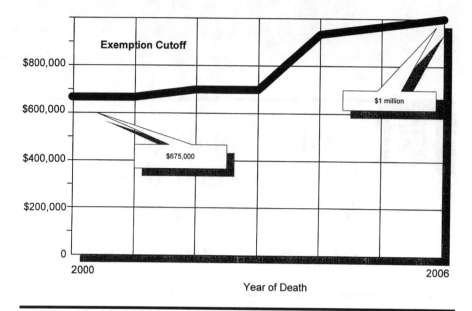

**Figure 15.1. The IRS and Estate Taxes.** Estates valued at more than $650,000 at the time of death must file an estate tax return with the IRS. Estates valued at less than that are exempt from federal estate taxes. The exemption will gradually increase to $1 million over the next six years.

We could all name the most basic elements of estate planning: *who* will get *what* upon your death, and *how* and *when* they will get it. Simple enough, right? Unfortunately, no, especially if the total value of your assets exceeds the current *unified credit* equivalent of $650,000 (indexed). Variables such as how you hold title to your assets, how you document your intentions, whether you have equity assets or tax-deferred assets, if you have a surviving spouse, and which of your assets provide retirement income are all major factors to address in estate planning and require examination of the many possible tax implications (Figure 15.1).

What we are suggesting takes a lot of effort and long-term planning with frequent reviews. Do-it-yourselfers can write their own wills or create trusts without the help and expense of professionals and specialists, and there are software packages, how-to books, and tutorials available to assist these ambitious individuals. However, even if they do not fall prey to procrastination or become overwhelmed by the task, chances are the results will not take advantage of all the intricacies of the tax laws. Or, as time goes by, necessary revisions to follow changes in the tax laws will not be made, as well as updates that reflect the changing financial circumstances of these do-it-yourselfers or their designated beneficiaries. All of their hard efforts, too, could be nullified if, for example, their beneficiaries die in the wrong order! In short, the money spent on the advice of a specialist is well worth the comprehensive consideration to details that an effective estate plan requires. Of course, you will still have to make decisions and supply the details.

## Your Heirs

Unless you prepare specific written documentation, the courts may include every relative and anyone you were ever married to as your beneficiaries. Interpretation varies by state law. So, the first step is for you to identify your beneficiaries, and then decide what you want them to receive from your estate. Give serious and honest consideration to your beneficiaries' needs. For example, if one of your three children has a debilitating disease, that child's needs are going to be different from the other two.

How do you want your beneficiaries to receive assets from your estate — by transferring the asset in a lump sum or by payments over a period of time? Each beneficiary could have different payout arrangements. Some people are concerned about spendthrift children or their children's spouses. In that case, specific instructions or distribution choices can leave them with more economic security and more money over time.

## Get It in Writing

Once you have determined who and what, you need to select the proper tools for transferring your assets. There are four basic ways to transfer property at your death; wills, trusts, beneficiary designations, and the way in which you hold title (ownership) to your assets determine how the distribution of your assets will occur. If you do not specify any of these correct forms of transfer, your assets after taxes will be transferred according to the statutes of the state in which you die or the states in which you own property. The most well-know document for this transfer is a will. Wills must go through a court process called probate, which slows down the transfer and is usually the longest and most expensive transfer method.

In Arizona for example, probate attorneys have said that the cost of probate is usually between 3 and 7% of the value of the estate. It is not that the attorneys charge this percentage, but the court fees, appraisal fees, and the attorney's hourly rate all add up. An advertisement must be run in the newspaper to allow all creditors to come forward against the estate, and there is at least a six-month lag time before everything can be settled.

Do not be fooled, however, into thinking that having a will is the last word on the subject! The other three methods of transferring property we already mentioned supersede your will. If you own real estate by "joint tenants with rights of survivorship" the asset will transfer to the surviving joint tenant without the will or probate. Conversely, if you are the sole owner and die, even if you are married, the asset goes through probate before it is transferred to the rightful heir.

Did you know your will can be contested? One example is a situation in New York state where a gentleman left his live-in girlfriend quite a chunk of his estate. The ex-wife and children have been fighting the validity of his will for four years. No one has seen a nickel, and the costs have been tremendous. The way you hold title to your assets and the manner in which you transfer your assets make a big difference in the effectiveness of your will.

## Ownership

Begin by checking how you own or hold title to all your existing assets to see if anything needs to be updated. Review everything periodically, because situations change. By taking care to assume ownership of every new asset correctly, your estate plan will work the way you wanted. This review should take place every time there is a major transaction or a change in your life, or no less than every two years. I also recommend a legal review periodically just to make sure you are taking maximum advantage of the current tax law.

Every time you add an asset to your estate, make certain to place it in the proper ownership and name your beneficiaries, if appropriate. Suppose you received a check for $20,000 and decided to invest it with Charles Schwab. You have already set up a trust, but when you went to open up the account, you forgot to bring the trust documents and your spouse was not with you, so you put the money in an account in your name only. Then, you put off taking care of properly transferring this investment and eventually forget about doing so. Your estate plan will not protect that asset. If you own something individually, even if you are married, the asset may go through probate before going to your spouse. If you own something as joint tenants or community property with rights of survivorship, the survivor can fill out the proper documentation and have 100% ownership.

Many people, after their spouse has died, think that putting their children on the title of their assets as joint tenants with rights of survivorship will result in an easier transfer; however, when we make the children joint tenants with rights of survivorship, we are making a gift. They have partial ownership now, and this can cause many problems. They must sign any documents making any changes, and the tax advantages at death are gone because you gifted it before death. Also, if one of the children is sued, part of your asset can be used to fulfill judgment against that person.

Suppose you own $1,000,000 of Microsoft stock, and you put a child on that account with joint rights of survivorship. You technically have given the child half of that account; in tax language, you have given a $500,000 gift. The basis of their half is what you paid for half the stock. If you had left it all to them at death, they would have avoided capitol gains tax on a sale, but because of your gift they will only save tax on half. When an asset is owned in a way where ownership is transferred automatically in a way different then stated in the will, the ownership provision applies and the will is not used.

## Trusts

Holding your assets in one or more trusts can serve many purposes, from avoiding probate to minimizing and eliminating certain taxes. It is not always tax smart to leave everything to your spouse. Couples frequently have what we call "sweetheart" wills. If he dies first, he gives everything to her, and if she dies first, she gives everything to him. That works with smaller estates where the value is less than the $650,000 tax-free exemption, But what if your estate is worth more than that?

If, instead, you put your assets into a proper trust so that at the first death, the estate is split in two, then the $650,000 *unified credit exemption equivalent* can be used for each individual. For example, in an estate worth $900,000, the first decedent's half is $450,000 — less than the tax credit equivalent of $650,000. Now, at the second death, the survivor's estate is only going to be $450,000, which is also less than the $650,000 exemption equivalent; therefore, you have no tax. The surviving spouse has access to and income from the decedent's trust, but it is not included in the their estate at death. When you use trusts, your will becomes a secondary backup document. Many are called "pour-over" wills (i.e., if I forgot anything, I want it to be poured over into my trust).

## Beneficiaries

Some assets allow you to designate your beneficiaries. When a beneficiary has been named, the asset will be transferred without reference to your will or

trust. The most common examples of assets that have a way to name beneficiaries are life insurance, IRAs, 401(k)s, and other retirement plans. In some
states, you can use transfer on death (TOD) or payable on death (POD)
designations on your accounts. Both designations will transfer the account to
your heirs automatically. Even though we can use ownership, trusts, and
beneficiaries to avoid probate, their use can cause other problems. Ownership
and beneficiary designations may be unequal to different heirs at the date of
your death and may not take advantage of all the tax laws.

## Uncle Sam

You have several different choices regarding how to transfer your assets to
your heirs, and every decision you make will have some tax consequences.
Aside from income tax, the estate tax effectively starts at 37%, and the
generation-skipping transfer tax (the tax you pay for skipping your children
and giving to your grandchildren) starts at 55%! But there are also some
exemptions and credits. Here are some facts that can help you in the initial
planning:

1.  First, the good news. Each of us has a $650,000 exemption (called the
    unified credit) which we can transfer without tax. Any gifts over
    $11,000 (indexed) a year go against the $650,000 total credit.
2.  More good news. At death, equity assets receive a "step-up in basis"
    valuation at the time of death. This saves on income taxes by stepping
    up the cost basis of the asset to the date of death for the new owner.
    Examples of these are stocks, real estate, or a family business. Any
    asset for which the value is likely to grow (for which you would
    typically pay capital gains taxes when you sell it) would qualify for a
    step-up in basis. When the new owner sells the asset, they are only
    liable for the capital gains taxes on any growth from the date of death.
    One exception is if ownership is transferred through joint tenancy
    with rights of survivorship. In that case, the surviving owner's cost
    basis is the original basis on their share of the asset and the stepped-
    up value on the share of the asset transferred at death.
3.  Some bad news. Qualified retirement vehicles such as IRAs, 401(k)s, and
    Keogh plans and tax-deferred annuities are income-tax deferred, which
    means there is still income tax due on the balance left in these types of
    accounts. When those assets are transferred to your heirs, they are
    potentially liable for income tax and estate tax on the same money.

4. Bonds, certificates of deposit, savings accounts, and other cash assets have little to no capital gain and are just a basic transfer of cash to the heirs.
5. The death benefit from a life insurance policy is generally 100% free of income tax, although there are some exceptions for business uses. Life insurance will be subject to estate tax if you own it. To avoid estate tax, the policy should be owned by your heirs or should be in an irrevocable life insurance trust designed to avoid the tax.

## How To Make Yourself Look Smaller to the IRS

A major goal for estate planning is to position your wealth so as to make it appear smaller to the IRS to lessen the tax liability when you die. One of the easiest ways to lower your estate value is to leave everything to charity. Then, in the eyes of the IRS, your estate is worth zero. Another way is through gifting. If you start gifting $11,000 a year now to your children, the gift and all of its growth are not included in your estate.

The $650,000 exemption you have does not require you to die to use it. You can give the amount before you die and set up an irrevocable trust and invest it for your heirs. (Keep in mind that irrevocable trusts will actually diminish the size of your estate in the eyes of the IRS, as *irrevocable* means you cannot get it back, you cannot undo it, and you cannot change it.) The $650,000 and all the growth are outside your estate. It will not be taxed at your death. Irrevocable trusts are commonly combined with life insurance. If I buy $1 million of life insurance and I pay the premiums, when I die, the IRS wants their part of the million. If a trust (of which my brother is the trustee and the beneficiaries are my children) buys life insurance on my life, when I die there will be no income tax or estate tax on that million dollars of insurance.

A charitable trust, a form of irrevocable trust, is a way to retain an income from your estate and get some tax advantages by making the charitable gift now. We will cover the ways to use charitable giving in the next chapter.

The qualified personal residence trust (QPRT) is a way to irrevocably give away your house to your children over a period of years, usually ten years or longer, for a fraction of its worth today. Because you are not giving a gift today but ten years out into the future, the value of that asset is significantly less in the eyes of the tax man. All the growth of that asset is outside of your estate and transferred to the children after the term of the trust.

We briefly mentioned the generation-skipping transfer tax — the tax you pay for giving your assets to your grandchildren instead of to your children.

Each person, however, has $1 million exemption. If you set up a trust, put $1 million in it, and fill out form 709 for the IRS, this $1 million is always exempt from the generation-skipping transfer tax. If that $1 million grows to be $10 million before you die, the entire $10 million is free from the generation-skipping transfer tax because you allocated it that way when you gave the $1 million.

## Which Assets You Should Leave Behind

The money you have invested in qualified, tax-deferred retirement plans is the money you should spend while you are alive. Your heirs inheriting the IRAs could possibly have to pay estate tax, income tax, and the generation-skipping transfer tax, if applicable. Instead, leave untouched the assets with favorable tax treatment — stocks, homes, family farms, life insurance, bonds, and cash.

Individual retirement accounts are a very powerful way to shelter income tax but the tax has to be paid eventually. Any withdrawal of funds prior to age 59-1/2 is subject to a penalty, and distributions must commence by age 70-1/2 based on the IRS minimum distribution formula. At the required beginning date (April 1 following the year you turn 70-1/2), you make an irrevocable choice of how to calculate life expectancy for your minimum distribution. This choice and the resulting order of death of the IRA holder and his or her beneficiaries can result in either a positive long-term result or disastrous tax results. The basic rule is that your IRA must be distributed over a period based on your life expectancy, or the combination of your life expectancy and that of your beneficiaries. If you do not name a beneficiary or your beneficiary is going to be your estate or a charity (which do not have a life expectancy), the calculation must be based on your life expectancy, if you have started making distributions.

## Retirement Income Distribution

There are actually two options for calculating minimum distributions. One is the annual recalculation of life expectancy, and it does not matter whether it is one or two people. Obviously, as you get older, your life expectancy will go down; however, you do not lose a full year in life expectancy for every year you get older. For example, it might only decrease from 19.8 to 19.3 years even though you have turned one year older, thus stretching out the length of time you have to take out your IRA.

The other calculation is the "term certain" payout, which reduces by one full year each year. The advantage to this is that if the participant dies prior to full distribution, the beneficiaries have the remainder of that payout period to take the distributions, thus spreading out the taxes.

The biggest problem is that in using recalculation of your life expectancy, your recalculated life expectancy at your death will be zero. Your heirs will have to liquidate the entire account in the next year and pay income tax on the entire amount. Only your legal spouse can roll your IRA into their own and make a new election on calculating the minimum distribution. If your spouse dies first, you cannot make a new election. In fact, the planholder has to take out at least as fast as previously. For example, suppose the planholder remarries and his new bride is 29. Even though the new wife has a longer life expectancy, the payout period remains the same. The election made at the required beginning date is irrevocable. He also could not add any children as beneficiaries and lengthen the payout period. Conversely, if he married an older person, the law would require a recalculation to shorten his payout period. Now let's say that this planholder's wife survives him. She is required to have the same minimum payout; however, she does have the option of rolling his IRA into a new IRA in her name and making a new election with new beneficiaries. Only in this case could she lengthen the period for the payout.

Over and over again, we see successful clients with large assets flooding their qualified plans with more money every year to take advantage of the tax shelter, but it can create a huge tax problem later. Depending on how much money we have and how much is in IRAs, we may have to reconcile ourselves to the idea that we should spend our IRA while we are alive and leave those assets which receive a more favorable tax basis to our heirs.

## Other Precautionary Measures

A will goes into effect when you die — it is not a document that can take care of you when you are living. A will does not help in the event that you become incompetent. If you were to become disabled or incompetent and could not manage your own financial affairs or even be able to make your healthcare decisions, a properly documented plan on how you want things carried out will ensure your intentions without disruption. A *durable power of attorney* is usually used for financial matters; the term *durable* means it will last. It is sometimes also called a *springing* power of attorney, as most people do not just grant an open power of attorney; instead, they make a provision for the trust to spring into effect when needed, and it is both durable and long lasting.

Some institutions will not accept the durable powers of attorney and the healthcare powers of attorneys if they are outdated. It is important to know the "rules" and stay on top of any changes. Some states are updating their laws, giving people more options and ways in which they can use those documents. For the healthcare directive or healthcare power of attorney, you can set up your own parameters to determine incompetence, such as specifying that if two doctors agree that you are mentally incompetent, then the power of attorney springs into effect.

In the case of a husband and wife, everything is usually owned as joint tenants with rights of survivorship and the spouse automatically makes healthcare decisions. What would happen if your spouse is already gone? If you have not designated a guardian and a conservator in writing and do not have a power of attorney in place, even your own children will have to go through court to take care of you. The best scenario for an incompetent person is to have a guardian and a conservator and have all their money in a trust where it can be managed for them without disruption.

## Summary Checklist

- Who will get your money at death?
- Do they receive a lump sum or payments over a specified period of time? List each beneficiary and any requirements.
- Which of your assets are better to leave to your heirs and which should you spend before you die?
- How will your money be managed if you become incompetent or disabled and cannot manage our own financial affairs?
- Who will make your healthcare decisions?
- What if you could have your cake and eat it too — with all the frosting?

Does that last item sound tempting? Do you want to find out how you can direct your "social capital" yourself, rather than sending it to Washington, D.C.? Then read the chapter about the charitable remainder trust.

# 16 Charitable Giving

I n addition to the self satisfaction that comes from making a financial gift to a cause you believe in, charitable giving also offers the donor several tax benefits. There are many techniques available for someone who is interested in charitable or planned giving, and one of the most popular is a charitable remainder trust (CRT). Who should consider using such a trust? Anyone who has a charity or other qualifying organization they would like to help, anyone who is facing a federal estate tax problem (that is, someone whose wealth exceeds the unified credit exemption equivalent of $650,000, as of 1999), and anyone who may have large capital gains on stock or other property and wants to avoid paying tax on those gains.

Here is the question everyone should ask themselves when they do charitable planning. If you have $1 million to give away, and you only have a choice of three ways in which you can direct the money (to family, government, or charity) how would you distribute that $1 million? Some people prefer that nothing go to the government, but others appreciate everything they have received from the government and are content paying the government something, just not at the rate at which the government wants to collect.

All the various taxes one pays contain a component called social capital. This refers to money that is used to fund the welfare system, Social Security, the military, and other social programs. Fully 60% of your state taxes go to the federal government for social reform. Accordingly, your local legislators only deal with 40% of the budget because 60% is spent before they even get it. When you utilize a charitable remainder trust, you can direct where that

1-57444-258-9/00/$0.00+$.50
© 2000 by CRC Press LLC

social capital goes instead of the government doing so. If you prefer, you can give instructions that 100% of it stay in your community or state. Most people feel this is preferable to sending it to Washington, D.C. and having it come back at perhaps 10¢ on the dollar.

Let's start by briefly reviewing federal estate taxes. In 1999, a person is entitled to pass the first $650,000 in wealth on to their heirs without any estate taxes. This is possible because current law provides a unified credit to every person which can be applied against any tax due. It is called a unified credit because it can be applied against either estate or gift taxes. If someone were to make a gift of more than $650,000 in a given year or have more than $650,000 passing at their death, their heirs would have to pay taxes on the excess starting at a rate of 37%. The unified credit is indexed so that it reaches $1 million in 2006.

What if you own low-basis, non-qualified stock or other property? These items receive a stepped-up basis when the owner dies, which means the capital gains tax is eliminated if it is held until death. However, by using a charitable remainder trust, you can give the property away while you are alive, avoid the capital gains tax, and still receive a lifetime income stream from it.

Rather than look at the social capital aspect, let's focus on the money you can keep control of if you set up a charitable remainder trust. You do not get to keep the money, but you do get to keep control of it and direct where it goes. This allows people to aid their local Special Olympics, American Lung Association, Ronald McDonald House, or any other qualified organization they feel strongly about instead of having their funds go toward a distant or even foreign charity for which they have no affinity. If you recycle your money into your own local community, the benefits will remain in your local community.

The conventional approach to wealth planning is keeping more of what you earn and leaving your family more of what you keep. This approach ignores the part that you cannot keep, but with a charitable remainder trust that is exactly the part that you address and gain control over — the social capital that is paid in estate taxes. Some people refer to this as "zero estate tax planning" because you can zero out your estate taxes. For example, if you have a $2 million estate, you would pay over $500,000 in estate taxes. By using a charitable remainder trust coupled with a wealth replacement trust, your estate tax could be zero, and the entire $2 million could go to your family — if that is what you so desire.

So what is a charitable remainder trust? A CRT is a tax-exempt trust which can pay you and your spouse an income for life; at your death, the remaining trust assets go to a charity of your choice (see Figure 16.1). Here is how a charitable remainder trust works. The donor makes a contribution to a CRT,

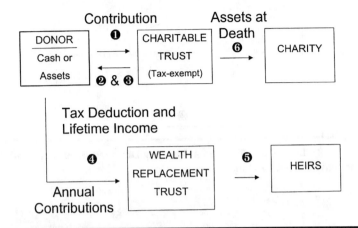

Figure 16.1. How a Charitable Remainder Trust Works

Figure 16.2. Donors Make a Contribution to the CRT

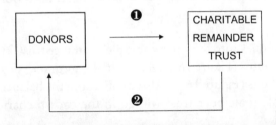

Figure 16.3. Donors Receive Tax Deductions for their Contributions

which is a tax-exempt organization (Figure 16.2). In return, they receive a charitable income tax deduction, which they can use to reduce their taxes that year; if they cannot use the entire deduction during the first year, they can carry it forward five more years (Figure 16.3). The trust sells the asset(s), pays no tax, and invests the proceeds (Figure 16.4). The trust then pays the donor an income for the rest of his or her life, or jointly over the donor and spouse's lives, if they prefer. If a CRT is coupled with a wealth replacement trust, the

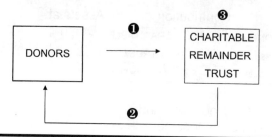

**Figure 16.4. CRT Invests the Assets in a Specially Designed Investment and Provides Lifetime Income Stream to Donors**

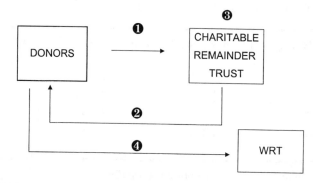

**Figure 16.5. Donors Direct Money into Wealth-Replacement Trust To Fund Life Insurance**

donor directs money into the irrevocable life insurance trust (ILIT) to pay the insurance premiums (Figure 16.5). At death, the insurance proceeds are paid to the donor's heirs (Figure 16.6). Also upon death, the balance of the money in the charitable remainder trust will go to the chosen charity or charities (Figure 16.7).

Consider the case of Bill and Brenda Braxton, both in their mid-60s. They transfer $500,000 of highly appreciated ($120,000 cost basis) telephone stock into a CRT. For that charitable contribution, the Braxtons immediately receive an income tax deduction of $126,000. The trust sells the stock, thereby converting it to cash. Because the trust is a non-taxable entity, there is no capital gains tax paid so more money is available for the trust to invest. The Braxtons receive a lifetime annual income stream from the trust equal to 8% of the trust assets. Upon their deaths, whatever assets remain in the trust go to a named charity.

In addition to the CRT, the Braxtons also elect to create a wealth replacement trust, an irrevocable life insurance trust, in the amount of $500,000.

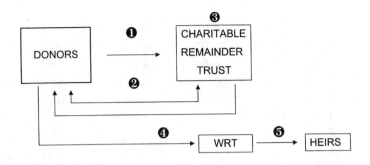

**Figure 16.6. At the Second Death, the Heirs Receive Tax-Free Insurance Proceeds**

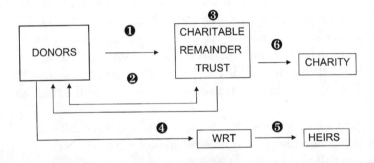

**Figure 16.7. At the Second Death, the Charitable Remainder Trust Assets Go to Charity**

Although it costs them about $6000 a year to fund it, the Braxtons will be receiving $40,000 annually from the CRT, leaving them with $34,000 per year for living expenses. The key is the increased cash flow the Braxtons have due to two intertwined items: First, because the CRT pays no taxes, it has more dollars to invest, thereby creating a bigger "pie" of which the Braxtons receive 8%. Second, the charitable deduction the Braxtons received means less taxes paid by them personally and increased cash in their pocket. When the Braxtons die, the money in the CRT goes to the designated charity or charities, and the $500,000 in the ILIT goes to their heirs income- and estate-tax free at both the state and federal levels.

Because Bill and Brenda needed the money to live on, they thought their only alternative was to sell the $500,000 of stock piece-meal or, in a worst case scenario, all in one year. If they sold their stock all in one year, they would have to pay almost $80,000 in taxes ($500,000 full market value – $120,000 basis = $380,000, times a 20% tax rate) which would bring their total down to about $420,000. An 8% return on their net proceeds would generate approximately $33,000 per year compared to the $40,000 per year from the CRT. Further, when the Braxtons died, because a portion of their estate would be taxed at a minimum of 37% estate tax, they would give another $155,000 of that $420,000 to the federal government, so their children would only net about $265,000. However, by putting their money into a charitable remainder trust and setting up a ILIT, Bill and Brenda now can have their cake and eat it too — with all the frosting. They have got an income for life, and they are still going to leave their heirs the full $500,000. As you can see, a CRT can increase your income and reduce your taxes.

The Braxtons also have a $126,000 worth of income tax deductions spread out over the next five years. The tax savings those deductions generate can assist in funding the premiums on the life insurance policy in the ILIT. In addition to increasing their income and reducing their taxes, a CRT can also diversify (see Chapter 7) their assets. Look at what happened with the Braxtons — they no longer have two or three different stocks; instead, they have a diversified portfolio (inside the CRT) providing them an income. The use of a variable annuity as an investment vehicle can further the flexibility of the CRT.

The Braxtons might also set up a special type of CRT called a net income with makeup provisions charitable remainder uni-trust (NIMCRUT). This type of trust allows the receipt of income to be controlled to a degree. Bill could work for about two more years and simply let the money accumulate inside the trust (by using a variable annuity contract, there will be no taxes until the money is withdrawn from it). Then, he and Brenda will start receiving income from the CRT. The result is they are going to get more income and not pay income tax until the money is received.

Why haven't people heard about this? If CRTs are so good, why aren't more people using them? Well, unfortunately, many people have a perception that CRTs are only for wealthy people, so there has been an emotional barrier for people to use them, as many people are afraid that they will give away all their money and their heirs will not get a cent. This mistaken notion is partially due to the lack of quality advisors who understand the technique. Fortunately, with the advent of computers and specially designed software, more people are going to be made aware of how CRTs can benefit them.

We all have four competing goals to balance effectively when we plan our futures — lifestyle, education, retirement, and inheritance. So, how do you maintain your lifestyle today and still give away those assets? How do you structure your retirement plan differently from the conventional way, holding onto adequate retirement funds but passing some of your assets or gross estate on to your children? You do that through charitable giving. The misconception is that when you give it away, it is gone forever; you lose control of it, and you never benefit from it. The charitable remainder trust is now coming of age because of increased awareness, a better quality of legal and technical resources, and consumer-oriented products.

What do you do if you have over $1 million in qualified money? The normal, conventional plan is to use a rollover IRA when the spouse will be the primary recipient of qualified money. When the plan participant dies, the spouse can roll the money over into a rollover IRA. When the money is taken out, the spouse must pay income tax on it. When the money goes to heirs (upon the spouse's subsequent death), it is subject to four different taxes, including estate taxes and state and federal income taxes. One alternative is to take the IRA account and name the charitable remainder trust as a primary beneficiary. As long as the spouse is the primary beneficiary of the trust, the only tax to be paid is income tax as the money is received by the spouse. When the spouse dies, the money goes to a charity.

If you had a $2 million estate, of which $1 million is in a qualified plan, you have got some serious estate tax and income-tax problems. By utilizing a CRT, you can split an IRA and contribute less than the entire $1 million to the trust (you could put in $500,000 or $600,000 or $700,000). The spouse would receive the income from the trust, and you could make a gift to charity. You could also create your wealth replacement trust. You could even use a last-to-die policy, because it is 40% less expensive than a regular life insurance policy. Your children will receive the insurance proceeds income tax free.

In general, you cannot complete this sophisticated charitable planning on your own. There are, however, places you can go to get help. Almost any large charity will do it for you. The disadvantage is that the charity is going to pay you a 5 to 6% return, and the charity is going to take 100% of the balance of the money. In the previous illustration of the Braxtons putting $500,000 into a trust, they would receive an 8% return ($40,000 a year). If the portfolio is earning 9% or 10%, guess who gets the difference? The charity. Because you are only taking 8% out, while the trust is earning 10%, the difference is going to accumulate at 2% a year. And when you die, all that money goes to charity. The charity is going to want to keep the payout rate really low, and if they are doing the paperwork for you, which they will do, they will also want to be the beneficiary of at least in most cases 50% of the remainder, if not all of it.

Let's look at another advantage of setting up your own CRT (as opposed to setting one up through a charity). If you set the CRT up at a relatively young age, such as 55 or 60, what happens if, before you die, they find a cure for the cause of the charity that you give the money to and you decide you want to change charities? Or, what happens if you now have a grandchild with a birth defect and now you want to steer money toward that particular charity? A CRT can be designed to be flexible enough to let you change the beneficiary, if you so choose.

To summarize, with a CRT you get increased income, reduced taxes, diversified assets, and wealth building for yourself. At the same time, you are giving a charitable gift to an organization or cause you care about, and your heirs are going to receive more money (if you also use an ILIT) than they would if they received their inheritance in a more conventional way.

## The Private Foundation

As you can see, a CRT is a very flexible tool that can be used to satisfy a variety of goals; however, suppose you want to continue your charitable intentions beyond your death. One option would be to put money into a foundation rather that giving money either outright to a charity or into a CRT. You can even have your children be advisors to the foundation, and, as advisors to the foundation, they can take an annual fee, perhaps as high as 2 to 3% of the total assets. The old wealth in the United States, like that of the Rockefellers and the Kennedys, has utilized private foundations for years.

The technique is extremely useful and very powerful. A donor can accomplish significant goals with a properly designed private foundation. For example, it has been said that Eli Lilly has the largest foundation in the world, and they have given a matching grant to every county in Indiana. Think of the concept of giving every county $100,000 in matching funds. We have some really poor counties in each state. If you give a county $100,000 in matching funds, they could build community centers, swimming pools, ballparks, etc. Just think of the interest earned by that money and what it could do. Think of all that wealth staying right there in the county and in the state.

## The Community Foundation

A community foundation is not an independent foundation, but a part of an umbrella foundation. Many communities have these. You could decide, for instance, that you would like to provide $200,000 to graduates from state colleges who want to be writers. Because you would prefer not to assume all the administration expenses, the compliance work, the filing of IRS forms, and other responsibilities and cost, you would want to join an existing foundation. When you join with a community foundation, they will administer

### Table 16.1. Advantages of Giving Through a Family Foundation

- Demonstrates family commitment to charity
- Increases ease of making gifts of appreciated assets to charity
- Gives greater family control over the gift's disposition or management
- Creates prestigious jobs for children
- Insulates you from personal-funding requests
- Gives your family a vehicle for leveraging giving
- Protects family wealth

the money for you and simply charge you a small fee for the paperwork. The fee is based upon volume — the more money they get, the less they charge.

Some people are hesitant to leave their money to charity; on the other hand, many people fear leaving their children too much money and spoiling them. By using either a private or community foundation, your children can sit on the board and you can pass your philanthropic philosophy on to your children and the generations to come. Suppose you have a handicapped child who has been active in the Special Olympics. You are very concerned about helping kids with special needs, and you want your own children to stay involved in that area. A private foundation or community chest would provide an ideal way to keep them involved, provide money to a cause you care about, and create a family legacy (see Table 16.1).

Seek competent financial advisors. When you put $500,000 in a trust, an advisor may receive a commission for selling the stock and for the investing in variable annuity accounts (if that is what is used). They also earn a commission for the sale of the insurance in the wealth replacement trust. It takes a lot of knowledge to implement these techniques successfully, and very often it will take months to structure these plans. As these CRTs are detailed and complex, you are strongly urged to seek a licensed registered investment advisor and a knowledgeable legal and tax counsel. In the remaining chapters, we will show you how to protect your assets, find a good advisor, teach your children about managing their money, and how to put all this information together.

# Part V.
# Protecting Your Assets

# 17 Protecting Your Assets

F inancial planning would not be complete without some discussion about insurance. People purchase all kinds of insurance, but we recommend trying to cover the most probable or the most devastating situation. This section is not designed to make you any money; it is designed to protect what you have.

First, let's examine automobile insurance, particularly liability insurance. Under the liability section of auto insurance, most people have coverage limits with designations such as $50,000, $100,000, $50,000. What that first $50,000 means is that if you get into an accident, the maximum for personal injury that the policy will pay is $50,000. If you are at fault in an accident, and someone is injured and sues you for $500,000, where does the other $450,000 come from? It comes from your retirement plan, from your mutual funds, your assets, or 25% of your income for the rest of your life. The coverage is not enough.

The next $100,000 is the maximum paid per incident. Once again, if you cause an accident and hurt three people, and they sue you for $50,000 each, or $150,000, the maximum your policy pays is $100,000. Obviously, that is not enough, either.

The next last is $50,000, which relates to property damage. Considering car prices today, we recommend you raise that coverage to the maximum. Buying insurance over and above the minimum is incrementally very inexpensive. The maximums are something like $250,000, $500,000, $250,000, which is a good start, but if someone sues you for more than your coverage, what should you do? We recommend buying an *umbrella* policy that will increase your liability up to $1 million. Now you have got something that can protect you. Most individuals should probably have much more coverage, and it is very inexpensive.

Another issue is homeowner's insurance. If you own a home, then obviously you have homeowner's insurance. If you do not own a house and are renting, you should consider buying renter's insurance. Homeowner's and renter's insurance covers theft or fire and other things, but many people do not realize that liability coverage is included, as well — anywhere from $100,000 to $300,000 worth of liability insurance. What that liability insurance really covers is what we call *unintentional acts*. For example, suppose you have a garage sale. When you open the door, and people come rushing in, someone slips and wants to sue you because he got hurt. Such an incident is covered under liability in your homeowner's or renter's insurance. Now suppose you are at a barbecue in the park and you accidentally knock over a grill. Unfortunately, it burns somebody, who then sues you. This situation, too, would be covered by your liability insurance. If one of your kids accidentally hits another in the head with a baseball bat and that child's mother sues you, you can rely upon your liability insurance. If your dog bites someone, that, too, will be covered by your liability insurance. People think these things will never happen to them, but they do.

The umbrella policy that you paid an extra $200 for that covers the liability in your car will also bring your liability insurance on your home up from $300,000 to $1 million, as well. Hence, the name umbrella coverage; it covers both for no extra charge. But, you have to increase the underlying limits to the maximum before the umbrella coverage will take effect.

If you are playing golf and hit somebody with your ball, you could lose your entire estate. All that work that you put into picking the right mutual fund or stocks or day-trading can be lost over something that simple. It is not probable, but it is very devastating if it does occur. And, of course, if you own a business, you will certainly need to have liability insurance for the business.

One way to make insurance more affordable is by having a higher deductible. The difference in premium could cover increased maximums or increase the umbrella. Protect the larger exposure, rather than the small, few hundred dollar things that most can afford. When you are starting out and have few assets, you do not worry about these things and you see it as a cash-flow drain. But, once you start accumulating a few things, you start to worry about losing it all.

Now that we have taken care of the car and home, the next area of concern is the general area of disability. Most people feel that their largest asset is their home; automobiles and investment portfolios are the other assets. Your largest asset, however, is your ability to earn an income. Without income, without cash flow, you can no longer keep the plates spinning. This becomes the starting point for insurance because it is a most probable situation and the most devastating.

Becoming disabled prior to age 65 is four times more likely to occur than dying prior to age 65. Your chances of becoming disabled before the age of 65 are 12.5%, and 48% of all foreclosures are due to a prolonged disability. Foreclosures occur because of a death only 3% of the time. It takes at least one, if not two, people to work to pay the mortgage. And, if one of them is disabled, what happens? Following is a brief description and guideline to a disability policy. (We find the fine print troubling to deal with and it is best to consult a professional to purchase this.)

1. The *waiting period*: The amount of time that you are basically self-insured before the insurance company starts accruing a benefit — a period of 60 or 90 days or longer is customary. The longer the waiting period, the lower the cost.
2. The *benefit amount:* The amount of money an insurance company is obligated to pay you as a result of loss of income due to an injury or sickness. As a rule, you need at least 60% of your current wages.
3. The *benefit period*: The length of time the insurance company is obligated to pay you. You may purchase almost any length of time, but you should consider purchasing five years or longer.
4. *Own occupation definition:* This is a good definition to have contained in your insurance contract. This provision states that you must be able to do your own occupation as stated on the application; other-wise, the insurance company is obligated to pay you, even though you may have other income.
5. *Residual disability:* This provision contained in your insurance con-tract provides for a proportional benefit to be paid as a result of proportional loss of income due to a covered sickness or injury.

There are two basic types of disability: people who are working and people who are retired. People who are no longer working require long-term care. Long-term care insurance will be the only insurance that will guarantee that you and your spouse still live together if one of you becomes disabled. If you have a long-term care policy and one of you needs it, you can get care and the other one still has a life.

Forty-three percent of Americans will spend some time in a nursing home. With today's technology and life expectancy, this number is only going to increase. If a couple reaches the age of 65, there is a good chance that one of them will live to age 90, with a 70% chance of one of you having to use a nursing home. The impact on your financial condition can be devastating: 56% of couples will be impoverished after one of them requires a facility for a period of longer than six months. The average cost is increasing at twice that of the inflation rate and is currently $142 per day, or over $50,000 per year. Most elderly in this situation become wards of the state or become indigent. There is already legislation now to require care by their children if the parents do not have enough money to pay for long-term care. We are looking at the first generation for whom it is going to cost more to care for their parents than for their children.

People think a life insurance policy of $100,000 or $200,000 is enough, but it isn't. Life insurance is designed to cover one of two things: to pay off any debts that are owed upon a death, and/or to replace the deceased's income. Coverage of $1 million sounds like a lot of money, but the proceeds from a $1 million policy invested at a 6% return provides about $60,000 a year, and Social Security will possibly pay roughly $12,000 a year. Someone who was making $60,000 and to whom Social Security will now pay $12,000 may only need to replace $48,000 without tapping the retirement plans. A smaller policy of approximately $750,000 worth of insurance invested at a 6% return will pay about $48,000 a year.

The next question is how long are you going to need coverage? Say you have kids and the youngest is 5 years old. In order to support those children until the youngest is somewhere in the neighborhood of 25 years old, you think you have about a 20-year period during which you might need that million dollars of coverage. After that, what would you need to have all that life insurance for? The problem is, you still may not have enough money in your retirement plan.

In the previous chapters, we talked about the variable universal life policy, the one that grows money tax-deferred and comes out tax free and also has a death benefit. If it has a death benefit of $300,000 and you need $750,000, you could buy a term insurance policy for the balance. Term insurance is a major category of life insurance for which the amount of time is specified. This term can be 1, 5, 10, 15, 20, or 30 years, until age 65. It makes a promise that if you die within that term, the insurance company is obligated to pay your beneficiary the death benefit. The insurance company will give you a very low rate for a period of 5, 10, or 15 years, but after that period, you must re-qualify. If you do not, your term rates could grow as much as three or four times. If you need the insurance for a longer period, term may not be the type of insurance you are after.

The other broad category of life insurance is permanent, which has two aspects to it: the mortality charges (or death benefit side) and the accrual side, where any excess or any mortality charges go into a side account and are invested in various funds (whether long-term bonds or mutual fund-like accounts). That cash value then allows for the policy cost to be reduced over a period of time and people are able to afford this policy for their entire lives.

As you grow older, your cost of dying is going to increase, and your cost of term insurance will go up dramatically once you are over the age of 50. Less than 2% of death benefits are paid on term insurance. For long-term benefits, universal life insurance is far better and more cost efficient with a decreasing form of protection and an increasing form of cash value. Universal life insurance is flexible. You can increase or reduce the death benefit. You also can increase or reduce your deposit based upon the contract. The downside risk is that if you do not pay the premiums, you may lose your death benefit. Many consumers who want to get a far better rate of return than a bond or a mortgage will buy a variable product.

The two types of variable products are variable life or variable universal life insurance. Variable life insurance works like whole life insurance. It will give you a level death benefit and will guarantee the death benefit for the life of your contract; however, you must pay your premiums. It will not guarantee your side accounts or the sub-account investments. Variable universal life insurance has become very popular since the 1986 tax laws. It can be used in risk management for protection, or it can be used quite creatively (as we have seen previously) for maximum accumulation and tax efficiency. Second-to-die life insurance is also becoming very popular. You will probably need an advisor to help you pick the one that really fits your needs.

Insurance will also help in business equalization, such as for a buy/sell partnership, because of the significant impact on cash flow if something should happen to one of the partnership's key players. And, insurance reduces the IRS costs. Life insurance is the cheapest substitute for taxes we can find. Purchasing life insurance probably requires as much professional help as any other investment, as you need to compute how much income you need, what cash flow structures you have to replace, and what your goals are. Until you have a proper risk management study done for you, you may be buying too much or too little. The rule of thumb is five or six times your earnings. That is very, very rough. Only a competent advisor can accurately help you determine how much and what kind of insurance to buy.

# 18 How To Select an Advisor

An advisor has to take on the role of a flight navigator. The individual or couple still has to be the pilot, but the advisor takes on the role of telling you where you are at any given time, just like a navigator would. An advisor will also keep you informed about the speed and direction you are taking, but ultimately, you are still in control. The problem is that some factions of the investment community want you to be a passive passenger (i.e., "I'm the pilot, so just sit down and I'll get you there!"). Assuming a passive position in investing is like not taking responsibility for your own health, and we all know how essential that is.

There once was a tanker truck that got lost on a rural road. The driver was so busy trying to find where he was going that he drove under a bridge that was a little too low, and the truck got stuck. He called the police, the fire department, and a tow truck. They were all running around with winches and devices trying to pull the truck out from under the bridge, with no success. Then, a 12-year-old boy who had been watching walked to the scene and asked an officer what was going on. When the officer told him they were trying to get the truck out, the 12-year-old boy asked, "Well, Officer, why don't you just let some air out of the tires?"

The moral of our story is that sometimes you are so close to a problem that you cannot see the solution. We often compartmentalize our thinking, so it is important that you find an advisor who can stand back and look at the entire picture objectively, an advisor who will tell you what you need to hear as opposed to what they want you to hear.

# Rule One

Do not follow blanket advice. Do not believe everything you read in newspapers or magazines. Every local newspaper has a money-makeover column. Recently, in the *L.A. Times*, a particular couple got a thumbs-up for the way they are handling their savings. He was making $56,000 a year, and she was making $50,000 a year. Well, because that relates to about .001% of the people in this country, the scenario was absolutely worthless to most people. Nobody knows what the goals of these people are, and what they have accumulated is not what you have accumulated, so if you follow the advice some reporter has written about this couple, you could make a drastic mistake.

# Rule Two

Do not listen to advertisements. Today, broker/dealers are buying banks, blurring the distinctions, and there does not seem to be any clear indication of where to find reliable advice. Advertising on CNBC is geared toward what the advertisers promote as being normal activities of most people — they are all on-line and trading. Unfortunately, these advertisers are playing off people's emotions of fear and greed. If they can arouse either one of those emotions, they can create some kind of impetus for action. It is all self-serving: "Don't pay full commission … Subscribe to my newsletter for $29 a month." "Don't pay high fees to brokers … buy my trading software." Our personal favorite right now is the pager that allows you to plug in your stock symbols; when one of those particular stocks hits a specified price, the pager alerts you to call your broker up and do something with it. Everybody is trying to hit that home run. What good is it if you save $5 dollars on a stock trade and lose your principal?

# Rule Three

Do not be a market timer. It just doesn't work (see Figure 18.1). You would have to be right exactly 70% on the down and exactly 70% on the up in order to exceed just holding the assets. Even most experts cannot do that. For your own protection, it is very important that you avoid investing as a result of phone, mail, or Internet solicitations. The Securities and Exchange Commission (SEC) is under-staffed as far as following up on complaints of Internet fraud. Sadly, today it all seems to come down to greed. You hear stories about people losing their life savings, because somebody knew how to manipulate them by hitting their greed button.

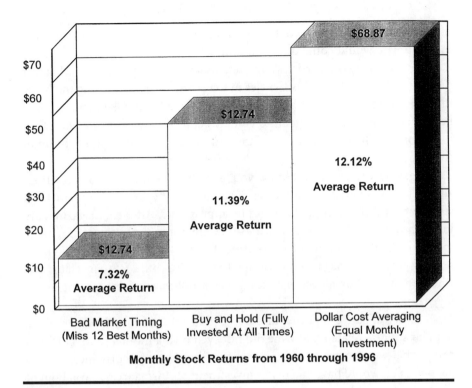

**Figure 18.1. Risk of Poor Market Timing**

## Rule Four

Never give somebody discretionary trading authority. Advisors should contact their clients before they make any transactions if they feel movements are needed. Never make out a check to the planner for an investment.

## Rule Five

Do not believe everything you read in an investment newsletter or magazines. Current law does not control investment newsletters, but there is talk about setting up some type of controls. When someone charges a fee for a newsletter, that is construed as payment for advice. Unfortunately, there are no credentials or prerequisites required. A person does not even have to be in the investment business or have any particular experience to write an investment newsletter or column. When someone is in print, their word is just kind of blankly accepted, and these people are not even held accountable. On the other hand, if an advisor were to make an erroneous statement, every licensing authority would come down on him.

Writers of magazine articles and even books can pretty much say whatever they want. Back in the 1980s, articles in magazines were expressing the belief that the entire country was going to go to hell in a handbasket, and you had better sell your stocks and get into gold. If people followed such advice, they lost money, which demonstrates how important it is that you rely upon someone who can be held accountable for bad advice.

Magazine writers cannot know you, and they are not able to apply their advice to your particular situation. You can do the best you can to try a strategy yourself, but it just may not be appropriate. After all, magazines are in business to sell advertising space — they are not in the business of rendering advice that will be necessarily correct for you. We always take delight in reading advice in a magazine article and then finding out a few pages later that whoever the author is recommending has a full-page advertisement in the magazine.

One investigative reporter discovered that 90% of the 60 writers for a popular money-related magazine did not even own a mutual fund. During a course that we give, we talk about this and about past performance. We tell people, "You would have had better investment performance had you bought whatever they told you to sell. Most of the journalists you are listening to are right out of college." One time a local newspaper columnist came up to one of us after a session and agreed with our characterization of most financial writers. These journalists do not really care about the technical aspects of what they are writing, as long as they feel they have produced a well-written article. They interview people, but the people they interview have a hidden agenda.

People spend more time planning a two-week vacation than they do planning their finances. But the reality is that we never have a chance to go back, so take the time you need now to plan your financial future.

## How To Select an Advisor

Question potential advisors thoroughly to make sure that you have information that is correct and unbiased. First of all, there should not be a name of an insurance company or brokerage company foremost on the advisor's card. Be wary when they suggest their own proprietary products.

Because of high turnover in this industry (we know of one company that hired 400 people, only to have one still around after four years), you will be safer dealing with a person who actually has an office and is not doing business over a kitchen table, for which the likelihood of that salesperson being around to help you 20 years from now is not too great.

It is advisable to deal only with registered investment advisors, because they can give non-commissioned advice and therefore are free to recommend one investment over another. Also, the advisor has to employ more than one strategy. We think a common mistake many people make is that they ignore some of their other investment options. There is no one strategy that will get you to where you want to go.

We have talked about the problems of the 401(k) and about taxes, planning, and a lot of other aspects of investment throughout this book, so we think that people who finish this book will realize that it takes more than one strategy to get them where they want to go. If you read magazines, they are going to give you the same advice that everybody else gives, which is to invest in a 401(k) and pay an extra amount or do bi-weekly payments to pay off a mortgage. But that is not necessarily the best advice for the majority of people.

Check on individuals with the National Association of Securities Dealers (NASD) or other regulatory boards if they have initials after their names. You can check with whatever regulatory board governs a particular designation to make sure that there is no record of complaints or disciplinary action against that person. The two common designations for financial planners are Registered Financial Consultant (RFC) and Certified Financial Planner (CFP), which is geared more toward financial planning.

Other designations mean that these individuals are probably proficient in additional areas, and any type of additional training should go to that individual's credit because it means they took the extra time to learn more about that particular field or subject. Also, a lot of advisors will be licensed for insurance, and you can check with your state's department of insurance to make sure they do not have any valid complaints or disciplinary actions against them.

Financial planning is not just investing. We think that is a fallacy many people have. Financial planning is not only concerned with the investment aspects, but also with making sure you are not hung out to dry when it comes to a particular risk.

A financial advisor can help you develop strategies that are multifaceted, and they can help you change strategies that perhaps were more effective for a different generation, switching you over to new strategies that are more appropriate for you. Your advisor also can help you make sure your taxes are not going to be so far out of whack that you end up paying more taxes during retirement than you did while you were working.

Implement a number of the strategies covered in this book — systematic withdrawals, dollar cost averaging, etc. and also take a look at a couple of different alternatives, depending on your individual situation. You are not going to get advice contained in this book in a magazine because it is a little too much out of the mainstream, but it may be appropriate for you.

## Problems

Many investors feel uncomfortable dealing with the financial services industry due to the transactional nature of the broker's or advisor's compensation. Many feel that the recommendations they receive are suspect due to the inherent conflict of interest in a commission sale. Many investors also feel unsure of how to discern how their portfolios are performing, and their monthly brokerage statements are intimidating. Tracking performance can be especially troublesome if there is more than one brokerage account involved. There is just so much information to come to grips with that the potential first-time investor often avoids taking any action at all.

Most investors feel they need an effective filter, so they subscribe to such publications as *Money, Forbes, Fortune, Business Week,* or *The Wall Street Journal.* Frequently, these periodicals contain conflicting recommendations, even though they draw upon the same data. In today's information age, one huge challenge is dealing with information effectively and using it to your advantage.

The difference between working with a good or merely an average financial advisor will make a significant difference to your success. Many stockbrokers, planners, and financial advisors make the language about investing much more complex than it needs to be. This just creates noise and confusion. Many professionals unconsciously (or consciously) change their voices when speaking to a client, literally becoming "the voice of authority". The timber in their voices deepens, and their stories are well rehearsed. But, just because someone sounds the part does not mean he or she is giving you information to rely upon.

## The Advice Givers

Try to think of all the various professionals out there selling investments as being like different divisions of the armed services. You have the Army, Navy, Marine Corps, and Air Force. All have a similar objective and often even use the same type of equipment; they just carry out their missions differently. To the public, this can be confusing, and rivalries among the various factions can result. The New York stockbrokers think they are at the top of the pecking order, bank representatives believe they sell on hallowed ground, and independent fee-only financial advisors sense they are close to nirvana. Yet, they all may be selling the exact same investment product or offering the same service, and the joint mission they all share is to provide a service to the public. Unfortunately, not all advisors share this sense of mission. In fact, some have changed their titles to "financial planner" simply to gain a marketing advantage. Often these individuals desire to sell you a product, not assist you.

## Stockbrokers

Most investors have a good relationship with their traditional Wall Street brokers; in surveys, these brokers score high marks. People feel secure when they see the plush offices, dark wood paneling, and concentrated activity. They do not realize that much of that activity revolves around cold calling and sales. Most stockbrokers attempt to add value by following traditional investment strategies, such as trying to pick exceptional securities, stocks, or mutual funds or even worse, by predicting which way the market is going. Academic studies, however, have conclude that these two strategies — stock picking and market timing — do not work over the long term.

These active strategies entail investigation and analysis expenses, increase general transaction costs, and involve capital gains taxation. These judgment calls may also involve the acceptance of a relatively high degree of diversifiable risk. The extra costs and risks can be substantial and must be justified by realistically evaluated return expectations.

Most of the big firms also have their brokers sell so-called proprietary mutual funds, which are their in-house packaged versions of already available investment products, but now the firm is biased towards these particular products over others. According to a recent publication, one firm allegedly began restricting access by its brokers to outside mutual fund vendors in an effort to increase sales of its proprietary mutual funds. According to the magazine article, the goal of the company's regional managers is for brokers to reach a minimum sales ratio of 40% proprietary funds/60% outside funds. Currently, proprietary funds account for only about 20% of the company's mutual fund sales. To help push in-house funds, the company recently targeted those branches below the minimum ratio and sent them a restricted list of outside fund vendors allowed into those branches. Although the brokers are compensated equally for selling in-house and outside funds, brokers say the pressure to sell the firm's funds has been immense.

While many brokers resent the pressure to sell in-house funds, industry observers say that a target ratio of 40/60 is far below those of other major houses. It has been reported that at Merrill Lynch proprietary funds constitute about 50% of mutual fund sales, and at Morgan Stanley Dean Witter (MSDW) branch managers are required to maintain a minimum sales ratio of 75% proprietary funds to 25% outside funds. MSDW is also the only major firm that compensates its brokers more for selling in-house products by paying them 20% less for selling outside funds.

## Brokerage Firms

The big Wall Street firms are called full-service, meaning they offer a wider variety of financial products than discount brokerages while charging considerably higher fees. Products they offer include stocks, bonds, derivatives, annuities, and insurance. A full-service stockbroker solicits business and is paid mostly by commissions. These houses also offer investment advice and research. A recent study by Prophet Market Research and Consulting in San Francisco shows that brokers continue to suggest investments without knowledge of their investors' financial backgrounds or objectives. Of the 300 brokers audited from 21 of the nation's largest full-service firms, 42% made investment recommendations without learning the potential investors' tax situations, 32% without knowing their financial status, 25% without knowing what securities they held, and 21% without knowing what the investors' financial objectives were. Furthermore, 9% of brokers studied from regional firms and 5% of brokers from national firms made recommendations without uncovering any qualifiers. In other words, they were there for one thing and one thing only: to sell stock.

## Discount Brokerages

Discount brokerages usually do not offer the full range of services provided by full-service brokers. They do not offer any advice or research — they simply transact trades, no frills. Because they manage fewer products than their full-service counterparts, discounters charge considerably lower fees. Discounters also often offer on-line computer order entry services. Those that have live brokers generally pay them a set salary to execute trades. The brokers do not solicit and are not paid commissions. Discount brokerages make money by doing business in volume, competing mostly on price and the reliability of their service. If they have the lowest prices and the best service, they get the most trades.

Which broker should you choose? You should first determine what types of services you need. If you require considerable research backup and advice, you should go to a full-service broker. If you are happy doing your own homework and do not need such advice, a discount broker is preferable.

## Investment Consultants

Investment consultants normally work for Wall Street firms but specialize in consulting with investors about their investments and charge fees for services rather than charging commissions on transactions. Consultants are only going to make more money if you make more money — so you are on the same side of the fence. You also know in advance what your costs are going to be. Investment consultants specialize not only in consulting but also in helping to educate investors about the capital markets. They take a much broader approach and maintain a macro-perspective of global, small cap, and large cap equities. They provide educational materials and attend training sessions. They help investors set financial goals and come up with comprehensive plans, rather than simply trying to sell particular investments.

## Bank Investment Representatives

For decades, consumers have named banks as their most trusted source of financial products and advice, the primary reason being that bank savings and CDs are backed by the FDIC. Traditional bankers, however, knew little about investments, financial planning, or diversification, and bank employees were basically trained in making loans, taking deposits, and issuing credit cards. Then, a few years ago, banks decided to offer investments as well as savings. After all, banks already had the customers, so it was a natural extension to hire and train sales representatives and offer investment products. These bank advisors have the same securities licenses as other brokers and many have gone through traditional Wall Street training programs. Somewhat objectionable, though, is the banks' use of mostly third-party investment products, meaning investments manufactured outside the bank which utilize active investment management strategies and market timing.

# What You Should Look For

Now you need to find a consultant who understands investing. Here is a list of questions to ask and what you should be looking for:

1. What is this person's education and certification with independent associations?
2. Does this person have fee-based clients? Only registered advisors are legally allowed to charge fees.
3. What investment vehicles does this person offer? Mutual funds? Individually managed accounts? Annuities?
4. Who is the typical client?
5. Where does this person obtain research? Who is this person's provider? What is this person's selection criteria?
6. How often does this person suggest rebalancing your portfolio?
7. How often would you like to meet with the advisor?

The following professional designations confer some assurance of thorough training and high standards of conduct, but these designations only tell you the consultant has had some extra training. It is still up to you to do your own homework.

## *Financial Planning*

Figure 18.2 presents the results of a survey of 4212 consumers who were asked which type(s) of financial advisors they consider reliable for investment advice. Consumers considered financial planners most reliable for this type of advice in nearly all demographic segments, while insurance agents were considered least reliable.

You still need to be aware that more than 200,000 women and men call themselves financial planners, including accountants, attorneys, stockbrokers, sales representatives, self-styled money managers, credit counselors, and the Internet junkie down the street. This still does not mean they understand the concepts represented in this book.

There are several kinds of financial consultants:

1. The Certified Financial Planner (CFP) is a designation of the Certified Financial Planner Board of Standards (based in Denver) that is granted to those who complete an approved course, pass an exam, and meet work-experience requirements.

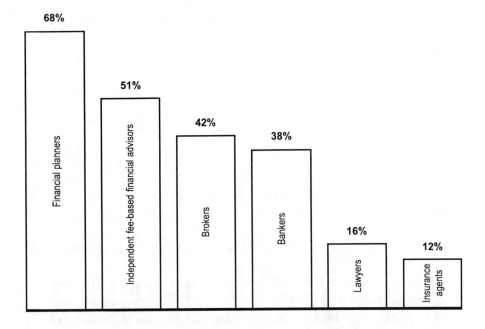

**Figure 18.2. Most Reliable Source of Financial Advice.** (Adapted from Dalbar Series on Personal Financial Advice, Report 8, 1996, Dalbar, Inc., Boston, MA.)

2.  The Certified Public Accountant/Personal Financial Specialist (CPA/PFS) is a designation of the American Institute of Certified Public Accountants (based in New York) that is given to CPAs who pass an exam and meet work-experience requirements.
3.  The Chartered Financial Consultant (ChFC) is a designation of the American College (Bryn Mawr, PA) given to those who complete a ten-part course of study.

## Investment Analysis

Investment analysis designations include:

1.  Chartered Financial Analyst (CFA), a designation of the Association for Investment Management and Research (based in Charlottesville, VA) given to those who pass a rigorous three-level exam (each level of exam must be taken one year apart) administered by the association and covering investment principles, asset valuation, and portfolio

management. Candidates must also have three years of investment-management experience.

2. Chartered Investment Counselor (CIC), a designation of the Investment Counsel Association of America (based in Washington, D.C.) given to those holding CFAs and currently working as investment counselors.

## Where To Turn

These professional organizations will provide you with select lists of financial planners in your area (in addition, please see the list of advisors to this book).

1. The American Institute of CPAs lists CPA/PFS planners (888-999-9256).
2. The Institute of Certified Financial Planners provides a list of financial planners with CFP designations (303-759-4900; www.cfp.board.org).
3. The Licensed Independent Network of CPA Financial Planners (LINC) lists members who are CPA/PFS fee-only planners in public accounting firms (800-737-2727).

The exact role an advisor plays is up to you. You may opt for an advisor who analyzes your financial condition, strategizes with you on the best route forward, and sends you on your way — in other words, someone who empowers you to take action on your own.

# 19 Teach Your Children To Manage Money

How to manage money is one of the most important lessons you can teach your children. Children who are excluded from open discussions of family financial affairs or sheltered from the financial realities of life can sometimes develop distorted ideas about money. They may make extravagant demands, often creating unnecessary squabbles about money, simply because they are not informed about the family's financial resources. When these children grow up, they may be ill-equipped to manage their own finances or unable to exercise good judgment in financial matters.

The key is to teach your children to think about money and financial management from a positive point of view. Of course, introducing your children to money management is a very personal matter, and you as the parent must decide what is best for your child. Here are some tips you may find helpful:

*Be open with your children about money matters.* Many families hold regular conferences, children included, to review finances. Every family member should be encouraged to speak out freely about his or her own priorities or goals. This way you can illustrate that priorities need to be made and that trade-offs are sometimes necessary for effective use of money. Even a fairly young child, for instance, should be able to understand that paying for shelter and groceries takes a higher priority over a new bike or a trip to an amusement park. Attending these sessions can give your children a sense of involvement and a greater willingness to work toward meeting family financial goals.

1-57444-258-9/00/$0.00+$.50
© 2000 by CRC Press LLC

*Give your children regular allowances.* You can begin when they reach school age, and be sure to include at least some money they are free to spend as they like without accounting to anyone. That way your children gain experience in deciding how to spend their own money. A recommended way to start is by giving a young child a small amount of money every day or two for little toys or treats. As the child gets older, you can spread out the payment periods and increase the size of the allowance and the purpose for which it is used. The child can have a greater voice as the years go by in determining what the allowance should be. A teenager, for example, might receive a monthly allowance that covers school lunches and supplies, hobbies and entertainment, and clothing. This can teach the child to plan and to save for necessities and special purchases and to shop carefully for good buys. Giving an occasional advance against an upcoming allowance may be appropriate, but if your child overspends constantly, work with him or her to bring spending in line with available income.

*Teach your children the value of working for extra money.* Children should learn at an early age that money must be earned. You do not want to pay your child for every routine household task, of course, but you might consider paying for special household chores, above and beyond the allowance.

*Encourage your children to save for special goals.* You might begin with a piggy bank and advance to a passbook savings account so that each child can see first-hand how money deposited regularly can earn money through interest — and grow faster. A child can open a savings account at any age, but remember that banks generally require a Social Security number for all depositors. Once a child has a passbook account, he or she should have the freedom, within reason, to withdraw funds at will when necessary.

*Introduce your children to checking accounts when they are old enough.* Opening checking accounts for your children when they are in their midteens is one way for them to learn about simple banking transactions — how to make deposits, how to write checks, and how to balance checkbooks.

*Teach your children to the basics of investing.* Because money management is sometimes more involved than balancing your checkbook or opening a passbook savings account, you should also try to involve your child in a goaloriented investment, such as for their college tuition. By actually owning a stock, a child can watch the stock market fluctuate, learn how investments help the growth of the American economy, and gain an understanding of basic investment principles. And, as a stockholder, your child will periodically receive information on his or her investment, including an annual report, that may be interesting as well as educational.

*Teach your children about credit when they are mature enough.* Credit has become such a substantial part of the American way of life that teaching your children to use it properly is an important element of their financial education. Many stores permit teenagers to use family credit accounts with their parents' consent. You should supervise their use of credit closely, of course, to make sure they keep credit purchases modest and pay bills promptly.

*Set a good example.* This is the best way to teach your children the principles of sound money management. No matter how much training you give them, many of their attitudes toward money will be influenced by the way you spend and save.

# 20 Putting It All Together

## Principle 1: Pay Yourself First and Eliminate Debt

P ay yourself before anybody else! As selfish as that might seem, it is a sound approach. Perhaps the most important piece of advice is to pay down your consumer debt and then pay the equivalent of those monthly interest payments to your investment program.

## Principle 2: Get Started Now and Build a Core Savings Program

Overcome the hurdle of getting started. Start small, but be consistent. Put the money into a savings vehicle where you cannot spend it. You will be encouraged by how quickly your weekly or monthly contributions begin to add up. Challenge yourself to increase the amount frequently. Become a saver first, then build that savings into an investment program. If you think you cannot find a large amount of money to invest, you can start out by saving just $6 a day. Taking just $6 a day (the cost of lunch), invest and re-invest in an index fund compounding over time at 16%. In 5 years, this account will be worth $19,000; in 10 years, $60,000; in 15 years, $150,000; in 20 years, $350,000; and, in 25 years, this account would be worth just under $1 million.

1-57444-258-9/00/$0.00+$.50
© 2000 by CRC Press LLC

## Principle 3: Remember the Mortgage Myth

See Chapter 14.

## Principle 4: Evaluate Your Future Needs

Determine your financial and personal needs and time frames. The most important element of an investment plan is matching your investment program to your own personality and implementing a clear plan. Commit the plan in writing.

## Principle 5: Manage Your Investment Expectations

Look past all the hype and maintain realistic expectations. Do not panic and sell if your mutual funds prices go down. In fact, it is wise to expect fluctuations and ride them out. Use a drop in the stock market as an opportunity to average your cost downward (dollar cost averaging). Upgrade your knowledge about investing. Education is the key to simplifying all the investment advice and products available and knowing how to apply the advice to a particular situation.

## Principle 6: Add Time!

Become a long-term investor. Lengthen time horizons for investments. The problem is that every investor has expectations of immediate gains, but those expectations are not compatible with being a long-term investor. Instead of running down the road in hopes of finding the pot of gold at the end of a rainbow, why not be standing where the next rainbow appears?

## Principle 7: Diversify

Diversification enhances returns. To the extent that you take advantage of effective diversification, you will increase the expected rate of returns of your portfolio over time. We learned from Harry Markowitz, Nobel Prize winner in economics, that while almost all diversification is good, there is effective diversification and ineffective diversification. If your investments all move together, you have ineffective diversification. It is as if you did not diversify.

Investments that do not move in tandem result in effective diversification of your portfolio due to the overall risk of the portfolio being less than the average risk of its components.

## Principle 8: Teach Your Family About Investing

Providing for your family is at the heart of everyone's financial concerns, but who said it was up to you alone? Do not operate in a vacuum, leaving those you care about in the dark. There is no better way to provide for your loved ones' future than to teach them to help themselves. Not only does this empower them as participants, but it also gives them a better appreciation of your efforts.

## Principle 9: Find an Investment Advisor

For many investors, having a qualified investment advisor on their financial team to ensure they stay on track will add substantial value.

## Epilogue

Now what do you want to do? Some of you are going to put this book on the shelf, and some of you are going to put it in the trash. But here is the reality. It makes sense. It is not about buying a product; it is about structuring your life to provide the best benefit possible for you. Be warned that misuse of this book could be hazardous to your financial wealth. Someone picking out all the products mentioned in this book and contacting a discount broker could overlook something important that might jeopardize their goal. Instead, we encourage you to find an advisor who subscribes to the theories that have been outlined here, one who really cares about your values and your goals. It can make a world of difference.

We might call it the "investment myth" — when television shows or magazines say investing is easy and that you do not need a pro to help you anymore. Just get up in the morning and tune in! Go to the Motley Fool on-line site, and pick up on a suggestion. Then you will be able to buy the hot stocks, right? Well, maybe, in a rising market, but what is going to happen when the market takes more than a 60-day downturn and stays down for an extended period of time? People do not realize that money is made over time — it is not a result of timing the market.

Most of us work a 40-hour week, and most people are at work when the stock market is doing its volatile thing. It is not realistic to believe that you can do your investment homework at night after working 8 or 9 hours and then be able to invest meaningfully and in such a way as to preserve your assets. The stock market is a rising tide, and a rising tide raises most boats. This tide has given a false sense of security to a lot of people who need to take a step back and reconsider their choice to be amateur day traders. Can you imagine if we created a work force of only day-traders? It would change the entire face of American business. Why bus dishes when you can day-trade? Why work the assembly line when you can day-trade instead? Why go to college when you can day-trade? What happens when the tide recedes and we have no one trained to bus tables or work on automobiles? Investing is not easy, and that is a very important point to understand. The readers of this book have to understand that it does take a systematic approach. Day-trade if you want, for some things, but you still need a systematic, long-term objective of putting the money to work to achieve the best net return possible.

Let's leave you with one last thought. Unless you are tax efficient, your long-term partner is the tax man. Some advisors say they can help, but they are doing your taxes one year at a time. Do you pay your CPA for 20 years' worth of tax efficiency? No. Your tax man will be around for a very long time, and we have attempted to show you how to fight back.

# Appendixes

# Appendix A.
# Understanding How
# Mutual Funds Work

This section is not about which is the best mutual fund or the top mutual fund; rather, we will discuss the basic trading structure or vehicle you should use. Think of a mutual fund as a financial intermediary that makes investments on your behalf. The mutual fund pools all its investors' funds together and buys stocks, bonds, or other assets on behalf of the group as a whole. Each investor receives a certificate of ownership and a regular statement of his or her account indicating the value of the shares of the total investment pool. A mutual fund, in other words, is an investment company that makes investments on behalf of its participants who share common financial goals.

Mutual funds continually issue new shares of the fund for sale to the public. The number of shares and the price are directly related to the value of the securities that the mutual fund holds. A fund's share price can change from day to day, depending on the daily value of its underlying securities. The main reasons people invest in mutual funds are their convenience, the professional knowledge accessed, and the opportunity to earn higher returns through a combination of growth and reinvestment of dividends. To understand why mutual funds are so popular, let's examine just how mutual funds work.

1-57444-258-9/00/$0.00+$.50
© 2000 by CRC Press LLC

## How Mutual Funds Work

The manager of the mutual fund uses the pool of capital to buy a variety of stocks, bonds, or money market instruments based on the advertised financial objectives of the fund. These objectives cover a wide range. Some funds follow aggressive policies, involving greater risk in search of higher returns. Others seek current income and no risk. Because each mutual fund has a specific investment objective, the investor has the ability to select a variety of funds to meet asset allocation and diversification needs.

When you purchase mutual fund shares, you own them at *net asset value* (NAV). This is the value of the fund's total investment, minus any debt, divided by the number of outstanding shares. For example, if the fund's investment value is $26,000, with no debt and 1000 shares outstanding, the NAV would be $26 per share. The NAV is not a fixed figure, because it must reflect the daily change in the price of the securities within the fund's portfolio. In a regular mutual fund which includes thousands and often millions of shares, the NAV is calculated on a daily basis without commissions, in full and fractional units, with values moving up or down along with the stock and bond markets.

The biggest mistake that most investors make when buying mutual funds is looking first (and sometimes only) at the prior performance of the fund or paying too much attention to the current bond fund yield. Fund costs are an equally important factor in the return that you earn from a mutual fund. Fees are deducted from your investment, which, combined with other charges, depress your returns.

## Fees

Because of the large amounts of assets being managed, investment companies are able to offer economies of scale, or competitive fee schedules, to their customers. The management fees charged depend on the complexity of the asset management demands. Foreign equity management requires substantially more research, specialized implementation, and transaction costs than the management of a U.S. government bond fund. Asset management fees reflect those differences. Equity mutual fund fees are higher than bond mutual fund fees. Fee comparisons are particularly important. Remember to compare the proverbial apples to apples — in this case, similar equities to equity mutual funds and similar bonds to bond mutual funds (see Table A.1).

### Table A.1. Fee Comparisons of Various Mutual Funds

| Mutual Fund | Annual Performance | Management Fees | Net Performance |
|---|---|---|---|
| Foreign equities | 12.50% | 1.25% | 11.25% |
| U.S. large cap | 12.50% | 1.00% | 11.50% |
| U.S. small cap | 13.00% | 1.20% | 11.80% |
| Investment-grade bonds | 7.80% | 0.65% | 8.50% |
| High-yield bonds | 9.25% | 0.75% | 8.50% |
| Foreign bonds | 9.25% | 0.90% | 8.35% |

## Keeping an Eye on Costs

You can put more money to work for you in your investment by keeping a careful eye on costs. It is simply common sense — lower expenses translate into higher overall returns. The goal of any investor is to keep acquisition costs as low as possible. There are three basic kinds of costs.

### Sales Charges

Sales charges (or loads) are commissions paid on the sale of mutual funds. In the past, all commissions were simply charged up front, but that has changed. There are now several ways that mutual fund companies charge fees. The sales charge is called a *load* and is subtracted from the initial mutual fund investment. A no-load fund does not have this charge, although other fees or service charges may be buried in its cost structure. Do not be misled; nearly all mutual funds have a sales charge. Some are hidden, some are not. Let's talk about the ones that you can see.

A *front-end load* mutual fund charges a fee when an investor buys it. Loaded mutual funds can also have a *back-end load* (deferred sales charge) and are sometimes known as B-shares. This option has higher internal costs. If you decide to redeem your shares early, usually within the first five years, you pay a surrender charge, as illustrated in Figure A.1. A customer who redeems shares in the first year of ownership would typically pay a 5% sales charge. The amount would drop by an equal amount each year. After six years, the shares could be redeemed without further charge.

For large investments, you should never purchase B-share mutual funds. There are brokers out there who will tell you it is better to invest in B-shares,

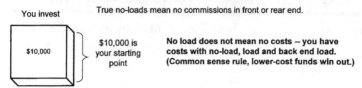

**(NO-LOAD) MUTUAL FUNDS**

True no-loads mean no commissions in front or rear end.

**Sales loads are commissions paid to brokers and financial advisors who sell mutual funds. They typically range from 4 percent to as high as 8.5 percent of the amount you invest.**

**FRONT-END (LOAD) MUTUAL FUNDS**

**BACK-END (LOAD) MUTUAL FUNDS**

**Some no-load mutual funds have redemption fees that scale down the longer you hold them. The broker/advisor is paid his commission by the mutual fund company. If you leave the fund earlier than the schedule, that percentage will be subtracted from your proceeds.**

Figure A.1. No-Load and Load Mutual Funds

as you will not pay an up-front fee. If you invest a large amount, you will get a breakpoint with an A-share mutual fund and your annual costs will be lower. Following is a summary of the different kinds of mutual fund shares:

1. A-share mutual fund commissions are payable all at once.
2. B-shares have a contingent deferred sales charge. They are more popular with brokers because you do not pay any up-front load, but every year they take out the equivalent of 1% to pay the broker.
3. C-shares typically have even higher internal expenses and pay the selling broker up to 1% per year based on the amount of the assets. This fee comes directly from your investment performance. The C-shares may have no up-front fee, but there is a possible 1% deferred sales charge in the first year (sometimes longer) and higher annual expenses (up to 1% extra per year).

### Table A.2. Commission Schedule for Typical Mutual Fund

| | Sales Commission as a Percentage of | |
| --- | --- | --- |
| Purchase Amount (A-Shares) | Public Offering | Net Amount Invested |
| Less than $50,000 | 5.00% | 5.26% |
| $50,000 but less than $250,000 | 4.00% | 4.17% |
| $250,000 but less than $500,000 | 3.00% | 3.09% |
| $500,000 but less than 1,000,000 | 1.00% | 1.01% |
| $1,000,000 or more | 0.00% | 0.00% |

Table A.2 illustrates the commission schedule of a typical mutual fund. You will notice that the offering price is different from the net amount invested column. The offering price, known as the *ask* price, is greater than the fund's NAV (net asset value). The NAV is identified as the amount per share you would receive if you sold your shares.

No-load mutual funds do *not* mean no cost. Some no-load funds charge a redemption fee of 1 to 2% of the net asset value of the shares to cover expenses mainly incurred by advertising. Buying a no-load mutual fund is like doing your own plumbing work. You can save money if you know what you are doing, but if you do not have the required time and expertise, you can make a serious mistake. We highly recommend working with an investment advisor who can offer the same no-load funds. (A reminder: When you call the toll-free number of the mutual fund company with a question, you are serviced by an employee of the mutual fund company, and the advice you receive may be biased.)

## Operating Expenses

Fees pay for the operational costs of running a fund — employees' salaries, marketing, servicing the toll-free phone line, printing and mailing costs, maintaining computers for tracking investments and account balances, accounting expenses, and so on. A fund's operating expenses are quoted as a percentage of your investment; the percentage represents an annual fee or charge. You can find this number in a fund's prospectus in the fund expenses section, usually entitled "Total Fund Operating Expenses". A mutual fund's operating expenses are normally invisible to investors because they are deducted before any return is paid and are automatically charged on a daily basis.

# Other Things You Should Know

## Dividends

Dividends and capital gains (the profits from a sale of stock) are paid in proportion to the number of mutual fund shares you own. So, even if you invest a few hundred dollars, you get the same investment return per dollar as those who invest millions. The problem is you will have to pay taxes on this amount even if it is reinvested, but you can use a variable annuity to defer those taxes until you plan to spend the money.

## Prospectus and Annual Report

Mutual fund companies produce information that can help you make decisions about mutual fund investments; for example, all funds are required to issue a prospectus. You can now find the prospectus for many mutual funds on the Internet. You can take a look at a fund's past performance and see what asset class it falls in. The prospectus, a legal document, is reviewed and audited by the U.S. Securities and Exchange Commission (SEC).

## Statements

Any mutual fund in which you participate will send you a year-end statement itemizing income you have received. You should save this sheet along with other records of dividends, tax-exempt interest, and capital gains distributions, as well as records of the amounts received from the sale of shares for tax purposes.

## Full-Time Professionals

When you invest in a mutual fund, you are hiring a team of professional investment managers to make complex investment judgments and handle complicated trading, recordkeeping, and safekeeping responsibilities for you. People whose full-time profession is money management will sift through the thousands of available investments in order to choose those that, in their judgment, are best suited to achieving the investment goals of a fund as spelled out in the fund's prospectus.

Full-time professionals select the portfolio's securities and then constantly monitor investments to determine if they continue to meet the fund's objectives. As economic conditions change, professionals may adjust the mix of the fund's investments to adopt a more aggressive or defensive posture. Having access to research analysis and computerized support, professional management can help identify opportunities in the markets that the average investor may not have the expertise or access to identify.

## Diversification

Diversification is one important characteristic that attracts many investors to mutual funds. By owning a diverse portfolio of many stocks and/or bonds, investors can reduce the risk associated with owning any individual security. To go it alone, you would need to invest money in at least 8 to 12 different securities in different industries to ensure that your portfolio could withstand a downturn in one or more of the investments. A mutual fund is typically invested in 25 to 100 or more securities. Proper diversification ensures that the fund receives the highest possible return at the lowest possible risk, given the objectives of the fund.

Mutual funds do not escape share price declines during major market downturns. For example, mutual funds that invested in stocks certainly declined during the October 27, 1997, market crash when the Dow Jones plunged 554.26 points. However, the most unlucky investors that month were individuals who had all of their money riding in Asian mutual funds. Some fund shares plunged in price by as much as 30 to 40% that month. Widely diversified mutual funds were impacted the least.

## Low Initial Investment

Each mutual fund establishes the minimum amount required to make an initial investment, and then how much additional is required when investors want to add more. A majority of mutual funds have low initial minimums, some less than $1000.

## Liquidity

One of the key advantages of mutual funds stems from the liquidity provided by this investment. You can sell your shares at any time, and mutual funds have a ready market for their shares. Additionally, shareholders directly receive any dividend or interest payments earned by the fund. Payments are usually made on a quarterly basis. When the fund manager sells some of the investments at a profit, the net gain is also distributed, but net losses are retained by the fund. Inside the mutual fund, when the dividends or capital gains are disbursed, the NAV is reduced by the disbursement.

## Audited Performance

All mutual funds are required to disclose historical data about the fund through their prospectus — returns earned by the fund, operating expenses, and other fees and the fund's rate of trading turnover. The SEC audits these disclosures. Having the SEC on your side is like having a vigilant guard dog focused on the guy who is responsible for your money. Remember that all mutual funds are registered investments. This does not mean that the SEC recommends them, but it does mean they have reviewed them for abuse and fraud.

## Automatic Reinvestment

One of the major benefits of mutual funds is that dividends can be reinvested automatically and converted into more shares.

## Switching

Switching, or an exchange privilege, is offered by most mutual funds through so-called family or umbrella plans. Switching from one mutual fund to another accommodates changes in investment goals, as well as changes in the market and the economy. Again, this switching between mutual funds creates tax implications. For instance, if you redeem a Franklin Growth and Income Fund and buy a Franklin NY Municipal Bond Fund, you have to pay taxes on the gains you earned.

## Low Transaction Costs

When an individual investor places an order to buy 300 shares of a $30 stock ($9000 investment), he or she is likely to get a commission bill for about $204, or 2.3% of the value of the investment. Even at a discount broker, commissions are likely to cost between $82 (0.9%) and $107 (1.2%). A mutual fund, on the other hand, is more likely to be buying 30,000 to 300,000 shares at a time. Their commission costs often run in the vicinity of one tenth of the commission you would pay at a discount broker. While the commission you would pay as an individual might be $0.35 a share, the mutual fund might only pay $0.05 a share, or even less. The commission savings can (and should) mean higher returns for you as a mutual fund shareholder.

## Flexibility in Risk Level

An investor can select from among a variety of different mutual funds, finding one that has a risk level he or she is comfortable with and having goals that match his or her own:

1.  *Stock funds.* If you want your money to grow over a long period of time, funds that invest more heavily in stocks may be most appropriate.
2.  *Bond funds.* If you need current income and do not want investments that fluctuate in value as widely as stocks, more conservative bond funds may be the best choice.
3.  *Money market funds.* If you want to be sure that your invested principal does not drop in value because you may need your money in the short-term, a money market fund or a guaranteed fixed-interest investment may best fit your needs.

## Virtually No Risk of Bankruptcy

A demand for money back (liabilities) exceeding the value of a fund's investments (assets) cannot occur with a mutual fund. The value can fluctuate, but this variation does not lead to the failure or bankruptcy of a mutual fund company. In fact, since the Investment Company Act of 1940 was passed to regulate the mutual fund industry, no mainstream fund has ever gone under.

In contrast, hundreds of banks and dozens of insurance companies have failed in the past two decades alone. Banks and insurers can fail because their liabilities can exceed their assets. When a bank makes too many loans that go sour at the same time and depositors want their money back, the bank fails. Likewise, if an insurance company makes several poor investments or underestimates the number of claims that will be made by insurance policyholders, it, too, can fail. But mutual funds are held in separate accounts and are not part of an insurance company's assets.

## Custodian Bank

A custodian is a separate organization holds the specific securities in which a mutual fund is invested independent of the mutual fund company. The employment of a custodian ensures that the fund management company cannot embezzle your funds or use assets from a better-performing fund to subsidize a poor performer.

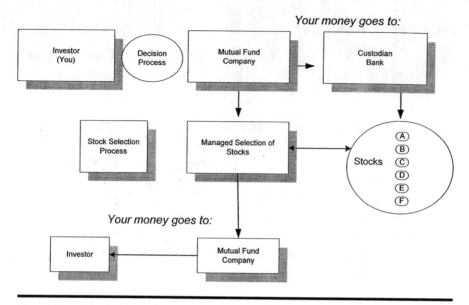

Figure A.2. Relationship of Various Parts of a Mutual Fund

## How Do These Various Parties Work Together?

(See Figure A.2.) After you have written your check to the mutual fund, the mutual fund company sends that check on your behalf to an organization functioning as a *transfer agent*. Here, your investment is recorded and processed, and the real safeguards come into play. The agent transfers the money, not to the mutual fund's portfolio manager (the individual or firm that makes the investment decisions, technically known as the *investment advisor*), but to a custodian bank. Once that custodian bank receives the money, it notifies the mutual fund that new money is available for investment. The fund manager checks a daily account balance sheet and new monies are invested according to the mutual fund's investment policy.

The requirement of the Investment Company Act of 1940 for independent custody for each mutual fund's assets has turned out to be the key provision that has sheltered the industry from potential trouble for half a century. Separate custody means a mutual fund's parent company can go belly-up without any loss to the fund's shareholders, because their assets are held apart from other funds and apart from the parent fund. Contrast this business structure with the far less restrictive setup between, for example, individual investors and a real estate promoter or investors and a stockbroker who may have direct access to his clients' accounts. In any number of notorious incidents, individuals in such a position have taken the money and run.

The limited partnerships of the 1970s and 1980s were excellent examples of poor business structure. During those years, many unregulated and unregistered limited partnerships were formed and investors sent their money directly to the limited partnership company, and an unscrupulous promoter could simply write himself a check. Financial scandals were numerous.

A money manager of a mutual fund has no direct access to his investors' cash. The fund manager only decides how to invest shareholders' money. The custodian who controls the underlying securities allows them to be traded or exchanged with other institutional investors only after getting proper documentation from the manager. The upshot of independent custody is that it is very difficult for a fund manager to use the money for his own purposes.

The Investment Company Act added other layers of investor protection, as well. Independent accountants must regularly audit every fund. A fund's board of directors, who serve as modern-day trustees, negotiate prudent contract terms with the fund's service providers and generally oversee the operation. The SEC has the power to inspect funds and bring enforcement action against those that break the rules. In addition, mutual fund firms have legions of compliance lawyers (essentially, in-house cops) paid to make sure that portfolio managers, traders, and others follow the rules.

### A Code of Conduct

Under SEC rules, fund managers are required to abide by strict codes of conduct. The codes require advance reporting of personal securities transactions so that there can be no conflict of interest between a manager's personal trades and what he does with his fund's securities. A manager otherwise could "front-run" his own fund, personally buying or selling securities before the fund trades in them, to his gain and possibly the fund's loss. To avoid such potential for self-dealing — that is, favoring one fund at the expense of another — the SEC has set down strict guidelines for when funds in the same company trade a security between one another rather than on the open market.

## Major Types of Mutual Funds

The number of mutual funds has nearly tripled since 1980. In the current universe of mutual funds, there are portfolios that suit most investment risk objectives. Likewise, the number of options has skyrocketed. There are funds that invest in high-quality growth stocks, or smaller aggressive growth stocks, or stocks that pay high dividends. Mutual funds that invest in corporate and government bonds are also available.

Many fund management companies offer a number of different types of funds under one roof, often referred to as a family of funds. A fund might include a growth stock fund, an aggressive growth stock fund, a fund that invests in stocks and bonds, a tax-exempt bond fund, a money market fund, and perhaps many others. Most mutual funds permit customers to exchange from one fund to another within the group for a small fee, if their personal investment objectives change.

Following is a description of how, roughly, the $2 trillion currently invested in mutual funds breaks down. Despite endless variations, there are basically three broad categories of mutual funds: those aimed at providing immediate income, those oriented toward long-term growth or appreciation, and those that stress tax-free returns. The fund's objectives will be stated at the opening of the prospectus, indicating whether the fund emphasizes high or low risk and stability or speculation. Funds generally fall into one of nine major types: growth, growth and income, income, bond, money market funds, tax-free, metals, foreign, and specialized.

## Stock Funds

Stock mutual funds invest only in stocks (also called equity funds.) Following are the various types of stock funds.

### Growth Funds

These stock funds emphasize growth. Dividend payouts will typically be low. These funds stress capital appreciation rather than immediate income. A typical growth fund would be the Vanguard S&P 500 index fund. This is a fund that consists of U.S. large cap stocks and has as its primary objective to equal the return of 500 largest U.S. stock companies. According to Morningstar, as of June 30, 1996, the average growth mutual fund had returned 12% over the last 10 years, but only 9.4% after tax (assuming maximum brackets). This reduction in returns is due to dividend and capital gain distributions made by the funds, which are taxable to investors.

### Aggressive Growth Funds

Aggressive growth funds invest in smaller, lesser known companies, giving these companies time and room for enough upward movement to perform spectacularly during a bull market. As the name implies, these funds are invested for maximum capital gains, capital appreciation, and performance. This type of portfolio can be highly volatile and speculative in nature. The old adage of "high risk, high return" would fit. Historically, the more aggressive funds or small cap funds have outperformed the larger blue-chip growth funds. You should be aware, though, that these returns also come with higher volatility, meaning the roller coaster ride has much bigger dips.

## Balanced Funds

These portfolios stress three main goals: income, capital appreciation, and preservation of capital. This type of fund balances holdings such as bonds, convertible securities, and preferred stock, as well as common stock. The mix varies depending on the manager's view of the economy and market conditions. The theory here is that the manager will have a better crystal ball than you at home, as they make big bucks and sit in front of a computer terminal all day looking at graphs. We generally do not believe in these funds unless they have a static ratio of stocks to bonds. We normally look for the manager to keep 60% in stocks and 40% in bonds. Because they are diversified into both bond and stock markets, these funds are most appropriate for investors who can only afford one fund.

## Growth and Income Funds

Combining stocks and bonds, this type of fund makes a serious effort at capturing both modest income and a long-term rise in the stock market. The manager is typically looking for blue-chip companies that pay high dividends. Another strategy is to place a large percentage of the portfolio in equities and a portion in fixed income to generate the dividends. The concept of these funds is that they will have lower volatility and a more predictable and consistent return.

## Income Funds

Their advertised investment objectives are safety and income, rather than capital appreciation, but we are skeptical. Income funds invest in corporate bonds or government-insured mortgages; if they own any stocks at all, these are usually preferred shares. The danger lies in chasing higher yields and not look at the risks.

## Utility Funds

Utility funds invest in stocks in utility companies around the country. Like bonds, utility stocks generate high income. Utilities are defensive investments in services that are needed, no matter how bad things get. The concept here is that everyone needs electricity, gas, water, etc. The problem is that we may need them, but sometimes the amount of regulation on these companies and the cost of distributing energy can negate the benefit of constant demand. Utility funds need to be treated as risk-based investments like any stock mutual fund. We would feel better recommending that you just buy your local utility company.

## Specialty Funds

Specialty funds are also known as sector funds because they tend to invest in stocks in specific industries. We advise that sector funds not comprise a large percentage of any portfolio. Investing in stocks of a single industry defeats a major purpose of investing in mutual funds — you are giving up the benefits of diversification. A sector fund would be something like the India Fund or a gold fund. They can be used to build a portfolio, but only in small amounts. Specialty funds tend to carry much higher expenses than other mutual funds. The only types of specialty funds that may make sense for a small portion (10% or less) of your investment portfolio are funds that invest in real estate or precious metals.

## Gold Funds

A gold fund is a cost-effective way to participate in a possible increase in the price of gold. Some funds invest only in South African stocks owning shares of mining firms. The down side is that gold can be highly volatile. These types of funds can help diversify your portfolio because they can do better during times of higher inflation — not today.

## Global Equity Funds

International and global funds focus their investments outside of the U.S. The term *international* typically means that a fund can invest anywhere in the world except the U.S. The term *global* generally implies that a fund can invest anywhere in the world, including the U.S.

## Hybrid Funds

Hybrid funds invest in a mixture of different types of securities. Most commonly, they invest in bonds and stocks. These funds are usually less risky and volatile than funds investing exclusively in stocks. Hybrid mutual funds are typically known as balanced or asset allocation funds. Balanced funds generally try to maintain a fairly constant percentage of investment in stocks and bonds.

## Asset Allocation Funds

Asset allocation funds tend to adjust the mix of different investments according to the portfolio manager's expectations. Depending on the manager, these could also be called market timing funds. The only problem is, no one can accurately predict the actions of the market.

## Bond Funds

Bonds are essentially IOUs. When you buy a bond, you are lending your money to a corporation or government agency. A bond mutual fund is nothing more than a large group (pack) of bonds. Most bond funds invest in bonds of similar maturity (the number of years that elapse before the borrower must pay back the money you lend). The names of most bond funds include a word or two to provide clues about the average length of maturity of their bonds.

For example, a short-term bond fund concentrates its investments in bonds maturing in the next few years. An intermediate-term fund generally holds bonds that come due within 7 to 10 years. The bonds in a long-term fund usually mature in 20 years or so. In contrast to an individual bond that you buy and hold until it matures, a bond fund is always replacing bonds in its portfolio to maintain its average maturity objective. Bond funds are useful when you want to live off dividend income or when you do not want to put all your money in riskier investments such as stocks and real estate (perhaps because you plan to use the money soon).

## Global Bond Funds

Global bond funds invest in foreign as well as U.S. bonds. Historically, global bond funds have outperformed domestic bond funds, but you do assume additional risk.

## Money Market Funds

Money market funds are the safest type of mutual funds if you are worried about the risk of losing your principal. Money market funds are like bank savings accounts in that the value of your investment does not fluctuate. This type of fund could be used as your core saving strategy.

## Index Funds

Think of these funds as baskets of stocks representing the various stock market indexes. The S&P 500 index fund is by far the most common index fund for both institutional and individual investors. It tracks the performance of the S&P 500 index, a capitalization-weighted index of 500 large U.S. stocks. It is estimated that over 95% of all retail indexed monies are invested in S&P 500 index funds. Following is a list of the indexes:

1.  The Wilshire 5000 includes all 5000 stocks on the New York Stock Exchange Annex, as well as over-the-counter (OTC) stocks. The Wilshire essentially takes the entire market as an index.

2.  The NASDAQ 100 is the National Association of Securities Dealers index of stocks traded over the counter via its automatic quoting system (NASDAQ). The NASDAQ 100 measures price changes in 100 of the largest OTC industrial stocks.

3.  The S&P 500, also known as the S&P composite index, consists of companies listed on the New York Stock Exchange plus a few of the American Exchange and over-the-counter stocks. Also, 7% of the stocks are non-U.S. companies and investment companies which can be affected by currency translations. One of the downsides of the S&P 500 is that the companies are chosen by committee, rather than by market efficiency.

4.  The Schwab 1000 index, possibly a better index, makes it possible for you to invest in 1000 American companies with just one investment. It includes common stocks of the 100 largest publicly traded U.S. companies measured by market capitalization, which represents 82% of the U.S. stock market value. It is a broader index and a broader diversification which is not selected by a committee or Charles Schwab, but according to a formula of market capitalization. The fund invests in large and mid-size growth companies and is designed to track the broad U.S. stock price in dividend performance in order to keep pace with the market.

5. Morgan Stanley EAFE (Europe, Australia, and Far East) index is actually two sub-indexes of 1000 stocks traded in Europe and the Pacific Basin and is the most commonly used index for mutual funds that invest in foreign stocks.

## Asset Class Mutual Funds

For a moment, think of mutual funds as being like a huge auto mart that offers everything from everyday, economical cars to sports cars that go fast but soon need a mechanic. There are lemons among them. You have to be wary of the seductive luxury cars with lots of extras that drive up the price. Asset class mutual funds are composed of financial instruments with similar characteristics. Unlike managers of index funds, asset fund managers actively manage costs when buying and selling for funds.

The most important attributes of asset class mutual funds include:

1. *Low operating expenses:* An important study of retail equity mutual funds by Elton and Gruber[1] found that the more expensive a fund is, the worse it performs on average. Low expenses is one of the main reasons to use asset class mutual funds.
2. *Low turnover:* Active mutual fund managers do a lot of trading — this is how they think they are adding value. As a result, the average retail mutual fund has an annual turnover rate of 86%, which represents $86,000 of traded securities for every $100,000 invested. High turnover is costly to shareholders because each time a trade is made there are transaction costs involved. These costs include commissions, spreads, and market impact costs. These hidden costs may amount to more than a fund's total operating expenses. Retail mutual funds have high turnover because they are under tremendous pressure to perform. Good short-term performance leads to a bonus for the manager and a flood of new money for the fund. If they are performing poorly, they often try to make up ground by changing the composition of their holdings. If a mutual fund sells a security for a gain, they must make a capital gain distribution to shareholders. This is because mutual funds are required to distribute 98% of their taxable income each year, including realized capital gains, to stay tax-exempt at the corporate level. No mutual fund manager wants to have his or her performance reduced by paying corporate income taxes.
3. *Low trading costs:* These are composed of commissions, bid/ask spreads, and market impact costs.

The four major equity asset classes are

1.  U.S. large company stocks
2.  U.S. small company stocks
3.  International large company stocks
4.  International small company stocks

These four equity asset classes represent more than 5000 different stock positions in 14 different countries. U.S. large stocks include domestic companies with capitalizations of over $50 million; small stocks, under $50 million. Academic research shows that large and small company stocks have a low correlation with each other. The two types of bond funds are fixed income and international fixed income. When the equity markets decline, fixed income securities will dampen the fall.

## U.S. Equity Asset Class Mutual Funds

U.S. equity asset class funds and pure index funds have portfolios that are market-capitalization weighted. In other words, the fund manager allocates money to U.S. companies based on the size of their markets, measured by market capitalization.

## International Equity Asset Classes

Global investing is a hot topic on Wall Street and among money managers, many of whom for various reasons would rather have U.S. investors park their funds at home. They, therefore, discourage international investing for their clients. These clever managers and advisors have even come up with ways that investors can seemingly play markets abroad using domestic assets. This theory holds that the way to make a global play — without taking on true global securities exposure — is to buy the stocks of U.S. multinational firms doing a great deal of business abroad.

This idea seems clever upon first glance, but there are difficulties. What most undermines this concept is that stocks of multinational firms tend to follow the movements of their local markets rather than the international market. This is true regardless of the degree to which their operations are globally diversified. For example, Colgate gets about 80% of its revenues from foreign operations, yet its stock price still closely follows the U.S. market. Because stocks of U.S. multinational firms are so highly correlated with the U.S. market, they lose their diversification power.

It has become conventional wisdom that you should put some of your money in international equities. The two reasons most often given for this recommendation are

1.  Foreign stocks have historically outperformed U.S. stocks.
2.  Foreign stocks provide good diversification due to their low correlation with U.S. markets.

While it is true that international stocks measured by Morgan Stanley Capital International's EAFE index have outperformed the S&P 500 since 1970, this occurs only because foreign currencies have outperformed the U.S. dollar. In local currency terms, the returns of foreign and domestic stocks are about equal.

Because the international and U.S. equity markets have a low correlation, they do not tend to move together. Given the data, our desire for true global diversification, and our belief that U.S. and foreign stocks have equal expected returns, we believe you should include foreign stocks in your portfolio to reduce risk.

Most international asset class funds and pure index funds have portfolios that are market-capitalization weighted. In other words, the fund manager allocates money to countries based on the size of their markets, measured by market capitalization. Currently, Japan is the largest of any market outside the United States. Therefore, an international fund that is market-capitalization weighted will allocate more money to Japan than any other country. This approach probably puts too much money in Japanese stocks. The overweighting occurs because, in Japan, it is common for companies to invest in the stocks of other companies. These cross-holdings are counted twice, which overstates the market capitalization of Japan relative to the rest of the world.

## Fixed Income Asset Class Mutual Funds

Fixed income securities are an important part of a comprehensive portfolio because they provide stability to counterbalance the high volatility of equities. While they have lower expected returns than stocks, they add value to the portfolio by reducing overall volatility. Bonds are the primary tools for focusing your portfolio on your target risk level. A higher allocation to bonds reduces portfolio risk and a lower allocation to bonds increases portfolio risk.

A bond represents a loan to an issuer, such as the U.S. government or a major corporation, usually in return for periodic fixed interest payments.

These payments continue until the bond is redeemed at maturity (or earlier, if called by the issuer). At the time of maturity, the investor receives the face value of the bond. Many investors buy long-term bonds because they normally have higher current yields than shorter term bonds. Investors consider them safe, but in reality long-term bonds have many different kinds of risk. These risks include reinvestment risk, call risk, purchasing power risk, liquidity risk, and interest rate risk.

The major risk you face with long-term bonds is interest rate risk. The prices of bonds move in the opposite direction of interest rates; when interest rates rise, the prices of bonds fall, and vice versa. For example, consider a newly issued 20-year Treasury bond with a 6% coupon. If, over the next 12 months, interest rates increase by 2%, new 20-year Treasury bonds will be offered with 8% coupons; therefore, the old 6% bonds will be worth less than the new bonds, as the new bonds have higher coupons. This inverse relationship between interest rates and bond values is an important risk of fixed income investments, as it can create significant volatility, especially for long-term bonds.

To give you an idea of the volatility of long-term bonds, consider the historical rates of total returns on 20-year Treasury bonds over the last several decades. During the 1980s, long-term bond investors enjoyed one of the best decades ever, with gains averaging 12.7% per year. Bond prices soared during this decade due to declining interest rates. Because of these high returns, long-term bonds became very popular in the late 1980s and early 1990s, as investors tend to place too much importance on their most recent experiences, a phenomenon that psychologists refer to as *cognitive bias*. We call this misplaced emphasis *rear view mirror* investing, as it is like trying to drive a car forward while only looking where you have been through the rear view mirror. It is crucial to analyze all statistical evidence available when making financial decisions.

In contrast, consider the decade of the 1950s. This was the worst decade for long-term bond investors because they experienced an average annual return of –0.1%, including reinvested interest. Most investors do not realize that the volatility of long-term bonds is close to the volatility of common stocks. The historical data show that long-term bonds do not actually provide the low risk that many fixed income investors are seeking.

The higher risk of long-term bonds would be acceptable if investors were sufficiently rewarded with higher rates of return. Eugene Fama of the University of Chicago has studied the rates of return of long-term bonds from 1964 to 1996 and found that the term premium for longer-term bonds is not reliable. His research shows that long-term bonds have wide variances in their rates of return and, most importantly, that bonds with maturities beyond 5 years do not offer sufficient reward for their higher risk.

The predominant investors in the long-term bond markets are institutions, such as corporate pension plans and life insurance companies. These investors are interested in funding long-term obligations, including fixed annuity payments or other fixed corporate responsibilities. In general, they are not concerned with volatility of principal or with the effects of inflation, as their obligations are fixed in maturity date and amount. You, on the other hand, should be concerned with inflation, as well as volatility. This is because you are an individual living in a variable rate world. There is a limit to the amount of volatility with which you feel comfortable.

Given the data, you should own fixed-income investments to provide stability to your portfolio, not to generate high returns. High returns should come from equities. Fixed-income securities can help offset the risk of your equity holdings and, therefore, lower the risk of your overall portfolio. You can best do this by using short-term, fixed-income securities rather than long-term bonds. Short-term bonds have less volatility and a lower correlation with stocks and are a better choice for your portfolio. They will allow you to invest a larger percentage of your money in stocks while maintaining low portfolio risk.

## International Fixed-Income Asset Classes

This asset class includes foreign government bond markets — the markets of Japan, the United Kingdom, Switzerland, The Netherlands, Germany, and France. They have credit quality equal to the U.S., according to debt ratings by Moody's and S&P.

## The Emerging Market Asset Classes

Many institutional investors now recognize emerging markets as a separate and distinct asset class. The term *emerging markets* refers to the stock markets of the world's developing countries whose economies are growing fast enough to deserve the term "emerging". It is important to keep in mind that while these markets may be defined as emerging, the companies whose stocks are being purchased are well-established companies in these countries. The countries must have well-organized markets that provide ample liquidity and also have a developed legal system that protects property rights and upholds contractual obligations. Typical holdings are national banks, land developers, and telephone companies of various countries. Our current country choices include Indonesia, Turkey, Argentina, Malaysia, Philippines, Portugal, Israel, Mexico, Brazil, Thailand, South Korea, and Chile.

These emerging countries are experiencing rapid growth and improvements in their political, social, and economic conditions. You might conclude that the higher rates of economic growth in these countries should lead to higher stock returns. This is a common message communicated by the financial press and investment professionals. While it is true that emerging market countries have higher economic growth rates than the developed world, this alone does not mean their stock returns will be higher, because the stock prices already reflect the market's expectations of high growth.

What is not so widely understood is that emerging market returns are *not* due to faster economic growth. Higher returns are a reward for accepting higher risk. Emerging market investing involves substantial risks including political instability, extreme market volatility, lack of liquidity, dramatic currency devaluation, high transaction costs, and regulatory risk. And, because of a lack of reliable information, low accounting standards, and very poor financial disclosure, investors should avoid these funds unless they are a small part of an overall asset class portfolio.

Even though investing in emerging markets seems risky, you may be surprised to see that the volatility of the emerging markets asset class is actually less than that of U.S. small company stocks. You might also be surprised to see that international small company stocks and U.S. small cap have approximately the same standard deviation or risk level (see Table A.3).

## The Rating Game

The mutual fund rating game works much the same way as the old dating game on television. Investors use ratings of mutual funds that are listed in newspapers and magazines as a guide to help them pick funds that are the right ones for the portfolio. Choosing an A-rated fund is a quick and easy way to choose a fund, but are these ratings actually useful? Let's consider mutual fund ratings in *The Wall Street Journal* as compiled by Lipper Analytical Services. Lipper awards an A to funds whose returns are in the top 20% of their category. The next 20% get a B, and so on, through C, D, and E.

For the period ending December 31, 1997, the Vanguard Index 500 was awarded an A, the highest rating possible, while the Vanguard Index Small Company Fund was only worth a C. This meant that the Vanguard Index 500 Fund was ranked in the top 20% of all similar funds, and the Vanguard Index Small Company Fund only ranked in the middle of its peer group. Likewise,

### Table A.3. Expected Returns/Standard Deviation

| Asset Class | Expected Return | Standard Deviation |
|---|---|---|
| Money market | 4.90% | 3.30% |
| Fixed income | 6.70% | 3.90% |
| U.S. large | 13.60% | 20.30% |
| U.S. small | 19.40% | 38.50% |
| International large | 13.60% | 20.30% |
| International small | 19.40% | 38.50% |
| Emerging markets | 16.00% | 29.00% |

for the last three years, the Vanguard Index European Fund earned the highest rating of A, while the Vanguard Index Pacific Fund only got a D for the previous 12 months. So something is odd or wrong with these ratings.

All of these funds are pure index funds. They simply track the performance of the predetermined market index. How can one fund deserve an A when the others get a D or C? The index funds have the lowest cost, and they are widely diversified. They should consistently rank modestly above average compared to other funds in their peer groups. Accordingly, they deserve no better and no worse than a B rating. The only possible explanation for the Lipper rating is that Vanguard funds are not benchmarked properly and are not matched to their correct peer groups.

Because index funds should be the easiest of all funds to rank, they simply mirror broad market segments and disclose exactly what is in their portfolios. Active managed funds are much harder to classify than index funds because they have changing styles, moving asset allocations, and other complications. If Lipper cannot classify index funds correctly, how accurate can other ratings be? Good ratings bring money into mutual funds, bonuses to managers, and so on. Naturally, managers will do whatever they need to do to improve their ratings.

For example, a recent study[2] found that mutual fund managers increase the risk level of their portfolios in the middle of the year if they are not ranked among peer group performance leaders. If they were successful and their funds' rankings improved, the managers would be given bonuses and the fund would get increased assets from investors. If the gamble failed, the fund would perform worse than it would have if no changes had been made, but because funds are a winner-take-all industry, fund managers feel it is worth the gamble to take that kind of risk. The mutual fund rating game is a loser's game.

# A Barometer of Ups and Downs

When the stock market is said to be up 10 points, what is usually meant is that the venerable Dow Jones Industrial Average (DJIA) went up 10 points. The DJIA is based on the average prices paid for 30 blue-chip stocks. The up-and-down fluctuations of the New York Stock Exchange has been recorded since 1896, and general upward and downward movements of stock prices are symbolized on Wall Street by bulls and bears.

# The Dow Jones Industrial Average

Most investors have never heard of most of the original companies in the widely watched Dow average, which reflects the U.S. economy. Only one stock, General Electric, remains from the original 12 chosen in 1896. When the average ended its first day at 40.94, 12 years before Henry Ford made his first Model T, the average included such stalwarts as U.S. Leather and Tennessee Coal & Iron. If it had not changed over the years, the average would not be an accurate barometer of the economy. It is true that there are only 30 companies, but they are 30 of the best-known and largest companies.

Narrow as it is, the Dow Industrial Average is easily the most popular gauge of the U.S. stock market. The public follows the Dow more than academics or even the Wall Street crowd. All three television networks acknowledge the popularity of the Dow as a yardstick by citing it on their nightly news reports. The Dow Industrials are big brand names and in that way have become synonymous with the fortunes of U.S. stocks generally. Investors who want to know if stocks are up or down ask about the Dow the same way customers ask for a soft drink or facial tissue — we ask for a Coke or a Kleenex.

Rival stock-market averages and indexes do not have the Dow's cachet, which was even more the case in the 1930s. They watched the stocks, but the Dow in most people's minds was *the* indicator of what the market was doing. Dow Jones, publisher of *The Wall Street Journal*, helps ensure that the Dow Industrials stay prominent. The biggest newspaper in the country, with a daily circulation of 1.8 million readers, the *Journal* usually manages to mention its average when writing about the stock market. Of late, the Dow Industrials have beaten the broader S&P 500 index, the 70-year-old benchmark which gauges 500 stocks. Since the current bull market began in October 1990, the Dow has surged over 144%, topping the S&P 500's 129% gain.

To understand the importance of the Dow Jones Industrial Average, investors must return to the closing years of the 19th century. Charles Dow was ahead of his time. When he decided in 1896 to create the industrial average, he sensed where the country was going. At the time, the NYSE did very little trading of industrial shares, which were considered too low brow and speculative (much like we would consider junk bonds today). At that time, the only stocks regarded as being investment grade were railroads and utilities. By giving investors a measuring instrument, Dow helped popularize stocks in general.

Big business was relatively unknown before 1880, when most companies were family owned. The next 25 years saw the creation of national businesses, companies such as General Electric and U.S. Steel, which is when Charles Dow began to recognize the growing importance of manufacturing and the opportunities available to investors. The Dow average's popularity grew because investors needed a way to compare their gains with the overall stock market.

Professional money managers think of the Dow as a crude average because no allowance is made for the size of a company. The prices of all 30 stocks are added up, but instead of being divided by 30, the total is multiplied by a divisor that is adjusted to maintain historical continuity. That method does not take into account that a 10% rise in International Business Machines (IBM), whose shares have sold for $109, has a far greater impact on the broad market than a 10% move in Bethlehem Steel's $12.75-a-share stock. By contrast, the S&P 500 index is weighted by a company's size and is the benchmark by which mutual fund managers usually measure their performance.

The Dow seldom changes the composition of its average unless forced to do so by a merger, acquisition, or spin-off. No change has been made in the Dow industrials in the five years since Walt Disney, Caterpillar, Wal-Mart, and J.P. Morgan & Co. were added to the average, replacing Navistar International Corp., Primerica Corp., USX Corp., and Woolworth. Others think the Dow Industrial Average will continue to evolve, perhaps by adopting leading NASDAQ stock market companies, such as Microsoft or Intel, which are regarded as proxies for the computer industry.

It is also possible that Dow Jones editors will broaden the average by enlarging it beyond 30 names. After all, they expanded the original list of 12 companies to 20 in 1920 and enlarged the average to the current 30 in late 1928. It has not been a static index. They have added companies and taken companies out. Generally, when they update the index, they add a company that's a little more responsive to what's going on in the economy.

The S&P 500 index, the Value Line composite index, and the New York Stock Exchange composite index are ostensibly more accurate indices and are also more widely followed. These are broader based, which should make them somewhat more accurate in a large market. Because the DJIA consists of only 30 large companies, it may not truly reflect market performance.

## Signs of a Bad Fund

What if you are in a mutual fund that is not performing according to its or your stated goals? We do not want to be going against our own advice on the subject of market timing, but this is an exception. Sometimes you just buy a bad fund. Let's look at the telltale signs of a bad mutual fund:

1. *Above-average expenses.* Those higher costs take a bigger bite out of the return earned by the stocks, meaning lower return to you. If your fund investment loses 3%, for example, and has a 2% annual expense ratio, you have actually sustained a 5% loss for the year. (You can find the expense ratio in your fund's prospectus.) Lipper Analytic says the average stock mutual fund has an annual expense ratio of 1.54%. The average fixed-income fund is around 0.96%.

2. *Poor communications.* Troubled funds often fall behind on providing information in a timely fashion. If information is not arriving on time, and you do not get a satisfactory explanation, it is appropriate to get nervous.

3. *Lack of discipline.* The best investments all take a consistent approach. The worst type of funds pursue whatever is hot. If your fund has changed its focus, or if the manager has changed his or her style, the fund could be chasing a hot sector, trying to enhance returns.

4. *Managers change.* If the managers keep leaving, there is something going on. The fund owes you an adequate explanation. They need to tell you what the new guy can do to help turn it around.

5. *Shrinking assets.* Funds get bigger when they are making more money, and they shrink when they lose. When investors lose confidence, the shrinking can be dramatic.

## Mutual Fund Names

Titles can mislead investors. There are some strict rules being proposed. When you hear names such as *Fidelity Magellan* or *Putnam Voyager*, what do they really tell you? Are they going on a voyage? No. You do not have a clue as to what these funds are investing in. Proposed federal regulation would

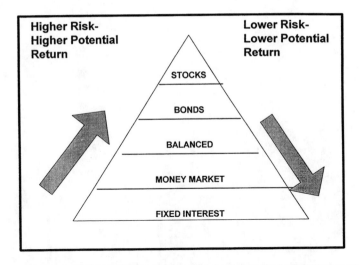

**Figure A.3. Relationship Between Risk and Return**

require mutual funds to have at least 80% of their assets in securities that match the name of the fund, instead of the 65% now required. So, for instance, ABC Japan fund would have 80% of its assets invested in Japan, instead of the 65% required now. The point is to prevent investors from being misled by fund names.

Now let's look at the underlying investments that make up these different mutual fund categories (see Figure A.3). Think of a pyramid. At the top of that pyramid would be stocks. If you combined stocks and bonds for less risk, they would make up the middle of the pyramid. Fixed-interest investments would be at the bottom of the investment pyramid, because of their low risk.

# References

1. Elton, E.J., Gruber, M.J., Das, S., and Hlavka, M., *Efficiency with Costly Information: A Reinterpretation of Evidence from Managed Portfolios,* The Society for Financial Studies, 1993.
2. Brown, Kelly, Van Harlow, and Laurel Starks, On tournaments and temptations: an analysis of managerial incentives in the mutual fund industry, *Journal of Finance,* March, 85–110, 1996.

# Appendix B.
# Understanding Stocks

E quity mutual funds are made up of many individual stocks. A stock is a security issued by a corporation or by a government as a means of raising long-term capital. The ownership is divided into a certain number of shares, and the corporation issues stock certificates which show how many shares are owned. The stockholders own the company and elect a board of directors to manage it for them. The capital a company raises through the sale of these shares entitles the holders to dividends and to other rights of ownership, such as voting rights.

Prices of stocks change according to general business conditions and the earnings and future prospects of the companies that have issued the stock. If the business is doing well, stockholders may be able to sell their stock for a profit. If it is not, they may have to take a loss when they sell. Large corporations may have many thousands of stockholders. Their stock is bought and sold in marketplaces called stock exchanges. A stock exchange occupies an important position in our country's financial system by providing a mechanism for converting savings into an investment portfolio. The stock exchange provides a primary or new-issues market, in which new capital can be raised by issuing financial securities, plus it also acts as a secondary market for trading existing securities which facilitates transferability of securities from seller to buyers.

1-57444-258-9/00/$0.00+$.50
© 2000 by CRC Press LLC

The shares of stock represent the value of the corporation. When the corporation has made a profit, the directors may divide the profit among stockholders as dividends, or they may decide to use it to expand the business. Dividends are paid to the stockholders out of the corporation's profits. When profits are used to expand the business, the directors and stockholders may issue more stock to show that there is more money invested in the business. This new stock will be divided among the old stockholders as stock dividends. Stocks are issued in two forms: common and preferred.

## Common Stock

Common stock represents true ownership shares in a company. Stockholders share directly in growing company profits through increasing dividends and an appreciation in the value of the stock itself. Holders of common stock are part-owners in the company that issued the stock. The purchaser of common stock receives not only a share of any dividends paid by the corporation, but also the right to vote for corporate directors who, in turn, choose the corporate officers and set the corporation's policies. When brokers use the term *stock*, they are normally referring to common stock, which will be the bulk of investments in most mutual funds.

## Preferred Stock

Preferred stock, like common stock, represents ownership or equity, not debt. Preferred stockholders have a claim on profits which precedes — or is preferred to — the claim of the common stockholder. The preferred stockholder has a right to receive specified dividends (for example, 10% of the face value of the preferred share) before the common stockholder can be paid any dividend at all.

On the other hand, the preferred stockholder does not have the possibility of realizing the large gains that a common stockholder might. While the common stockholder may hope for rising dividends if the corporation prospers, the preferred shareholder will at most receive the specified dividend. If the preferred stockholders do share with the common stockholders in dividends beyond the specified percentage, the stock they hold is called participating preferred.

Preferred stock may also be cumulative. That is, if there are no dividends given in a year, the preferred stockholders must be given double their dividend the next year. This is paid before anything is paid to the common stockholders. This principle continues for as many years as dividends are not paid.

## Price/Earnings Ratio

This is how you measure the value of a company by dividing the stock's market price by the company's earnings per share (EPS) over the past 12 months. Suppose a company is earning $1 a share and the public is buying the stock at $10. In this case, to determine the price/earnings ratio, you divide10 by 1, which tells us that the stock is selling at 10 times earnings (10P/E or 10×). If you invest in this company and pay $10 per share, theoretically you are paying one year's worth of earnings to own it. When the market is low, you will commonly see a price/earnings ratio of 10×; in today's bull market, though, the average is 25 to 30 times earnings.

## Dividend Payout Ratio

This is the ratio of a company's annual cash dividend per share to its earnings per share and can range from zero to 100%. A utility that pays out $4 in dividends for each $5 of earnings would have a payout of 80%. For the average large industrial company, the payout is normally above 50% and is even higher for the typical utility. The higher the dividend payout, however, the less room there is for dividend increases, as less profit is available to reinvest for future growth.

## Dividend Yield

This measures the annual dividend divided by the stock price. For example, if a utility's dividend is $4 and its stock sells for $50 a share, the yield would be 8%. When the EPS (in general) are high, yields will be low.

## Blue-Chip Stocks

These high-quality companies are typically large, old, and well established, such as those represented in the Dow Jones Industrial Average. Blue-chips are often considered income stocks by virtue of their fairly high dividend payouts. Many of the companies included in the S&P 500 would also qualify as blue-chips. Stocks can be lumped into any of several broad categories. These are general classifications, and a stock might simultaneously fit into two or more categories. For example, a blue-chip may also be classified as growth and income or defensive. And a growth company may be categorized as speculative.

## Where Are Stocks Traded?

The stock exchange is a marketplace where member brokers (agents) buy and sell stocks and bonds of American and foreign businesses on behalf of the public. A stock exchange provides a marketplace for stocks and bonds in the same way a commodity exchange does for commodities. Like a stockbroker, a bank investment representative receives a small commission on each transaction he or she makes.

To most investors, the stock market means the New York Stock Exchange. The New York Stock Exchange has been in existence for more than 200 years, and, needless to say, it has come a long way since 24 merchants and auctioneers met at the site of the present exchange to negotiate an agreement to buy and sell stocks and bonds issued by the new U.S. government, along with those of a few banks and insurance companies. It was not until 1817 that the exchange adopted an approved constitution, whereby it named itself the New York Stock and Exchange Board. The exchange did not cross the million-share daily threshold until 1886. Its slowest day ever was March 16, 1830, when only 31 shares changed hands. In 1997, the exchange witnessed the first day when 1 billion shares were traded.

There are also many other North American exchanges trading stock, ranging from the American Stock Exchange (AMEX) to the Spokane Stock Exchange. In addition, thousands of equities are not traded on any exchange but are sold over the counter (OTC). Prices for OTC stocks are readily available through the NASDAQ, an acronym for the National Association of Securities Dealers Automated Quotations system, the hottest market today. Many unlisted industrial securities are more speculative than listed ones.

A distinct difference between OTC stocks and exchange-listed equities revolves primarily around eligibility requirements. Each stock exchange has listing requirements that must be met before a company may take its place on the exchange floor. For example, before a stock can be listed on the NYSE, the company must have at least one million shares outstanding (available to the public). Those shares must be held by at least 2000 different stockholders, each of whom owns at least 100 shares. The company must also have earned a pre-tax profit of at least $2.5 million the year preceding the listing, and the pre-tax profits in the two prior years must have been at least $2 million each year. The AMEX and the regional exchanges have similar (though less stringent) listing requirements, but no such limitations exist for OTC listings.

## How Does a Stock Exchange Operate?

Federal and state laws regulate the issuance, listing, and trading of most securities. The Securities and Exchange Commission (SEC) administers the federal laws. Stocks handled by one or more stock exchanges are called *listed stocks*. A company that wants to have its stock listed for trading on an exchange must first prove to the exchange that it has enough paid-up capital, is a lawful enterprise, and is in good financial condition.

## How Do Stocks Trade on the Exchange?

Probably one of the most confusing aspects of investing is understanding how stocks actually trade. Words such as *volume, ask price, bid,* and *spread* can be quite confusing if you do not understand what they mean. Exchanges known as open auction markets include the New York Stock Exchange and the American Stock Exchange (composed of the Boston, Philadelphia, Chicago, and San Francisco Exchanges), which are both listed exchanges, meaning brokerage firms contribute individuals known as *specialists* who are responsible for all of the trading in a specific stock. *Volume* (the number of shares that trade on a given day) is counted by the specialists.

The specialists control stock prices by matching buy-and-sell orders delivered by floor brokers shouting out their orders. The specialists change the prices to match the supply-and-demand fundamentals. The specialist system was created to guarantee that every seller finds a buyer, and vice versa. This process may sound chaotic, but specialists do succeed in their function of maintaining an orderly market and matching sellers to buyers. In return for this service, the specialist charges the buyer an extra fee of 6.25¢ or 12.5¢ per share, depending on the price of the stock.

## Over-the-Counter Market

The NASDAQ stock market, the NASDAQ Small Cap, and the OTC Bulletin Board are the three main over-the-counter markets. In an over-the-counter market, brokerages (also known as broker-dealers) act as market makers for various stocks. The brokerages interact over a centralized computer system managed by the NASDAQ, providing liquidity for the market to function. One firm represents the seller and offers an *ask price* (also called offer), which is the price at which the seller is willing to sell the security. Another firm represents the buyer and gives a *bid*, or a price at which the buyer will buy the security.

For example, a particular stock might be trading at a bid of $10 and an ask of $10.50. If an investor wants to sell shares, he would receive the bid price of $10 per share; if an investor wants to buy shares, he would pay the ask price of $10.50 per share. The difference is called the *spread*, which is normally paid by the buyer but can be split between the two firms involved in the transaction. Volume on over-the-counter markets is often double-counted, as both the buying firm and the selling firm report their activity.

## Placing an Order

A person who wishes to buy stock places an order with his representative. The representative gets a quotation (price) by telephone and relays the order to the floor of the exchange. The partner negotiates the sale and notifies the brokerage house. The entire transaction may take only a few minutes. How do you do it, and what types of orders can you place? Let's look at the major types of orders.

1.  *Buy order.* The order you place when, obviously enough, you want to buy shares. Simply tell the broker how many shares you want to purchase.
2.  *Buy at market.* You instruct the broker to buy a specified number of shares at the prevailing market price.
3.  *Buy at a limit.* You instruct the broker to buy a specified number of shares, but only at a specified price or lower. For example, you might say: "Buy 100 shares of IBM at a limit of $50." In this case, you are only willing to purchase shares of IBM if you can do so at $50 or less.
4.  *Sell order.* An order you place when you want to sell shares.
5.  *Sell at market.* An order to sell your shares at the prevailing market price.
6.  *Sell at a limit.* An order to sell your shares only at the price that you specify or higher.
7.  *Sell at a stop limit.* You instruct your broker to sell your stock if it falls to a certain price (i.e., you instruct your advisor/broker to sell your IBM stock if it falls to $45, which would be a sell stop at $45).

# Shorting Stocks

Shorting a stock is the reverse of buying a stock. In effect, if you sell a stock by borrowing it from a broker hoping that its share price will go down, you are "short" the stock. The idea is to buy the stock back later at a lower price and then return the shares to the broker and keep the difference. Although shorting is not the place for the conservative investor, you should understand how it works.

The basics of the shorting transaction are straightforward. You first contact your brokerage in order to determine whether or not they can borrow shares of the stock you want to short. When you receive the borrowed shares, you immediately sell them and keep the cash, promising to return the shares at some future time. The plan is to eventually repurchase the shares at a lower price and return them, keeping the difference yourself. But, if the stock's price rises, you might have to buy back the shares at the higher price and thus lose money.

It is worth the time to understand how individual stocks makes up equity mutual funds and how they work. Just think of a mutual fund as the house, and the individual stocks and bonds are the people who live inside.

# Appendix C.
# Understanding Bonds

What is a bond? If you don't know, you are not alone. A recent survey indicated that more than 90% of the general public is in the dark in this area. In fact, the majority of people who have actually invested in stocks and bonds do not really understand what makes a bond different from all other types of investments.

A bond is the legal evidence of a debt, usually the result of a loan of money. When you buy a bond, you are in effect lending your money to the issuer of the bond. The issuer agrees to make periodic interest payments to you, the investor holding the bond, and also agrees to repay the original sum (the principal) in full to you on a certain date — known as the bond's maturity date. Interest rates can soar and you, the customer, will still be repaid the entire principal at maturity. Interest payments are certain, and there will be no volatility with the investment, while even a mutual fund with a stable net asset value (NAV) will be affected to some extent by changes in interest rates.

More important is what backs the bond. In the case of many corporate securities, nothing more is behind them than the full faith and credit of the companies that issue them. These bonds, usually called debentures, are probably the most common type of debt issued by industrial corporations today. Public utilities generally issue bonds with specific assets as collateral against the loan. These are called mortgage bonds or collateral trust bonds. Some utilities, however, issue debentures and some industrial corporations issue collateralized bonds.

1-57444-258-9/00/$0.00+$.50
© 2000 by CRC Press LLC

# Kinds of Bonds

There are three main categories of issuers of bonds: (1) the U.S. government or one of its agencies, (2) corporations, and (3) municipalities. While these three types of bonds have some different characteristics, they share a basic structure.

## U.S. Government Notes and Bonds

The U.S. government issues both Treasury notes (maturities of 2 to 10 years) and bonds (maturities over 10 years). U.S. government securities are considered to have no credit risk, and their rate of return is the benchmark against which all other rates of return in the market are compared. The government auctions U.S. government securities on a regular quarterly schedule. In a normal yield-curve environment, U.S. government Treasury notes typically have yields 50 to 250 basis points higher than yields on Treasury bills (maturities of a year or less), and the same spread lower than a U.S. government bond (100 basis points equal 1%). Notes are the most likely investment for an individual investor because of the maturity range. Institutional investors and traders actively trade the 30-year bonds.

## Corporate Bonds

Corporations of every size and credit quality issue corporate bonds, from the very best blue-chip companies to small companies with low ratings. Corporate bonds are not easy to evaluate, especially those with longer maturities when call provisions may apply and the credit outlook is less certain. Many investors simply choose to stay with shorter maturities or extremely sound companies such as utilities. Corporate bonds may be backed by collateral and are fully taxable at the federal, state, and local levels.

Yields are higher on corporate bonds than on a CD or government-issued or insured debt. The coupon is fixed and return of principal is guaranteed by the issuer if the investor holds it until maturity. If the investor sells the bond prior to maturity, the bond will be subject to market fluctuation. Investors who want to be able to check the prices of their bonds in the newspaper should buy listed bonds, preferably those listed on the New York Stock Exchange.

The fully taxable nature of corporate bonds (as opposed to municipals or Treasuries) has an effect on yield. Even when buying a AAA-rated corporate bond, you are still buying a security that has more risk than a U.S. government bond. For the risk you are taking, you should receive an additional 25 to 50 basis points in yield.

## Municipal Bonds

Municipal bonds are investment instruments used to finance municipal governmental activities. They are not always guaranteed by the municipality. Investors whose goal is simply to conserve capital and generate returns that keep up with inflation often look to municipal bonds with the idea that these bonds are fairly safe. Investors may believe this because municipal bond issuances often have language stating they are "backed by the full faith and credit" of the issuing authority. In addition to the safety that conservative investors think they are gaining in municipal bonds, investors may also believe these bonds' tax-free status offers additional rewards. The combination of safety and tax-advantaged reward seems irresistible to many who are not especially sophisticated about the securities markets and who are seeking simply to avoid making an investment mistake. Municipals may also attract many wealthy investors for the same reasons. They are not looking for growth. The largest part of Ross Perot's holdings are in municipal bonds, and I am guessing that if we asked him, he would say he is not concerned about growth.

We do not like municipal investments, because if rates fall and prices rise, you are not necessarily going to be able to take advantage of your good fortune because the municipalities may hurry to call the bonds away from you. And tax-free certainly does not mean risk-free. Remember the Orange County debacle of the early 1990s or the New York City municipal difficulties of the 1970s?

Municipal bonds have high trading costs. This is because there are large bid/ask spreads and significant market impact costs in the municipal marketplace. These additional costs eliminate the benefits of using an enhanced trading strategy, such as the matrix pricing strategy we use in our government and corporate bond portfolios. The turnover required would simply be too costly. Because of their high trading costs, municipal bonds are only suitable for buy-and-hold investors who want to hold longer maturity bonds or high-yield municipals.

Almost all municipal bonds have had a tough last few years, in part because the stock market continues to steal their thunder. According to the Investment Company Institute, for the first 5 months of 1997, the amount of investor dollars put in municipal bond funds shrank from $3.1 billion to $253 billion. The outflow had followed a similar decline in 1996. Today, municipals can offer rare tax breaks for small to medium-sized investors, which makes them particularly attractive in states with high income taxes, such as New York and California.

### Municipal Bond Funds

Municipal bond funds are nothing more than a large grouping of various municipal bonds. They may be appropriate when you are in high federal (28% and up) and state (5% or higher) tax brackets. Most municipal bond funds invest in municipal bonds of similar maturity (the number of years before the borrower, in this case the municipality, must pay back the money to you, the lender). The key advantage of a bond fund is management. Unlike individual issues, the fund managers can switch bonds from time to time within a fund. A bond fund is always replacing bonds in its portfolio to maintain its average maturity objective.

To determine if a municipal bond fund makes sense for you, compare your after-tax return to another type of bond fund. For example, if a municipal fund pays 5% vs. 6% on a corporate bond fund, which fund works better for someone in the 28% tax bracket? Divide 5% by 0.72 (100 minus the 28% tax bracket). The answer, 6.94, is your after-tax return. So the corporate fund needs to yield 6.94% to measure up.

## What Are the Risks of Bonds?

The main form of market risk for a bond is the risk of interest rates changing after a customer buys the bond — called the *interest-rate risk*. If market interest rates go up, the bond loses principal value; if market rates go down, the bond gains principal value. The longer the term of the bond, the more the price will be affected by changes in interest rates. Whether the U.S. government, a corporation, or a municipality issues the bond, the risk is similar. Bonds are also subject to *call risk*, the risk that the bond issuer will choose to redeem (call) the bond before the maturity date. The call provisions must be stated in the prospectus along with other special features, but a prospectus can be difficult to understand.

## A Look at Interest Rates

A bond's current value is directly affected by changes in the interest rates. The effect of higher interest rates on bonds is to lower their prices. Conversely, lower rates raise bond prices. The fluctuation is due to the fact that the price of the bond must offer a prospective purchaser current market rates.

## Buying a Bond Vs. Bond Fund

There is a lot to understand before buying an individual bond. It is a somewhat different process from buying stocks or mutual funds, because only a certain dollar amount of each bond is issued and that amount is almost certainly much smaller than the amount of equity issued. Large companies have millions of shares of stock outstanding, and all shares of common stock are the same. To buy a bond, on the other hand, the customer cannot simply consult *The Wall Street Journal*, pick a particular bond, and place an order. Buying a bond means finding the owner (such as an institutional trading desk) of a bond that meets your needs. Owners of individual bonds have much greater control over both their cash flow and tax consequences, as bond investors control when to take profits and losses based on their best interests. If it matters to an investor whether a tax gain is taken in December or January, a bond allows that choice.

An individual investor with less than $50,000 to invest in bonds is probably better off in a bond fund (called a unit investment trust), receiving the advantages of diversification, professional management, and significant cost benefits. Any institutional investor buys bonds more cheaply than a single individual, and the bonds in a mutual fund have been purchased at the institutional price. The institutional investor also pays a minuscule portion of total price in transaction costs, whereas transaction costs can be significant for an individual — and it gets worse if the individual must pay for safekeeping the securities. A bond fund does, however, have a management fee that might equal the transaction cost an individual would pay. The mutual fund pays dividends monthly, as it owns bonds with many different payment dates, whereas individual bonds pay out only semi-annually. Following is information an investor should consider before making a bond purchase:

1. Type of bond, purpose of bond, and issuer
2. Rating (for example, AA is better than A)
3. Trade date (date the bond is purchased in the market)
4. Settlement date (date the purchaser pays for the bond and interest starts accruing)
5. Maturity date (date the purchaser will be repaid the principal and last interest payment)

## Table C.1.  Bond Ratings

| Credit Risk | Moody's | S&P | Fitch Prime |
|---|---|---|---|
| Best Quality | Aaa | AAA | AAA |
| Excellent | Aa | AA | AA |
| Upper medium | AA | A+, A | A |
| Lower medium | Baa | BBB+, BBB | BBB |
| Speculative | Ba | BB | BB |
| Very speculative | B, Caa | B, CCC, CC | B, CCC, C |
| Default | Ca, C | DDD, DD, D | DDD, DD, D |

6. Interest payment dates (dates interest payments are made, usually semi-annually)
7. Coupon — fixed annual interest rate (interest income) stated on bond.
8. Price (dollar price paid for the bond; an offer price is the price at which the individual investor buys the bond, while the bid price is the price at which the individual can sell the bond)
9. Current yield (coupon divided by price, giving a rough approximation of cash flow)
10. Yield to maturity (measure of total return on the bond at maturity)
11. Par amount (face amount of the bond when it was issued, normally $1000)
12. Accrued interest (amount of interest, or coupon, income earned from the date of the last coupon payment to settlement date)
13. Whether the bond uses a 360-day or 365-day basis to calculate interest payments.

## Bond Rating Services

The two major independent rating services are Moody's and Standard & Poor's. Ratings are intended to help you evaluate risk and set your own standards for investment; lower rated bonds are considered speculative (see Table C.1). The price of any bond fluctuates in harmony with the rise and fall of interest rates in general and the stability of the underlying corporation or agency issuing the bond. Grades AAA through BBB are considered investment grade, although many advisors will confine their attention to bonds rated A or above. Ratings attempt to assess the probability that the issuing company will make timely payments of interest and principal. Each rating service has slightly different evaluation methods.

# Appendix D. Understanding Annuities

The way most people start saving for retirement income is through their employers' retirement plans. Eventually, however, these people either reach the point where they are putting in as much as they can or their employers do not have the type of retirement plans that allow them to put in as much money as they really need to save. So, people need to take a close look at other types of investment vehicles that are available to help them save money consistently and easily for the long term.

There is a lot of discussion about the one best vehicle, but what we really have to find is the vehicle that accomplishes our own personal objectives. Most people are not looking for the best overall return; they are looking for the simplest and most convenient way to save money. That is where the annuity (either variable or fixed-income) really shines, because of its simplicity. The annuity has many advantages, in that it offers an assortment of investment choices, tax planning flexibility, tax deferral, and an ability to meet various objectives and coordinate with other retirement plans.

Because no one can predict what the tax laws will be in the future, there is no way to make a fair comparison, purely from a tax standpoint, between investing in conventional stocks/mutual funds and investing in an annuity. When you invest in conventional mutual funds or stocks, you anticipate paying a capital gains tax in the future (currently at the 20% level). When you invest in an annuity, however, you expect all income or earnings derived from

1-57444-258-9/00/$0.00+$.50
© 2000 by CRC Press LLC

the annuity to be taxed at whatever your ordinary income tax level is at the time you take distribution. We have had a major tax law change every year for the past 10 years, so, for all we know, the capital gains tax could be abolished at some point in the future. For the moment, then, it is best to set future tax considerations aside.

What is more important is to understand what is happening right now in today's tax climate. First, let's look at portfolio turnover. With stocks or conventional mutual funds, selling a stock, trading a stock, rebalancing a portfolio, changing your holdings, or altering your asset allocation between different selections of stock or mutual funds triggers either a short-term or a long-term capital gain. And, that means that you are giving up a certain portion of your return each and every year. The variable annuity works differently, and one of its true benefits is that it allows you to rebalance, change your asset allocation, or change your investment strategy literally on a daily basis, and your taxes are all deferred.

There are three primary categories of annuities: *fixed*, *flexible-premium deferred*, and *single-premium immediate*. The fixed annuity is similar to a CD at the bank. Think of taking your CD or Treasury bill and putting a tax wrapper around it so you do not pay taxes on any of the earnings until the time comes when you need to take out the money. While a CD is guaranteed by a bank, the principal amount of an annuity is guaranteed by an insurance company, which means that you need to be concerned with the strength of the company that is backing the fixed annuity.

An investor can add to a flexible-premium deferred annuity on an ongoing basis as money becomes available. A sub-category of this type of annuity is the single-premium annuity, into which you put one lump sum.

The third type of annuity is the single-premium immediate annuity, which allows you to put in a lump sum of money in exchange for an income option that will pay you an income for either a specified period of time or for life. These are excellent annuities for somebody who needs to generate an income stream right away, who typically has never invested in anything other than CDs, and who has limited funds and is concerned about outliving the principal.

## Fixed Annuities

Amelia is a retired film editor who has accumulated $75,000 of total retirement savings. She knows that money has to last her for as long as she lives, so she selects a life insurance policy with a 10-year guarantee option. (There are many different payment periods, but a typical example would be a life policy with a 10-year guaranteed payment.) Amelia gives the $75,000 cash to the insurance company in exchange for the annuity, which will guarantee her a monthly income for as long as she lives, but for no less than 10 years, should she die sooner. That is a very popular option.

Insurance companies have designed these fixed annuities so that an individual who is 65 years old will get back the principal plus about 2 to 3% interest at the end of the specified period of time (the breakeven period). If they live longer, the net return increases significantly. For example, if the individual lives 20 years instead of 10, they will receive about a 7% rate of return. If the individual lives 25 years, that rate of return goes over 8%. So, as the investor lives longer, he or she is increasing the overall yield (with absolutely no risk) and can never outlive their income even if they are fortunate enough to live into their nineties or beyond. This is an excellent planning tool for those who have not saved as much for retirement as they would like, yet want to maximize their income and ensure that it lasts for a lifetime.

The disadvantage is that by exchanging their principal for a guaranteed return of income, they lock themselves into a fixed income amount that will not offset the effects of inflation. On the other hand, they probably would not have been able to counteract inflation with the small amount of money they had anyway. For individuals who have a difficult time managing money or who do not like to take on any risk, the fixed annuity is one of the best planning tools available. Individuals in this situation should learn to live on 90%, saving 10% for the future.

Unless the money to purchase the annuity comes out of a retirement plan, the income received will all be taxed as ordinary income. If you purchase an annuity with personal savings, then a portion of the monthly income received will not be taxed because it is a return of your original investment. For example, for the first 10 to 12 years, probably about 40 to 45% of the income you receive will be non-taxable because it is considered a return of your principal, and about 60% will be taxable as ordinary income.

## Tax-Deferred Annuities

A tax-deferred annuity is an interest-bearing contract between an investor and insurance company. When an investor purchases an annuity, the insurance company pays interest which is tax deferred until withdrawal. The investor may withdraw the money at regular intervals or at a specific period of time in a lump sum or through random withdrawals. These annuities allow people to accumulate money without paying current income tax on their earnings. This means that the amount can grow faster, due to the tremendous power of compound interest. Most deferred annuity contracts provide a greater deal of flexibility in regard to the timing of premium payments and benefit payouts.

One feature of an annuity that is unique and not found in any other investment vehicle is that the annuity provides a stream of income that the investor cannot outlive. Annuities offer protection against living too long. (This statement about living too long refers only to the person's financial situation.) Dollars in the annuity remain tax deferred until withdrawal, which is at the complete discretion of the owner of the annuity.

For example, if you have $10,000 to invest in a deferred annuity that is earning 5% a year, at the end of the first year your annuity will be worth $10,500. That full amount will be available to earn interest the following year. If, instead, you invest in a currently taxable investment that is also earning 5% and your marginal tax rate is 28%, at the end of the year, only $10,360 will be available for reinvestment. The remaining $140 will be paid to the government for income tax on the $500 you earn. This may seem like a small sum of money, but if this continues for 10 years, the difference between the values of the tax-deferred annuity and the currently taxable investment will be $2046! (Of course, taxes must still be paid when the earnings inside the annuity contract are distributed. If the annuity were cashed in after 10 years, the income tax would be $1761, assuming a 28% rate and no penalty taxes.)

## Immediate Annuities

An immediate annuity is one which begins paying benefits very quickly, usually within one year of the time purchased. By nature, it is almost always a single-premium purchase. The immediate annuity can be useful for an individual who has received a large sum of money and must count on these funds to pay expenses over a period of time.

### Single-Premium Annuity

A single-premium annuity is purchased with one premium, usually fairly large. The single-premium option may be used to purchase either a fixed annuity or a variable annuity. A single-premium annuity requires an initial lump sum deposit (generally a minimum of $1000 to $5000) and does not accept any future contributions.

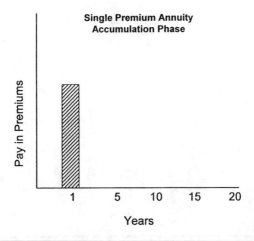

**Figure D.1. Single-Premium Annuity Accumulation Phase**

As an example, Bob recently received a settlement from an insurance claim — a lump sum of $150,000. He does not need the money currently, so he uses the funds to purchase a single-premium annuity for $150,000 and chooses to receive benefits at his retirement age by electing one of the income settlement options.

Other types of investors might include athletes, actors, or artists who receive a large payment at one time; they purchase single-premium annuities that begin paying benefits when their careers end. Another example would be a business owner who has recently sold his company. Once a single-premium annuity has been purchased, the annuity holder can choose to begin receiving the benefit payments from the annuity at any time. If it is an immediate annuity, benefit payments will usually begin within one year of purchasing the annuity; however, if the annuity is a deferred annuity, the annuity holder may delay the receipt of benefits for several years (see Figure D.1).

## Flexible-Premium Annuity

A flexible-premium annuity allows payments to be made at varying intervals and in varying amounts. Flexible-premium annuities can accept future contributions and often require a smaller initial deposit. This type of annuity is usually used for accumulating a sum of money that will provide benefits at some point in the future. As with a single-premium annuity, the flexible-premium annuity can also purchase either a fixed or variable annuity (see Figure D.2).

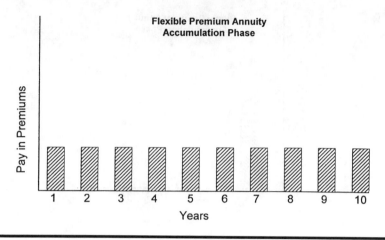

Figure D.2. Flexible-Premium Annuity Accumulation Phase

## Annuity Stages

There are two phases of an annuity. During the asset-building or *accumulation phase*, a variable annuity is generally more appropriate for a customer with longer time horizons to allow a substantial accumulation of wealth through equity investments on a tax-deferred basis. In the accumulation phase, you buy units similar to that of mutual fund shares. Unlike a mutual fund, however, the annuity does not pay out income or distribute any capital gains, so the customer accumulates unit values over a period of years. These also grow tax deferred, making the compound effect even more dramatic.

The payout, distribution, annuitization, or *benefit phase* is when the insurance company starts making a series of payments consisting of principal and earnings for a defined period of time to the investor or to the main beneficiary. Taxes are only assessed on the portion of each payment that comes from earned interest (except with qualified contracts).

The payout options include:

1. *Lifetime income.* The entire account value is converted to a monthly income stream guaranteed for as long as the annuitant lives.
2. *Lifetime income with period certain.* The income stream is guaranteed for a specified number of years, or for as long as the annuitant lives, whichever is longer.
3. *Refund life annuity.* The entire account value is converted to a monthly income stream guaranteed for as long as the annuitant lives. If the

annuitant dies prior to the principal amount being annuitized, the balance is paid to the beneficiary.

4. *Joint and survivor.* The income stream is guaranteed for as long as either annuitant lives (for example, you or your spouse).

5. *Fixed period certain.* The entire account value is fully paid out during a specified period of time.

6. *Fixed amount annuity.* Equal periodic installments are withdrawn until the account balance is exhausted.

Unlike regular life insurance, which pays out a lump sum upon premature death, the lifetime payout option ensures you against the danger of outliving your money. Once a guaranteed income option is elected, the investor cannot withdraw money or surrender his or her contract. The single exception to this is the immediate annuity, which does not actually pass through an accumulation phase, but moves immediately after it is purchased into the distribution phase.

## Parties to an Annuity

Generally, there are four potential parties to an annuity contract: the owner, the annuitant, the beneficiary, and the issuing insurance company. The rights and duties of each of these entities will be discussed in a general overview. The owner is the one purchasing the annuity, and the annuitant is the individual whose life will be used to determine how payments under the contract will be made. The beneficiary is the individual or entity that will receive any death benefits, and the issuing insurance company is the organization that accepts the owner's premium and promises to pay the benefits spelled out in the contract. The most common situation involves only three parties, as the owner and annuitant are usually the same individual. Thus, the three parties normally are the owner/annuitant, the individual or beneficiary, and the insurance company.

### The Owner

Every annuity contract must have an owner. Usually, the owner is a real person, but there is no qualification that the owner must be a real person, as there is with the annuitant. In most instances where the owner and the annuitant are the same person, the owner pays money in the form of premiums into the annuity during the accumulation phase (see Figure D.3). Also,

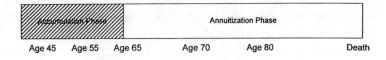

**Figure D.3. Annuity Phases**

the owner has the right to determine when the annuity contract will move from the accumulation phase into the payout or annuitization phase and begin making payments. Most annuity contracts do not specify a maximum age past which annuity payments cannot be deferred, but, in most annuities, the age will usually be well past retirement age.

## The Annuitant

According to the Internal Revenue Service, the annuitant is the individual whose life is of primary importance in affecting the timing and amount of payout under the contract. In other words, the annuitant's life is the measuring life (see IRA, Section 72-S6). The annuitant, unlike the owner and the beneficiary of the annuity contract, must be a real person (see Figure D.4).

## The Beneficiary

Similar to the conditions of a life insurance policy, beneficiaries of an annuity contract receive a death benefit when the annuitant dies prior to the date upon which the annuity begins paying out benefits. In effect, the payment of the death benefit allows the owner to recover his investment and pass it along to the beneficiaries if the annuitant does not live long enough to begin receiving annuity contract benefits. The death benefit is equal generally to the value of the annuity contract at the time of death.

The beneficiary has no rights under the annuity contract other than the right to receive payments of the death benefit. He or she cannot change the payment settlement options or alter the starting date of the benefit payments nor make any withdrawals or partial surrenders against the contract. The owner, under most annuity contracts, has the right to change the beneficiary designation at any time. In a very general sense, the insurance company that issues the annuity contract promises to invest the owner's premium payments responsibly, credit interest to the funds placed in the annuity, pay the contract death benefit in the event of the death of the owner prior to annuitization of

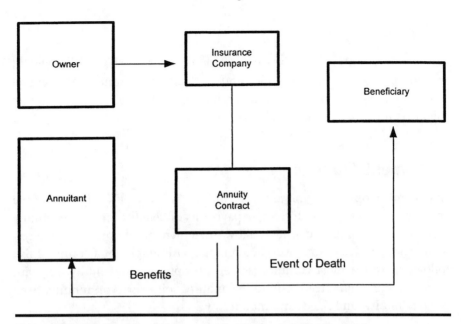

**Figure D.4. Relationship of Various Parties to the Annuity Contract**

the contract, and make benefit payments according to the contract settlement options selected by the contract owner.

The Internal Revenue Service requires that all annuities contain certain provisions in order to be eligible for the tax benefits associated with the annuity contract, but there is considerable variation between companies. For example, all companies have a maximum age beyond which they will not issue an annuity contract. If an individual is 80 years old, he or she will not be able to purchase an annuity contract from a company whose maximum age is, say, 75. Financial planners should request a sample contract for each annuity product they work with to maximize their understanding.

The financial strength and investment philosophy of the issuing company should be examined. To evaluate the financial strength, you could look at the AM Best companies, Moody's, Standard & Poor's, or Duff and Phelps. The rating services examine the items connected with the insurance company that are important in gauging the effectiveness and probability of the company's likelihood of performing in the future. It includes a list of information evaluating the company's profitability and capitalization and its liquidity. In addition, rating services examine the company's investment strategy and marketing philosophy, as well as its business practices and history.

## Premium Payments

Most annuity contracts require each premium payment to be at least a certain minimum amount. For example, under a deferred annuity, the contract might require a minimum monthly premium of $50, while another annuity might require a minimum single premium of $5000.

## Settlement Options

A settlement option in the annuity contract is the method by which the annuity owner can select to receive payments of benefits under the annuity contract. Most annuity contracts allow the settlement option to be changed with proper notice to the insurance company. Although not a complete list, following are the most common settlement options: life annuity, life with period certain guaranteed, refund life annuity, joint survivor annuity, fixed period annuity, and fixed amount annuity.

## Maintenance Fees

The annual contract maintenance fee generally ranges from $25 to $40.

## Insurance-Related Charges

Many fixed annuity contracts levy a charge against partial or full surrender of the contract for a period of years after the annuity is purchased. This charge is usually referred to as a surrender charge or a deferred sales charge. It can range from 0.5 to 1.5% per year of average account value. There are also no-load annuities that do not have surrender charges. The surrender charge is usually applicable to surrender made for an annuity for a certain number of years. Typically, a surrender charge is a percentage decreasing with each passing year similar to vesting. For example, a fixed annuity contract might provide the following surrender charges: year 1 surrender/withdrawal charges, 8%; year 2, 7%; year 3, 6%; year 4, 5%; year 5, 4%; year 6, 3%; year 7, 1%.

## Loans

Most annuity contracts do *not* offer the option of taking a loan against the annuity value.

# Death Benefits

There are certain standard provisions common to most annuity contracts. They require distribution after the death of the owner to be made in a particular manner as requested by the Internal Revenue Service. If the annuitant dies, the value of the death benefit is the greater of the amount originally invested in the contract or the annuity's account value. The death benefit is guaranteed never to be lower than the total amount invested in the annuity. In this sense, annuities look a bit like life insurance.

# Interest Rates

Typically, a fixed annuity contract will offer two interest rates: a guaranteed rate and a current rate. The guaranteed rate is the minimum rate that will be credited to the funds in the annuity contract regardless of how low the current rate sinks or how poorly the insurance company fares. Typically, the guaranteed rate is 3 to 4%. The current interest rate varies with insurance companies. The current rate might be 7%, and its guaranteed rate could be 4%. On the anniversary of the purchase of the annuity, the company notifies the owner of the new current rate. If, for some reason, the interest rate drops below the guaranteed rate, a bailout provision (or escape clause) allows the contract holder to fully surrender the annuity contract and not incur any surrender charges under the annuity contract.

For example, an annuity offering a bailout clause allows the contract to be surrendered if the current interest rate drops 1% below the interest rate of the previous period. Assuming that the prior interest rates were 6.5%, if the current rate for the next period falls below 5.5%, the annuity holder could surrender the annuity contract completely and not be subject to any contract charges. The 10% penalty tax on premature withdrawals may still apply to a surrender under the bailout provision.

# Competitive Return

Fixed annuities offer a competitive interest rate because their rate is more closely tied to the medium- or long-term maturities rather than typically lower rates of short-term maturities associated with products such as CDs. The current rate, which is actually the annualized rate, is usually guaranteed for one year, although other options may be available. At the end of the guaranteed period of the current or initial rate, the annuity will renew with a new rate that is the best rate the company can offer under the current economic conditions. The minimum guaranteed rate also applies, usually around 3 to 4%, which is the lowest rate possible regardless of where the current rates are, and that rate is also tax deferred.

As we have discovered, annuities have many different features and there are a number of factors to examine. For example, you should ask about penalties for early withdrawals. Are there graduated withdrawal charges over a period of years? How much can you withdraw at any one time without a penalty? In addition, if you are considering the purchase of an annuity, you should ask:

1.  What is the current interest rate, and how often does it change?
2.  What is the minimum interest rate guaranteed in the contract?
3.  Is there a bailout option that permits you to cash in the annuity, without withdrawal penalties (there may be tax penalties), if the interest rate drops below a specified figure?
4.  Are there front-end load charges or annual administrative fees? How much are they, and how will they affect your return?

The variable annuity holder may choose how to allocate premium dollars among a number of investment choices, including stocks, bonds, a guaranteed account, income, growth fund, and various funds called sub-accounts. Any funds placed in the guaranteed account of a variable annuity are credited with a fixed rate of interest in much the same manner as funds in a fixed annuity contract. There is a guaranteed interest rate and a current interest rate, and the current rate changes periodically. If it drops below the floor set by the guaranteed rate, then the annuity holder receives at minimum the guaranteed rate.

The variable annuity typically offers the annuity holder several different sub-accounts in which to invest all or a portion of the premiums paid into the annuity. The terms *sub-account, flexible account,* and *flexible sub-account* are interchangeable. When an annuity holder purchases a variable annuity, he determines what proportion of the premium payments, usually on a percentage basis, will be allocated or paid to the different variable sub-accounts. Once a percentage is determined, it remains in effect until the annuity holder notifies the insurance company that he wishes to alter the allocation arrangement. Many variable annuities offer an option known as dollar cost averaging, which provides a method of systematic transfer of dollars from one fund to another inside the variable annuity.

In contrast to the fixed annuity option, an annuity holder who elects to receive all or part of the benefit payments under the variable option would receive a check for the same amount each month. For a list of variable annuity products, see Table D.1

## What Is a Sub-Account?

A sub-account is a term that describes the mutual fund portfolio held inside a variable annuity. Variable annuities offer anywhere from 5 to 35 sub-account investment options. Mutual fund account managers select individual securities inside the sub-accounts; the investor then selects the most appropriate sub-account based on the security selection for his or her portfolio. If this sounds exactly like a mutual fund, for the most part it is. The same (or clone) mutual funds tend to have the same managers inside variable annuity sub-accounts, so the same criteria exist for choosing a mutual fund as for choosing a sub-account, and the same benefits also exist, such as professional money management, convenience, economies of scale, and diversification. Sub-account exchanges do not create taxable events and do not entail sales or transfer charges, Most companies do set limits, usually 12, on the number of annual exchanges before a transfer fee is charged. The variable annuity offers the added benefit of tax-deferred wealth accumulation. Sub-accounts usually include a list of the primary investment objectives, and it is relatively easy to determine what the fees are applied for. A sub-account is required to specify the primary group of securities held and the issuing insurance or mutual fund company.

## The Investment Flow of a Sub-Account

All investment funds flow through the insurance company into the various sub-accounts, depending on what has been chosen by the investor or investment advisor (see Figure D.5). Each sub-account has a specific investment objective. Choosing from among the various sub-accounts gives the investor a chance for diversification and the ability to select different portfolios to meet asset allocation and diversification needs. Sub-account managers purchase stocks, bonds, or cash which are valued daily as an accumulation unit, another name for fund shares of the mutual fund. Accumulation units are purchased by the contract owner at accumulation unit value (AUV), which is

**Table D.1. Directory of Variable Annuity Products**

| Company | Variable Annuity Products | Primary Markets | Telephone |
|---|---|---|---|
| AAL Capital Management | AAL Variable Annuity | Consumer or Broker NQ, IRA | 800-553-6319 |
| Aetna Life Insurance & Annuity Co. | Aetna Marathon Plus Growth Plus Multi Vest Plan Variable Annuity Account C Variable Annuity Account D3 | Consumer or Broker NQ, IRA, 401(k), TSA | 800-367-7732 |
| Aegon Financial Services Group — PL & H | Advisor's Edge Dimensional Marquee | Investment Advisor | 800-797-9177 |
| AIG Life Insurance Co. | AIG Life Insurance Variable Acct I Alliance Gallery I Variable Annuity II | Consumer or Broker NQ, IRA | 800-862-3984 |
| Alexander Hamilton Life | Allegiance Variable Annuity | Consumer or Broker NQ, IRA | 800-289-1776 |
| Allianz Life Insurance Co. | Franklin Valuemark II | Consumer or Broker NQ, IRA | 800-342-3863 |
| Allmerica Financial Life | Allmerica Select Resource Allmerica Medallion Execannuity Plus Separate Account (A,B,C,G,H) | Consumer or Broker NQ, IRA, 401(k), TSA | 800-669-7353 |
| American Enterprise Life | AE Personal Portfolio | Consumer or Broker NQ, IRA | 800-333-3437 |

| Company | Product | | Phone |
|---|---|---|---|
| American General Life | Separate Account D | Consumer or Broker NQ, IRA | 800-247-6584 |
| American International Life | Variety Plus | Consumer or Broker | 800-362-7500 |
| American Life Insurance Co. of NY | Variable Account A | Consumer or Broker NQ, IRA | 800-872-5963 |
| | American Separate Account No. 2 | | |
| American Partners Life Insurance | Privileged Assets Select Annuity | Consumer or Broker NQ, IRA | 800-297-8800 |
| American Republic Insurance Co. | Paine Webber Advantage Annuity | Consumer or Broker NQ, IRA | 800-367-6058 |
| American Skandia Life Assurance | Advisors Choice | Consumer or Broker NQ, IRA, 401(k) | 800-704-6201 |
| | Advisor Design | | |
| | Advisors Plan | | |
| | Alliance Capital Navigator | | |
| | Galaxy Variable Annuity | | |
| | The Lifevest | | |
| | Select | | |
| | Stagecoach | | |
| American United Life Insurance | AUL American Unit Trust | Consumer or Broker NQ, IRA | 800-634-1629 |
| Ameritas Variable Life Insurance | Overture Annuity II | Consumer or Broker NQ, IRA | 800-634-8353 |
| | Overture Annuity III Plus | | |
| Anchor National Life Insurance | American Pathway II | Consumer or Broker NQ, IRA | 800-445-7861 |
| | ICAP II | | |
| | Polaris | | |
| Annuity Investors Life Insurance | Commodore Mariner | Consumer or Broker NQ, IRA | 800-789-6771 |
| | Commodore Nauticus VA | | |
| | Commodore Americus | | |

**Table D.1. Directory of Variable Annuity Products (cont.)**

| Company | Variable Annuity Products | Primary Markets | Telephone |
|---|---|---|---|
| Banker Security Life Insurance | Centennial (P)<br>Centennial (Q)<br>The U.S.A Plan (P)<br>The U.S.A Plan (Q) | Consumer or Broker<br>NQ, IRA | — |
| Canada Life Insurance of America | Trillium<br>Varifund Annuity | Consumer or Broker<br>NQ, IRA | 800-905-1959 |
| Century Life of America | Members Variable Life | Consumer or Broker<br>NQ, IRA | — |
| Charter National Life | Scudder Horizon Plan | Consumer or Broker<br>NQ, IRA | 800-225-2470 |
| CNA | Capital Select Variable Annuity<br>Capital Select Equity Index Annuity | Consumer or Broker<br>NQ, IRA | 800-262-1755 |
| Connecticut General Life Insurance (CIGNA) | CIGNA ACCRU Variable Annuity | Consumer or Broker<br>NQ, IRA | 800-628-2811 |
| COVA Financial Services Life | COVA Variable Annuity | Consumer or Broker<br>NQ, IRA | 800-343-8496 |
| Dreyfus | Dreyfus/Transamerica Triple Advantage | Consumer or Broker<br>NQ, IRA, 401(k) | 800-258-4260 |
| Equitable Life Assurance | Accumulator<br>Equi-Vest<br>Equi-Vest Personal Ret Program<br>Income Manager Accumulator<br>Income Manager Rollover | Consumer or Broker<br>NQ, IRA, 401(k), TSA | 800-628-6673 |

| Company | Product | | Phone |
|---|---|---|---|
| Equitable Life of Iowa | Momentum | | |
| | Momentum Plus | | |
| | Rollover IRA | | |
| | Equi-Select | Consumer or Broker NQ, IRA, TSA | 800-344-6864 |
| Farm Bureau Life Insurance | Farm Bureau Life VA | Consumer or Broker NQ, IRA | 800-247-4170 |
| Fidelity Investments Life Insurance | Fidelity Retirement Reserves | Consumer or Broker NQ, IRA | 800-544-2442 |
| Fidelity Standard Life | Fidelity Standard Life Separate Account | Consumer or Broker NQ, IRA | 800-283-4536 |
| First Allmerica Financial Life | Allmerica Select (NY) | Consumer or Broker NQ, IRA | — |
| | Delaware Medallion (NY) | | |
| | Execannuity Plus (NY) | | |
| | Execannuity Plus (NY) | | |
| First Investors Life Insurance | Vanguard Variable Annuity Plan (NY) | Consumer or Broker NQ, IRA | 800-832-7783 |
| 1st Providian Life & Health | | Consumer or Broker NQ, IRA | 800-523-9954 |
| First SunAmerica Life | First SunAmerica ICAP II (NY) | Consumer or Broker NQ, IRA | 800-996-9786 |
| | First SunAmerica Polaris | | |
| First Transamerica Life | Dreyfus/Transamerica Triple Advantage | Consumer or Broker NQ, IRA | 800-258-4260 |
| First Variable Life Insurance | Vista Annuity/Capital Five VA | Consumer or Broker NQ, IRA | 800-228-1035 |
| | Capital No Load Annuity | | |
| Fortis Benefits Insurance | Fortis Masters VA | Consumer or Broker NQ, IRA | 800-800-2638 |
| | Fortis Opportunity VA | | |
| | Fortis Value Advantage Plus VA | | |
| | Fortis Benefits Insurance Co. | | |

**Table D.1. Directory of Variable Annuity Products (cont.)**

| Company | Variable Annuity Products | Primary Markets | Telephone |
|---|---|---|---|
| General American Life | G.T. Global Allocator | Consumer or Broker NQ, IRA, TSA | 800-233-6699 |
| Glenbrook Life & Annuity | General American Step Account Two AIM Lifetime Plus VA STI Classic VA | Consumer or Broker NQ, IRA | 800-776-6978 |
| Golden American Life Insurance | Fund For Life Golden Select (2D) Golden Select DVA Plus | Consumer or Broker NQ, IRA | 800-243-3706 |
| Great American RSV Insurance | Great American RSV VA Account C Great American RSV VAE | Consumer or Broker NQ, IRA | 317-571-3700 |
| Great Northern Insurance Annuity | Paragon Power Portfolio VA | Consumer or Broker NQ, IRA | 800-455-0870 |
| Great West Life & Annuity | Future Funds Series Account Maximum Value Plan (MVP) | Consumer or Broker NQ, IRA | 800-468-8661 |
| Guardian Insurance & Annuity | Guardian Investor Value Guard II | Consumer or Broker NQ, IRA | 800-221-3253 |
| The Hartford | The Director The Director I Dean Witter Select Dimensions | Consumer or Broker NQ, IRA 401(k) | 800-862-6668 |
| IDS | Flexible Portfolio Annuity IDS Life Flexible Annuity Symphony | Consumer or Broker NQ, IRA | 800-437-0602 |
| Integrity Life Insurance ARM Financial Group | Grandmaster II Pinnacle OMNI New Momentum | Consumer or Broker NQ, IRA, TSA | 800-325-8583 |

| Company | Product | Availability | Phone |
|---|---|---|---|
| John Hancock | Accumulator<br>Accommodator 2000<br>Independence<br>Independence Preferred<br>Declaration | Consumer or Broker<br>NQ, IRA | 800-732-5543 |
| Jackson National Life | JNL Perspective | Consumer or Broker<br>NQ, IRA | 800-873-5654 |
| Jefferson-Pilot Life | Allegiance<br>Alpha Flex<br>Jefferson-Pilot Separate Acct. A | Consumer or Broker<br>NQ, IRA | 910-691-3448 |
| Kemper Investors | Kemper Advantage III<br>Kemper Passport | Consumer or Broker<br>NQ, IRA | 800-554-5426 |
| Keyport Life Insurance | Keyport Preferred Advisor<br>Preferred Advisor | Consumer or Broker<br>NQ, IRA | 800-367-3654 |
| Life Insurance Co. of Virginia | Commonwealth Variable Annuity Plus | Consumer or Broker<br>NQ, IRA | 800-352-9910 |
| Lincoln Benefit Life | Investors Select<br>Investors Select Variable Annuity | Consumer or Broker<br>NQ, IRA | 800-865-5237 |
|  | American Legacy<br>American Legacy II<br>American Funds | Consumer or Broker<br>NQ, IRA, 401(k), TSA | 800-443-8137 |
| Lincoln National Life | LN Variable Annuity Multifund | Consumer or Broker<br>NQ, IRA, 401(k), TSA | 800-421-9900 |
| Lutheran Brotherhood | LB VIP Variable Annuity | Consumer or Broker<br>NQ, IRA | 800-423-7056 |
| Manufacturers Life | Lifetrust 1<br>Lifestyle Fixed | Consumer or Broker<br>NQ, IRA | 800-827-4546 |

## Table D.1. Directory of Variable Annuity Products (cont.)

| Company | Variable Annuity Products | Primary Markets | Telephone |
|---|---|---|---|
| MFS — Sun Life of Canada | MFS Regatta Gold | Consumer or Broker | 800-752-7216 |
| | MFS Regatta | NQ, IRA, 401(k) | |
| | Compass-3 | | |
| Mass Mutual | Flex Extra | Consumer or Broker | 413-788-8411 |
| | Flex Extra (2) | NQ, IRA, 401(k), TSA | |
| | Lifetrust | | |
| | Panorama | | |
| | Panorama Plus | | |
| | Panorama Premier | | |
| MBL Life Assurance | Dreyfus Series 2000 | Consumer or Broker | — |
| | Dreyfus Series 2000 (2) | NQ, IRA | |
| | Mutual Benefit VAC Account-2 | | |
| | Mutual Benefit VAC Account-3 | | |
| | Seligman Mutual Benefit Plan | | |
| | Portfolio Plus | | |
| Merrill Lynch Life Insurance | Retirement Plus (A) | Consumer or Broker | 800-535-5549 |
| | Retirement Plus (B) | NQ, IRA | |
| MetLife | The Preference Plus Account | Consumer or Broker | 800-553-4459 |
| | | NQ, IRA | |
| Midland National Life | Separate Account C | Consumer or Broker | 800-638-5000 |
| | | NQ, IRA | |
| Minnesota Mutual Life | Megannuity Multioption Flexible Annuity | Consumer or Broker | 800-443-3677 |
| | | NQ, IRA | |
| MML Bay State Life Insurance | Lifetrust 1 | Consumer or Broker | 800-272-2216 |
| | | NQ, IRA | |

| Company | Product | Distribution / Type | Phone |
|---|---|---|---|
| Monarch Life Insurance Company | Milestone | Consumer or Broker NQ, IRA | — |
| Mony Life Insurance Co. of America | Keynote The Moneymaster The Valuemaster | Consumer or Broker NQ, IRA | 800-487-6669 |
| Mutual of America Life | Mutual of America Separate Account 2 | Consumer or Broker NQ, IRA | 800-463-3785 |
| National Integrity Life | Grandmaster (NI) Grandmaster II (NI) Pinnacle | Consumer or Broker NQ, IRA, 401(k), TSA | 800-433-1778 |
| Nationwide | Best of Americas Vision Best of America III Best of America IV DCVA DCVA-TSA Fidelity Advisor Classic Fidelity Advisor Annuity Select MFS Spectrum Multi-Flex Nationwide Variable Account 3 NEA Valuebuilder Annuity Nationwide Life & Annuity VA (A) One Investors Annuity | Consumer or Broker NQ, IRA, 401(k), TSA | 888-867-5175 |
| New York Life | Facilitator (I) Facilitator (II) Lifestages NYLIAC VA I NYLIAC VA II (Qualified) | Consumer or Broker NQ, IRA, 401(k) | 212-576-6569 |

**Table D.1. Directory of Variable Annuity Products (cont.)**

| Company | Variable Annuity Products | Primary Markets | Telephone |
|---|---|---|---|
| New England Mutual Life | Zenith Accumulator | Consumer or Broker NQ, IRA, 401(k), TSA | — |
| North American Security Life | Venture<br>Venture Vision | Consumer or Broker NQ, IRA | 800-334-4437 |
| Northbrook Life Insurance Co. | Dean Witter Variable Annuity | Consumer or Broker NQ, IRA | 800-654-2397 |
| Northern Life | Northern Life Advantage | Consumer or Broker NQ, IRA, TSA | 800-870-0453 |
| Northwestern Mutual Life | NML Variable Annuity Account C | Consumer or Broker NQ, IRA | — |
| Ohio National Life Insurance | Top A (A)<br>Top A (B)<br>Top Plus (B) | Consumer or Broker NQ, IRA | 800-366-6654 |
| Pacific Corinthian Life | Pacific Corinthian Variable Annuity | Consumer or Broker NQ, IRA | 619-452-9060 |
| Pacific Mutual Life | Pacific Select Variable Annuity<br>Pacific Select Variable Annuity One<br>Pacific Portfolios | Consumer or Broker NQ, IRA | 800-722-2333 |
| Paine Webber Life Insurance | Paine Webber Milestones B<br>Paine Webber Milestones D | Consumer or Broker NQ, IRA | 800-552-5622 |
| Penn Insurance & Annuity | Pennant | Consumer or Broker NQ, IRA | 800-548-1119 |
| Penn Mutual Life Insurance | Diversifier II | Consumer or Broker NQ, IRA | 800-548-1119 |

| Company | Product | Availability | Phone |
|---|---|---|---|
| PFL Life Insurance | Endeavor Variable Annuity<br>Fidelity Income Plus | Consumer or Broker<br>NQ, IRA | 800-525-6205 |
| Phoenix Home Mutual | Big Edge<br>Big Edge Choice<br>Big Edge Plus<br>Templeton Investment Plus | Consumer or Broker<br>NQ, IRA | 800-243-4361 |
| Principal Mutual Life Insurance | Pension Builder Plus<br>Principal Variable Annuity | Consumer or Broker<br>NQ, IRA | 800-986-3343 |
| Protective Life Insurance | Protective Variable Annuity | Consumer or Broker<br>NQ, IRA | 800-456-6330 |
| Provident Mutual Life & Annuity | Market Street VIP<br>Market Street VIP (2)<br>Options VIP | Consumer or Broker<br>NQ, IRA | 610-407-1717 |
| Providian Life & Health | Marquee Variable Annuity<br>Providian Prism<br>The Advisors Edge | Consumer or Broker<br>NQ, IRA | 800-866-6007 |
| Pruco Insurance Co. of NJ | Discovery Select<br>Discovery Plus (NJ) | Consumer or Broker<br>NQ, IRA, 401(k) | 201-802-6000 |
| Prudential Insurance | Variable Investment Plan<br>Discovery Plus<br>Discovery Select | Consumer or Broker<br>NQ, IRA, 401(k) | 800-445-4571 |
| Putman | Capital Manager | Consumer or Broker<br>NQ, IRA | 800-225-1581 |
| Reliastar Life | Northstar NWNL Variable Annuity<br>Select Annuity II<br>Select Annuity III | Consumer or Broker<br>NQ, IRA | 800-621-3750 |

**Table D.1. Directory of Variable Annuity Products (cont.)**

| Company | Variable Annuity Products | Primary Markets | Telephone |
|---|---|---|---|
| SAFECO Life Insurance Co. | Spinnaker Q & NQ Flex<br>Spinnaker Plus<br>Mainsail<br>SAFECO Resource Account A<br>SAFECO Resource Account B | Consumer or Broker<br>NQ, IRA, 401(k), TSA | 800-426-6730 |
| Schwab | Schwab Variable Annuity | Consumer or Broker<br>NQ, IRA | 800-838-0650 |
| Security Benefit Life | Parkstone Variable Annuity<br>SBL Variable Annuity Account III<br>SBL Variable Annuity Account IV<br>Variflex LS<br>Variflex<br>T. Rowe Price Variable Annuity | Consumer or Broker<br>NQ, IRA, 401(k), TSA | 800-888-2461<br>800-541-8803 |
| Security First Life Insurance | Flexible Bonus<br>Investors Choice<br>Strive | Consumer or Broker<br>NQ, IRA | 800-284-4536 |
| Security Life of Denver | Exchequer Variable Annuity | Consumer or Broker<br>NQ, IRA | 800-933-5858 |
| Sun Life Assurance of Canada | MFS Regatta Gold<br>MFS Regatta<br>Compass 3<br>Compass 2 | Consumer or Broker<br>NQ, IRA | 800-752-7216 |
| TIAA | College Retirement Equities Fund | Consumer or Broker<br>NQ, IRA, TSA | 800-842-2776 |

| Company | Product | Availability | Tax Type | Phone |
|---|---|---|---|---|
| Templeton | Templeton Imm. Variable Annuity | Consumer or Broker | NQ, IRA | 800-292-9293 |
| Touchstone | Touchstone Variable Annuity<br>Touchstone Variable Annuity II | Consumer or Broker | NQ, IRA, 401(k) | 800-669-2796 |
| Transamerica Occidental Life Ins. | Schwab Investment Advantage<br>Dreyfus./Transamerica Triple Advantage | Consumer or Broker | NQ, IRA | 800-258-4260 |
| Travelers | Universal Annuity<br>Vintage<br>Portfolio Architect | Consumer or Broker | NQ, IRA, 401(k), TSA | 800-334-4298 |
| Union Central Life Insurance | Carillon Account | Consumer or Broker | NQ, IRA | 800-825-1551 |
| United Companies Life Insurance | Spectraselect | Consumer or Broker | NQ, IRA | 800-825-7568 |
| United Investors Life | Advantage II | Consumer or Broker | NQ, IRA | 800-999-0317 |
| United of Omaha Life Insurance | Ultrannuity Series V | Consumer or Broker | NQ, IRA | 800-453-4933 |
| USAA Life Insurance | USAA Life Variable Annuity | Consumer or Broker | NQ, IRA | 800-531-6390 |
| Vanguard (Providian Life & Health) | Vanguard Variable Annuity | Consumer or Broker | NQ, IRA | 800-522-5555 |
| Variable Annuity Life Insurance | Portfolio Directory 2<br>Independence Plus<br>Portfolio Director<br>Portfolio Director 2 | Consumer or Broker | NQ, IRA | 800-228-2542 |

**Table D.1. Directory of Variable Annuity Products (cont.)**

| Company | Variable Annuity Products | Primary Markets | Telephone |
|---|---|---|---|
| Western Reserve Life | Janus Retirement Advantage<br>WRL Freedom Attainer<br>WRL Freedom Bellwether<br>WRL Freedom Conqueror<br>CASE Reserve Variable Annuity<br>Meridian/INVESCO Sector VA | Consumer or Broker<br>NQ, IRA, 401(k), TSA | 800-443-9974,<br>ext. 6510 |

*Note:* NQ = Non-qualified (after tax); IRA = individual retirement account; TSA = tax-sheltered annuity.

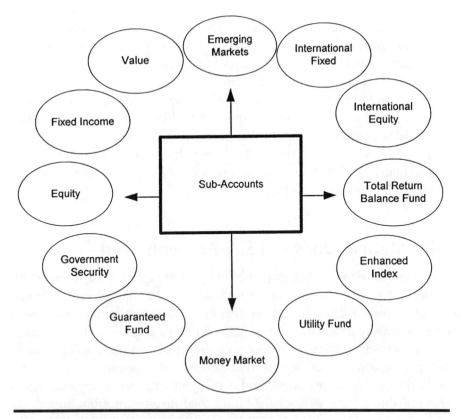

**Figure D.5. Typical Variable Annuity Investment Option**

very similar to the mutual fund equivalent known as net asset value (NAV), without commissions, in full and fractional units.

## Types of Sub-Accounts

Sub-accounts may be divided into several broad categories: asset classes seeking aggressive growth, asset classes seeking more stable growth, asset classes seeking low volatility by utilizing fixed-income bonds, a combination of these, and asset classes featuring money market rates. Within each of these classes, categories are further broken down.

Fixed-income accounts are established to decrease risk for those in need of meeting current income requirements. Fixed-income sub-accounts include government agencies, corporate rate bonds, high yield, foreign government corporate bonds, and certain other fixed-income choices. Equity or stock investing would be in funds for growth of principal. Because variable annuities are long-term investments, the equity sub-accounts will be most important to review. Other asset classes could include cash and cash equivalents, which would be more short term.

You still may have questions about sub-accounts and mutual funds, how they work, and what makes up a mutual fund. Think of a sub-account inside the variable annuity and a mutual fund as being the same thing. Although they are kept separate and the fund within each cannot be commingled, for ease of understanding how these work we will look at the predecessor to the sub-account, the mutual fund.

## How Mutual Funds and Sub-Accounts Work

The manager of the mutual fund uses the pool of capital to buy a variety of stocks, bonds, or money market instruments based on the advertised financial objectives of the fund. The mutual fund manager uses the investment objectives as a guide when choosing investments. These objectives cover a wide range. Some follow aggressive policies, involving greater risk in search of higher returns. Others seek current income and little risk.

When you purchase mutual fund shares, you own them at net asset value (NAV), which is the value of the fund's total investment minus any debt, divided by the number of outstanding shares. For example, if the fund's investment value is $26,000, it has no debt, and there are 1000 shares outstanding, the NAV would be $26 per share. In a regular mutual fund, which includes thousands and often millions of shares, the NAV is calculated on a daily basis, with values moving up or down along with the stock or bond markets. The NAV is not a fixed figure because it must reflect the daily change in the price of the securities in the fund's portfolio. In contrast, a variable annuity issues shares at accumulation unit value (AUV). The only difference between the two is that in a mutual fund you will sometimes pay higher than the NAV for shares that have front-end commissions, and in annuities this is not an option.

## Costs

It is simply common sense that lower expenses generally translate into higher overall returns. The goal of the smart investor is to keep his or her acquisition costs as low as possible. There are four basic kinds of costs.

## Sales Charges

Sales charges (or loads) are commissions paid on the sale of mutual funds. All commissions used to be simply charged up front, but that has all changed. There are now several ways that mutual fund companies charge fees. Annuities and mutual funds are similar if you compare the B-share mutual fund option. This option has no front-end sales charges but has higher internal costs. If you decide to redeem your shares early, usually within the first 5 years, you pay a surrender charge. This is very similar to annuity investing.

Some sales charges, as for B-shares, are levied on the back end as a contingent deferred sales charge. The load is charged when the investor redeems shares in the fund. A customer who redeems shares in the first year of ownership would typically pay a 5% sales charge. The amount would drop by an equal amount each year. After 6 years, the shares would be redeemed without further charge. For large purchases, you should never purchase B-share mutual funds, although there are less-than-ethical brokers out there who will tell you it is a better deal to invest in B-shares as you will not pay an up-front charge.

Class C-shares typically have even higher internal expenses but pay the selling broker up to 1% per year based on assets. This fee comes directly from your investment performance and is paid to the selling broker. C-shares may have no up-front fee, possibly a 1% deferred sales charge in year one (sometimes longer), and higher annual expenses (up to 1% extra per year).

No-load mutual funds do *not* mean no cost. Some no-load funds charge a redemption fee of 1 to 2% of the net asset value of the shares to cover expenses mainly incurred by advertising. Fee comparisons are particularly important. Every dollar charged comes directly from the performance of the sub-account. Remember to compare the proverbial apples to apples — in this case, similar equities to equities sub-accounts, and similar bonds to bonds sub-accounts.

## Operating Expenses

These are fees paid for the operational costs of running a fund. These costs can include employees' salaries, marketing and publicity, servicing toll-free phone lines, printing and mailing published materials, computers for tracking investments and account balances, accounting fees, and so on. A fund's operating expenses are quoted as a percentage of your investment; the percentage represents an annual fee or charge. You can find this number in the prospectus of a fund in the fund expenses section, entitled Total Fund

Operating Expenses or Other Expenses. The operating expenses of a mutual fund are normally invisible to investors because they are deducted before any return is paid, and they are automatically charged on a daily basis. Beware, though; a sub-account can have a very low management fee but exorbitant operating expenses. A fund that frequently trades will have more wire charges, for instance, than a fund that does not.

## Transaction Charges

Also known as execution costs, total transaction costs (or the cost of buying and selling stocks) have three components: (1) the actual dollars paid in commissions, (2) the market impact (i.e., the impact a manager's trade has on the market price for the stock which varies with the size of the trade and the skill of the trader), and (3) the opportunity cost of the return (positive or negative) given up by not executing the trade instantaneously.

For example, when an individual investor places an order to buy 300 shares of a $30 stock ($9000 investment), he or she is likely to get a commission bill for about $204, or 2.3% of the value of the investment. Even at a discount broker, commissions are likely to cost between $82 (0.9%) and $107 (1.2%). A mutual fund, on the other hand, is more likely to be buying 30,000 to 300,000 shares at a time, so their commission costs often run in the vicinity of one tenth of the commission you would pay at a discount broker. Where a commission might have been $0.35 a share, the mutual fund might pay less than $0.05 a share. The commission savings can (and should) mean higher returns for you as a mutual fund shareholder.

## Index Annuity

The newest annuity is a hybrid between a fixed annuity and a variable annuity and is referred to as an index annuity, which is ideal for individuals who want the specific minimum guarantees offered by a fixed annuity and also want to participate in the upside of the market, but do not want to take on the risk associated with making their own investment decisions on a variable annuity. Essentially, the insurance company is putting a percentage of the money into a fixed annuity account, while the balance is invested in options that are connected with the S&P 500. In a year in which the S&P 500 outperforms the fixed-income guarantees, the typical investor can enjoy a gain of 70 to 80% of the increase in the S&P 500; in a year in which the S&P 500 has a negative return, the investor receives the guaranteed fixed interest rate of the contract. Either way, the investor comes out ahead.

## Is an Annuity Right for You?

It really depends on what you are trying to accomplish. For the majority of people who are looking for a long-term supplemental retirement vehicle that will complement their 401(k)s and IRAs and give them simplicity, flexibility, and tax-deferral, annuities are definitely an investment vehicle they should consider. A qualified financial advisor can offer expert guidance in this area and help you select the types of annuities (see Table D.2, pages 242 and 243) that will accomplish your own personal goals and objectives.

**Table D.2. Sub-Accounts**

| Portfolio | Objective | Type of Investment | Asset Class Represented |
|---|---|---|---|
| Small cap value | Capital appreciation | Equity securities of small U.S. and foreign companies | U.S. small cap |
| Enhanced index | Total return modestly in excess of the performance of the S&P Index | Primarily equity investments of large and medium-sized U.S. companies | U.S. large cap |
| Domestic blue-chip | Primarily long-term growth of capital; secondarily, providing income | Common stocks of blue-chip companies | U.S. large cap |
| Utility fund | High current income and moderate capital appreciation | Equity and debt securities of utility companies | Energy |
| Money fund | Current income with stability of principal and liquidity | High-quality money market instruments | Cash |
| High-yield income bond fund | High current income and overall total return | Lower rated fixed income securities | High-yield fixed income |
| U.S. government securities | Current income | U.S. government securities | Short-term fixed income |
| Emerging markets | Capital appreciation | Equity securities of companies in countries having emerging markets | Emerging markets |
| Growth equity | Capital appreciation | Primary equity securities of domestic companies | U.S. large cap |

| | | | |
|---|---|---|---|
| Domestic small cap | Capital appreciation | Primarily common stocks, convertibles, and other equity-type securities with emphasis on small company stocks | U.S. small cap |
| International fund | Capital growth | Primarily equity securities of companies located outside the U.S. | International large cap |
| Value fund | Primarily long-term capital appreciation; secondarily, current income | Equity securities of medium to large companies, primarily in the U.S. | U.S. large cap value |
| International small cap | Long-term capital appreciation | Primarily equity securities of small and medium-sized foreign companies | International small cap |
| International equity | Capital appreciation | Equity securities of non-U.S. companies | International large cap |
| Small company growth | Capital growth | Equity securities of small U.S. companies | U.S. small cap |

# Appendix E.
# How To Read
# a Prospectus

The prospectus describes investment objectives, strategies, and risks. Spending time with a jargon-filled prospectus may not be enthralling, but it is a must-read for would-be first time investors and is required by the federal government as a protection for all investors. Any misstatements or omissions can lead to stiff penalties; thus, the tendency for legalese.

You will want to begin by identifying the type of asset class mutual fund you are interested in. You can then request a prospectus by calling or writing the fund or asking a broker or financial planner. When you receive it, check the date to make sure it is current; such documents must be updated at least once a year. Following are some of the things you should look for in a mutual fund prospectus.

## Minimums

If the minimum amount required to open an account is too high for you, read no further.

## Investment Objective

At the core of the prospectus is a description of the fund's investments and the portfolio manager's philosophy. The objective should outline what types

1-57444-258-9/00/$0.00+$.50
© 2000 by CRC Press LLC

**245**

of securities the fund buys and the policies regarding the quality of those investments. If the fund has more than 25% of its assets in one industry or holds bonds rated below investment quality, these policies must be included in the prospectus. A global equity fund, for example, earns a high level of total return through investments in world capital markets. A typical balanced fund strives to obtain income equally with capital growth, while the investment objective of a long-term municipal bond fund is to preserve capital by seeking a high level of interest income exempt from federal income tax.

## Performance

This bottom-line information on how funds have fared over the last decade shows you what you would have earned in per-share dividends and capital gains distributions and any increase or decrease in the value of that share during the year. The portfolio turnover rate reveals how actively the fund trades securities. The higher the turnover, the greater the brokerage costs of the fund.

## Risk

Different investors can tolerate various risk levels. In this section of the prospectus, the fund should describe the potential for risk. For instance, a fund that invests in only one portion of the economy may offer greater risk than a highly diversified fund, while a fund that invests in well-established companies may be less risky than one that favors start-up companies. Other risks are associated with certain types of funds or securities. Bond funds are susceptible to interest rate changes, while fixed-income savings and investment vehicles are subject to inflation risks.

## Fees

Management and accounting fees and the cost of printing and mailing reports to shareholders are internal charges that should be evaluated. Generally, a company that keeps its expenses (excluding sales fees) at 1% or less of its assets is considered a low-cost fund. A fund whose expenses are above 2% of its assets is viewed as a high-cost fund. Fees are required to be summarized in a table in the front of the prospectus. Other charges to consider are minimum fees for subsequent investments or fees for switching from one fund to another in the same family.

## Management

When you are putting money in a mutual fund, you are paying for professional management. Examine information about the fund's managers to evaluate their investment philosophy and to find out whether the portfolio is managed by an individual or committee.

## Services

This section will tell you if features such as check-writing or automatic investing are available.

## Buying or Selling Shares of a Fund

Look for information detailing how to get in and out of a fund and whether there is a charge for redeeming shares. Additional information, such as securities held in the fund's portfolio at the end of its fiscal year, is included in a Statement of Additional Information, also called Part B of the prospectus. Funds must provide this information free on request.

## Other Evaluation Tools

Other tools to evaluate mutual funds include news accounts and the fund's annual report. Make sure you are comparing apples to apples. Various magazines measure funds during different time periods and use different criteria, which could affect a fund's ranking.

## The Language of a Prospectus

A survey by the Investment Company Institute, the mutual fund industry's trade group, discovered that only half of the fund shareholders consult a prospectus before investing. The good news, though, is that there is a movement afoot to simplify the language used in a prospectus so that it is more useful to the typical investor. The Securities and Exchange Commission is demanding simplification of the language used in prospectuses and has recommended the creation of a clearly written, one-page summary to accompany each prospectus. The SEC new rules will force mutual funds to abandon legalese and rewrite their prospectuses, the important disclosure booklets that most people toss unread into the trash. SEC representatives will coach prospectus writers on how to translate common jargon and to write more effectively. We hope that by the time you read this book the SEC and the mutual fund companies will have fully adopted the use of plain English.

Fund companies began distributing the plain English prospectuses in 1998, which is good news. With more than an estimated 6000 mutual funds from which to choose, many investors feel overwhelmed when comparing possible investments, particularly when they have to wade through prospectuses that make no sense.

Fund companies also will being distributing a streamlined publication that includes a mutual fund's vital statistics. This is a victory for the consumer, at least for those who care enough to follow through and do their homework. The document will contain a 10-year bar chart, a fund performance, a table comparing performance to market index, and a description of the risk involved in the investment. A three- to six-page profile at the beginning of the document will also summarize the fund's fees, risks, and investment objectives.

# Appendix F.
# Retirement Plans

There are a number of special plans designed to create retirement savings, and many of these plans allow you to deposit money directly from your paycheck before taxes are taken out. Employers occasionally will match the amount (or a percentage of that amount) you have withheld from your paycheck up to a certain percentage. Some of these plans permit you to withdraw money early without a penalty in order to buy a home or to pay for education. For those plans that do not allow early withdrawals without a penalty, sometimes you can borrow money from the account or take out low-interest secured loans with your retirement savings as collateral. Rates of return vary on these vehicles depending on what you invest in, as you can invest in stocks, bonds, mutual funds, CDs, or any combination.

You can do it yourself or use an investment advisor. An investment advisor's job is to screen investment managers across the country and across investment disciplines to ensure compatibility with the investor's financial goals. They not only monitor the money managers on an ongoing basis, but they also help monitor and evaluate personal portfolios by providing a quarterly performance report.

Let's take a look at the different types of retirement plans and which one best fits your needs (Figure F.1).

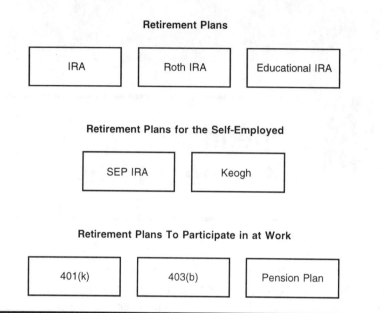

**Figure F.1. Retirement Plans**

# Individual Retirement Account (IRA)

Individual retirement account contributions may be deductible even if you or your spouse are covered by another retirement plan such as corporate pensions, SEP-IRA accounts, Keogh plans, or 401(k) company-sponsored plans. If your adjusted gross income is under $35,000 (single) or $50,000 (joint; both these amounts are indexed), you are allowed $1 in IRA deductions for each $5 below those limits. In other words, you can still get a tax credit for the full $2000 IRA contribution if your adjusted gross income is no higher than $25,000 (single) or $40,000 (joint) and you or your spouse are not covered by a pension plan or a Keogh.

## IRA Checklist

Consider putting money in an IRA if:

1.  You are among those whose contributions are fully deductible — couples filing jointly with gross income of less than $40,000, singles who make less than $25,000, or anyone not covered by a pension, profit-sharing, or other tax-advantaged retirement plan.

2.  You qualify for a partial deduction and are sure that you will not need the money in your IRA before age 59-1/2.

Contributing to a traditional IRA is probably not worthwhile if:

1.  You are ineligible for a deduction, especially if you think that your tax rate when you retire will be higher than now.
2.  You can use other tax-favored retirement savings plans, such as a 401(k).
3.  You do not want to worry about the lifelong burden of paperwork required to document a nondeductible or partially deductible IRA for the IRS.

The basic rules of contributing to any type of IRA (with the exception of educational IRAs which are really not retirement accounts) are based on taxable compensation. This includes wages, salaries, tips, professional fees, commissions, and self-employed income. Your annual contribution to all IRA accounts cannot exceed the lesser of your compensation or $2000, plus up to an additional $2000 for a non-working or low-earning spouse.

The IRA is simply a tax shelter, because all of the earnings in every type of IRA compound are completely tax deferred. For example, say you accumulate $50,000 in a deductible IRA by the time you reach age 40. If your account averages a 10% annual return for the next 25 years, you will generate $492,000 of earnings. And, if you withdraw that as a lump sum and pay a 30% average tax rate, you will net around $344,000. On the other hand, if you have that $50,000 in a taxable account, your earnings are subject to an average tax rate of 30% and you net only 7% per annum instead of 10%. At that rate, your $50,000 earns about $221,000 over the next 25 years, which reflects the benefit of compounding. You get an extra 3% provided by the IRA tax shelter.

Beginning in 1998, if one spouse actively participates in an employer-sponsored plan and the other does not, the spouse who does not participate may make a deductible IRA contribution, provided the adjusted gross income (AGI) on their joint return is $150,000 or less. The amount deductible is phased out with an AGI over $150,000, with full phaseout at $160,000 (see Table F.1 for the new phaseout ranges for IRAs).

For example, in 1998 Mary is an active participant in an employer-sponsored retirement plan, but her husband, John, is not. The combined AGI for Mary and John for the year is $200,000. In this situation, neither Mary nor John is entitled to make deductible contributions to an IRA for the year. If,

### Table F.1. New Phaseout Ranges for Deductible IRAs

| Year | Joint Return | Single, Head of Household |
|---|---|---|
| 1998 | $50,000–60,000 | $30,000–40,000 |
| 1999 | $51,000–61,000 | $31,000–41,000 |
| 2000 | $52,000–62,000 | $32,000–42,000 |
| 2001 | $53,000–63,000 | $33,000–43,000 |
| 2002 | $54,000–64,000 | $34,000–44,000 |
| 2003 | $60,000–70,000 | $40,000–50,000 |
| 2004 | $65,000–75,000 | $45,000–55,000 |
| 2005 | $70,000–80,000 | $50,000–60,000 |
| 2006 | $75,000–85,000 | $50,000–60,000 |
| 2007 and later | $80,000–100,000 | $50,000–60,000 |

in a future year, the situation is the same but the couple's combined AGI is $125,000, then John could make a deductible IRA contribution of up to $2000, but Mary could not make a deductible contribution.

Individual retirement accounts are also a great place to have an aggressive growth mutual fund because you want to strive for high returns to maximize the advantage of the tax-deferred compounding. Even though your stocks are riskier in the short run and there may be volatility over the long run, they participate in the growth of the economy.

## Educational IRAs

Educational IRAs limit contributions to $500 a year. As with other IRAs, the earnings compound tax free, but the money must be used for tuition or other allowable college costs. The IRS would penalize you if your child decides to buy a car with it instead. If the funds are used for any purpose other than education, income tax and a 10% penalty are slapped on the earnings. Also, when you cash in an educational IRA, you become ineligible for new tuition tax credits during that calendar year. And, finally, whether you are ready or not, you must withdraw any remaining funds by your youngest child's 13th birthday (I know that sounds silly...). Another idea for your children's education might be to set aside your spare change, unused dimes, and quarters every day. Once a month, write a check equivalent to the total to a mutual fund company. They will accept a contribution as small as $50 a month. If you earn 8% a year, in 10 years, your child could net $9064.

# Roth IRA

The new Roth IRA, first available in 1998, is a valuable new kind of IRA. It differs in that contributions are not deductible; however, distributions of funds held in the IRA for more than 5 years from the date you set up the Roth IRA will be totally tax free if used (1) for up to $10,000 of first-time home-buyer expenses, (2) after the occurrence of death or disability, or (3) after you reach age 59-1/2. The Roth IRA will be most valuable when it holds investments that compound at a high rate — such as growth stocks — for a long period of time. That is because the ultimate value of the compound investment returns will be distributed tax free instead of being taxed at normal rates, as are distributions from regular IRAs and other retirement accounts.

## Children's IRA Opportunity

A Roth IRA is an excellent investment account to open for children as soon as they have earned income. The extra years of compounding available to a child can produce a tax-free payoff that will give the child a big headstart on lifetime financial security. While a child must have earned income to open a Roth IRA, the IRA need not be funded with the child's earned income.

## Roth IRA for Yourself

You can make a full $2000 contribution to a Roth IRA if your adjusted gross income is less than $150,000 for a joint return or $95,000 for a single return. The contribution gets phased out from $150,000 to $160,000 (joint) and $95,000 to $110,000 (single). If your AGI does not exceed $100,000, you will be able to convert existing IRAs into Roth IRAs. To do this, you will first have to withdraw your IRA assets and pay the taxes on the gains. If you are converting after 1998, you must pick up all of the income in the year of conversion. Whether it will pay to convert a regular IRA to a Roth IRA will depend on several factors, such as:

1. Your current and expected future tax rates
2. The length of time you expect to keep your funds in the IRA
3. The rate of return that you expect to earn
4. Whether you can pay the tax due on the conversion from non-IRA funds

A Roth IRA offers other advantages in addition to the tax-free distributions, such as being able to withdraw the amount of your regular contributions to a Roth IRA at any time.

# Retirement Plans for the Self-Employed

## Keogh

This is a special type of IRA that doubles as a pension plan for a self-employed person. The self-employed person can put aside up to $30,000 a year, significantly more than the normal $2000 cap on an individual IRA. If you are self-employed, sock away 20% of your income, up to a maximum of $30,000, in a Keogh account plan. You can establish a Keogh plan with any bank, brokerage firm, or mutual fund. You may also want to explore the advantages of an SEP plan.

## Simplified Employee Pension Plan

A simplified employee pension (SEP) plan is like a giant IRA. SEPs were created so that small businesses could set up retirement plans that were a little easier to administer than normal pension plans. Both employees and the employer can contribute to a SEP. The SEP lets you contribute 13% of your net earnings from self-employment, up to $24,000, without the paperwork of a Keogh. The reason you do not hear more about these plans is that the brokers do not make money selling them. You can actually save more in an SEP account than you can in a 401(k). An SEP allows you to put away as much as 13.034% of pre-tax self-employed earnings or $24,000 a year, whichever is less. The nice thing about an SEP account is that you can wait until the last minute to invest in it, as the cutoff date for contributions to them is April 15th.

# Participate in Retirement Plans at Work

The 403(b) is the nonprofit version of a 401(k) plan. Local and state governments offer the 457 plan.

The 401(k) is like found money, as some employers will match your contribution, so your contribution and your employer's contribution could be compounding tax-deferred until you retire. Things have changed dramatically in the last few years. If you participate in a 401(k) retirement plan at work, you need to know that any investment mistakes you make come out of your retirement nest-egg. In other words, investment results are your responsibility and not those of the sponsor of the plan. This makes it even more important for you to understand your investment choices and make smart decisions.

The problem is that time does not permit you to absorb and evaluate the vast amounts of information required to make astute investment decisions. Meeting your personal production schedules, sales, or service commitments must take priority. All too often, these problems ultimately push you, the plan participant, to choose expedient, short-term solutions that seem reasonable but may not produce the results you desire.

Participants normally have the right to move their funds in a 401(k) plan from one alternative to another periodically. Daily switching (a feature offered by 401(k) service providers which gives the participant the freedom to transfer between investment options on a daily basis) offers plan participants the greatest control over their assets. Be aware, though, that by moving from equities to cash or fixed income and back you unknowingly become your own personal market timer. (Aside from everything in this book about market timing, this type of activity also causes you to get "whipsawed" by market moves you may not understand, to the detriment of your long-term investment success.)

The best approach is to decide upon one strategy and stick with it. Work with your 401(k) plan's financial consultant and develop a personal strategy, in the form of a statement of investment objectives for each alternative, and commit to it in writing. Such a statement should articulate clearly what the fund may and may not invest in, the expected long-term goals (in terms of performance and volatility), and the general approach to be taken by the manager (whether a private investment manager or a mutual fund manager) in achieving those results.

Most 401(k) plans have a long-term, systematic manner of monitoring any plan's investment progress. You should inquire into how your assets are to be monitored. If mutual funds are used as an investment vehicle, then you should be provided performance results periodically; otherwise, periodic meetings or telephone conferences with your financial consultant should be requested. Questions that should form the basis of such meetings include:

1. Is your manager continuing to apply the style and strategy that you understood would be used in the management of your assets?
2. Do you find the reporting clear, logical, and understandable? Does it show clearly what your plan owns?
3. Do you feel comfortable that your overall communications with the financial consultant are good and that your queries and needs are attended to promptly?

4. Is the performance of your 401(k) plan roughly in line with the performance you expected? Or, is the fund apparently doing much better or much worse than expected? Why is this the case? Is the explanation satisfactory?

5. If there are investment restrictions in your guidelines, are these being adhered to?

A financial advisor can be called upon to meet with participants to explain the advantage of various investment alternatives, as well as how the plan has progressed. This, of course, would be at the option or request of the sponsoring company. As a participant, you should understand that, over long periods of time, common stocks (although more volatile) tend to produce overall returns almost twice as high as high-quality bonds.

401(k) plans are much more attractive to many companies, because the company's investment committee is not directly liable for any losses sustained by the plan. Many employees like the sense of control they get from a 401(k) plan, but serving as one's own money manager can also be overwhelming to people who have trouble managing their own checkbooks, let alone their financial future. Unfortunately, with so much at stake, many participants feel intimidated about making investment decisions. That is why the most popular choice in 401(k) plans are low-risk, fixed-rate guaranteed investment contracts (GICs) offered by insurance companies.

Luckily for plan investors, back in the 1980s fixed-rate contracts were paying unusually high rates of around 9%. But, in the 1990s, interest rates came down. Participants coming out of a 5-year, 9% contract had to reinvest at lower rates, which meant they will be coming up short at retirement. Still, many investors who are given a choice with their retirement money prefer to play it safe with a fixed income, which is fine if it is the only way you can sleep at night. Don't forget, though, that there is a trade-off in results.

## Being Prepared To Make Investment Decisions

Faced with a number of investment decisions, an employee should get prepared:

1. *Step 1.* Identify investment goals.
2. *Step 2.* Select and set appropriate risk parameters and choose an option to meet your financial needs.
3. *Step 3.* Look at all the options, not just the guaranteed ones; remember that, in fixed-investment vehicles, low risk often means low return.

4.   *Step 4.* Get an investment advisor.
5.   *Step 5.* Monitor your investment manager's progress.

In most 401(k) plans, participants are offered short-term investment vehicles that neglect their long-term investment needs. This can spell trouble 20 years from now when many plan participants may learn, too late, the ruthless rules of investing. It is a sad fact that most 401(k) participants are not being properly advised and cannot be expected to make appropriate investment allocations or choices.

Beyond the minimum requirement of distributing a prospectus that offers the standard three investment choices, there is absolutely no incentive for employers to inform employees of investment options. This forces the employee participants to fend for themselves in the rough investment seas of the 1990s. In most cases, participants act as their own asset allocators or market timers, deciding each quarter — or sometimes each day — how much money should be invested in each class.

## Defined Benefit Pension Plans

In a defined benefit pension plan, the sponsoring company takes full responsibility for providing a guaranteed benefit for you as a participant. The sponsoring company shoulders all the investment risks and promises to make specific payouts. To many companies who have abandoned pension plans, retirement benefits generated from these plans did not seem worth the extensive amount of government paperwork and the fiduciary risk that the sponsoring company had to shoulder.

## Retirement Check Up

Pension miscalculations are a growing problem affecting people of all ages, not just retirement age. Any time people change jobs or take lump-sum pension cashouts, they are at risk. Women are especially vulnerable to pension mistakes because they tend to move in and out of the workforce more often than men. For the most part, pension mix-ups are not intentional, as federal pension laws are incredibly difficult even for expert number crunchers.

How would you know if there was an error which had been compounding for many years? How can you ensure that you will get what is rightfully yours when retirement arrives? It is up to you to keep track of your own pension.

Know your rights and monitor your retirement plan before the "golden years" creep up on you. Learn the details. Ask for a summary plan description. This will show how your pension is calculated. If you are in a workplace 401(k), get a description of your program from the administrator of your benefits plan. Also, an individual benefit statement will tell you what your benefits are currently worth and how many years you have been in the plan. It may even include a projection of your monthly check.

Check for obvious errors such as wrong years of service. If you are stashing money away in a 401(k), you will get periodic statements just as you do with your checking accounts. Save all your statements. You should keep any pension documents your company gives you over the years. Also, keep records of dates when you worked and your salary, as this type of data is used by your employer to calculate the value of your pension. Ask for professional help if you still think something might be wrong. Ask for the name of a qualified specialist in your area, or call the American Society of Pension Actuaries (703-516-9300) or the National Center for Retirement Benefits (800-666-1000).

## Nine Common Pension Mistakes

Most companies will not intentionally mishandle your fund; usually simple errors can be to blame if there is a problem. Here is what you should watch for:

1. The company forgot to include commission, overtime pay, or bonuses when determining your benefit level.
2. Your employer relied on incorrect Social Security information to calculate your benefits.
3. Somebody used the wrong benefit formula (e.g., an incorrect interest rate was plugged into the equation).
4. The calculations are wrong because you have worked past age 65.
5. You did not notify your workplace personnel officer of important changes that could affect your benefits, such as marriage, divorce, or death of a spouse.
6. The firm's computer software could be flawed.
7. Errors could result from the anticipated year 2000 problems; consult with your pension administrator to make sure that your financial records are not lost.
8. The company neglected to include your total years of service.
9. Your pension provider just made a basic math mistake.

You will want to complete a form requesting that the Social Security Administration send an accounting of your benefit payments, so you can know ahead of time how much you are going to be making when you retire. Also, request from your company that same information regarding your pension plan, if you have one. Subtract the total of those two amounts from what you would anticipate needing in retirement and the difference is going to be your investment goal.

## Last Notes on Retirement Planning

Qualified plans all have contribution limits, so what do you do if you are contributing the maximum amount into your retirement plans and will still have a shortfall? Avoid any get-rich-quick plan or the sure bets; they probably are not what they appear to be. Millions of dollars are lost each year to scams. What may appear as a potentially great conversation piece at a cocktail party may very well put you in a position of not being able to afford to attend the next one.

If you have at least 10 years before you need to receive retirement income, invest in variable annuities. If you have a need for the funds prior to this, use mutual funds. Variable annuities have expenses that mutual funds do not have and are also taxed differently. If you have less than 10 years before you begin distributions (notice we do not say 10 years until retirement), the cost and less favorable taxation of the annuity may negate the benefits of its tax deferral and the death benefit. You may have other sources of capital to use for retirement income, such as a 401(k), that would enable you to continue to defer the use of the annuity for income and maximize the benefit of the variable annuity.

# Appendix G.
# Social Security

Social Security cannot continue to exist in its present form, nor can Medicare, Medicaid, or Welfare. These and other entitlements heretofore politically sacrosanct will be drastically altered and benefits reduced. The handwriting is on the wall. Social Security can be likened to a giant pension fund that we all pay into. Theoretically, the assets taken in will grow to fund the liabilities that the fund will have down the road when you retire; however, Social Security was never set up to be a retirement plan. It was meant to be a safety net, a last resort.

Social Security originated in 1936 during the Depression years. Working people would pay a small portion of their wages into the Social Security system with the idea that the current working population would help support the retirees of that time. So, money went in and right back out again. It worked at first, because in 1937 (the first full year of operation) there were 33 workers for every one retiree. The annual contribution of a working person was only $30, so the system was workable. The problem is that, given the demographics of the following years, including the slowing down of the birth rate and the fact that wages grew more slowly, strains on the system started to build. Our political and economic system forced the Social Security system to become a pension plan for every American citizen.

## Table G.1. Social Security Benefits

| Your Age in 1988 | Individual/ Couple | Your Earnings ($) in 1987 | | | | |
|---|---|---|---|---|---|---|
| | | $20,000 | $25,000 | $30,000 | $35,000 | $45,000 |
| 25 | Individual | $11,796 | $13,548 | $14,568 | $15,600 | $17,652 |
| | Couple | 17,688 | 20,316 | 21,852 | 23,400 | 26,472 |
| 35 | Individual | 10,896 | 12,540 | 13,476 | 14,436 | 16,296 |
| | Couple | 16,344 | 18,804 | 20,208 | 21,648 | 24,444 |
| 45 | Individual | 9972 | 11,496 | 12,360 | 13,104 | 14,412 |
| | Couple | 14,952 | 17,244 | 18,540 | 19,656 | 21,612 |
| 55 | Individual | 9048 | 10,344 | 10,920 | 11,352 | 12,036 |
| | Couple | 13,572 | 15,516 | 16,380 | 17,028 | 18,048 |
| 65 | Individual | 8100 | 9216 | 9564 | 9792 | 10,056 |
| | Couple | 12,144 | 13,824 | 14,340 | 14,688 | 15,084 |

*Note:* These figures represent the approximate yearly income from Social Security benefits for a single person and for a worker and nonworking spouse of the same age when they become eligible for full Social Security benefits at age 65 or 67. All of the amounts in this table are Social Security Administration projections in 1988 dollars, based on continuous employment throughout an adult lifetime.

In 1960, there were 15 workers for every one person retired. It is estimated that in the year 2029, there will be 2.5 workers for every one person retired. You can see that something has to give. But, there is some good news! Check into your Social Security benefits. Obtain estimates of your future benefits based on what you have been credited for and what you will be credited for by the time you reach retirement age.

We do not want to debate whether Social Security will be here or not. We could have the same debate about your insurance company. What we have discovered, though, is that if one of the authors were to die today, his children and widow would receive almost $900 a month. If one of us were to become disabled, he would receive over $800 a month. When we figured the cost of how much insurance it would take to duplicate those benefits, Social Security began to look very good.

The point is that you may not even need expensive life insurance. You can take the money you would save by not buying it and invest it in a mutual fund instead of contributing it to an insurance company's coffers. Table G.1 shows how Social Security can build, and Figure G.1 shows how Social Security estimated the benefits of one of the authors.

Figure G.2 is a Request for Earnings and Benefits Estimate Statement. It will take you about five minutes to complete this form, and you really want to do so. If the government makes a mistake, you have only three years in order to correct it. Also, things may not be as they seem. One of our instructors had a student who worked for a small employer, and when she received her statement she discovered her employer had not been sending in the necessary contributions. The employer went bankrupt, and she lost three years of eligibility and contributions. You need to stay informed.

You can send this form to your nearest Social Security office or to the Social Security Administration; Wilkes-Barre Data Operations Center; P.O. Box 20, Wilkes-Barre, PA 18711-2030. Or, you can call 1-800-772-1213 or visit the Social Security website at hcdp://www.ssa.gov.

Facts, Credits, and Earnings
November 7, 1990

THE FACTS YOU GAVE US

| | |
|---|---|
| Your Name | |
| Your Social Security Number | XXX-XX-XXXX |
| Your Date of Birth | July 20, 1947 |
| 1989 Earnings | $45,000 |
| 1990 Earnings | Over $51,300 |
| Your Estimated Future Avg. Yearly Earnings | Over $51,300 |
| The Age You Plan to Retire | 70 |
| Other Social Security Numbers You've Used | None |

YOUR SOCIAL SECURITY CREDITS

To qualify for Social Security benefits and Medicare, you need credit for a certain amount of work covered by Social Security. The number of credits you need will vary with the type of benefit. Under current law, you do not need more than 40 credits to qualify for any benefit or for Medicare.

Our review of your earnings, including any 1989 and 1990 earnings you told us about, shows that you now have at least 40 Social Security credits.

YOUR SOCIAL SECURITY EARNINGS

The chart on the next page shows the earnings on your Social Security record. It also estimates the amount of Social Security taxes you paid in each year to finance benefits under Social Security and Medicare. If you have government earnings that help you qualify for Medicare, those earnings also are shown on the chart.

We show earnings only up to the maximum yearly amount covered by Social Security. These maximum amounts are shown on the chart. The chart may not include some or all of your earnings from last year because they may not have been added to your record yet.

YOUR EARNINGS RECORD

| Years | Maximum Yearly Earnings Subject to Social Security Tax | Your Social Security Taxed Earnings | Est. Taxes You Paid: Retirement, Survivors & Disability Insurance | Est. Taxes You Paid: Medicare Hospital Insurance | Your Medicare Qualified Government Earnings |
|---|---|---|---|---|---|
| 1963 | 4,800 | 1,276 | 46 | 0 | 0 |
| 1964 | 4,880 | 1,469 | 53 | 0 | 0 |
| 1965 | 4,800 | 1,040 | 37 | 0 | 0 |
| 1966 | 6,600 | 1,475 | 56 | 5 | 0 |
| 1967 | 6,600 | 1,255 | 48 | 6 | 0 |
| 1968 | 7,800 | 1,247 | 47 | 7 | 0 |
| 1969 | 7,880 | 2,110 | 88 | 12 | 0 |
| 1970 | 7,800 | 612 | 25 | 3 | 0 |
| 1971 | 7,800 | 1,574 | 72 | 9 | 0 |
| 1972 | 9,000 | 2,177 | 100 | 13 | 0 |
| 1973 | 10,800 | 1,442 | 69 | 14 | 0 |
| 1974 | 13,200 | 7,187 | 355 | 64 | 0 |
| 1975 | 14,100 | 14,100 | 697 | 126 | 0 |
| 1976 | 15,300 | 15,300 | 757 | 137 | 0 |
| 1977 | 16,500 | 16,500 | 816 | 148 | 0 |
| 1978 | 17,700 | 17,700 | 893 | 177 | 0 |
| 1979 | 22,900 | 22,900 | 1,163 | 240 | 0 |
| 1980 | 25,900 | 25,900 | 1,315 | 271 | 0 |
| 1981 | 29,700 | 30 | 1 | 0 | 0 |
| 1982 | 32,400 | 0 | 0 | 0 | 0 |
| 1983 | 35,700 | 4,020 | 217 | 52 | 0 |
| 1984 | 37,800 | 0 | 0 | 0 | 0 |
| 1985 | 39,600 | 39,600 | 3,603 | 1,069 | 0 |
| 1986 | 42,000 | 42,000 | 3,948 | 1,218 | 0 |
| 1987 | 43,800 | 0 | 0 | 0 | 0 |
| 1988 | 45,000 | 45,000 | 4,554 | 1,305 | 0 |
| 1989 | 48,000 | 45,498 | 2,757 | 659 | 0 |
| 1990 | 51,500 | | | | |

*Earnings were taxed for Hospital Insurance beginning 1966

Figure G.1a. Estimating Social Security Benefits

Estimated Benefits
RETIREMENT
You must have 40 Social Security credits to qualify for retirement benefits. This is the same number of credits you need to qualify for Medicare at age 65. Assuming that you meet all the requirements, here are estimates of your retirement benefits based on your past and any projected earnings. The estimates are in today's dollars, but adjusted to account for average wage growth in the national economy.

| | |
|---|---|
| If you retire at 62, your monthly benefit in today's dollars will be about: | $965 |
| The earliest age at which you can receive an unreduced retirement benefit is 66 years of age. We call this your full retirement age. If you wait until that age to receive benefits, your monthly benefit in today's dollars will be about: | $1,355 |
| If you wait until you are 70 to receive benefits, your monthly benefit in today's dollars will be about: | $1,855 |

SURVIVORS
If you have a family, you must have 21 Social Security credits for certain family members to receive benefits if you were to die this year. They may also qualify if you earn 6 credits in the 3 years before your death. The number of credits a person needs to be insured for survivors benefits increases each year until age 62, up to a maximum of 40 credits.

Here is an estimate of the benefits your family could receive if you had enough credits to be insured, they qualified for benefits, and you died this year:

| | |
|---|---|
| Your child could receive a monthly benefit of about: | $705 |
| If your child and your surviving spouse who is caring for your child both qualify, they could each receive a monthly benefit of about: | $705 |
| When your surviving spouse reaches full retirement age, he or she could receive a monthly benefit of about: | $945 |
| If more family members qualify for benefits (other children, for example), the total amount that we could pay your family each month is about: | $1,655 |
| We may also be able to pay your surviving spouse or children a one-time death benefit of: | $255 |

DISABILITY
Right now, you must have 21 Social Security credits to qualify for disability benefits. And 20 of these credits had to be earned in the 10-year period immediately before you became disabled. If you are blind or received disability benefits in the past, you may need fewer credits. The number of credits a person needs to qualify for disability benefits increases each year until 62, up to a maximum of 40 credits.

If you were disabled, had enough credits, and met the other requirements for disability benefits, here is an estimate of the benefits you could receive right now:

| | |
|---|---|
| Your monthly benefit would be about: | $895 |
| You and your eligible family members could receive up to a monthly total of about: | $1,340 |

These estimates may be reduced if you receive workers' compensation of public disability benefits.

IF YOUR RECORDS DO NOT AGREE WITH OURS
If your earnings records do not agree with ours, please report this to us right away by calling the 800 number shown below. We can usually help you by phone. When you call, have this statement available along with any W-2 forms, payslips, tax returns or any other proof of your earnings.

IF YOU HAVE ANY QUESTIONS
If you have any other questions about this statement, please read the information on the reverse side. If you still have questions, please call 1-800-937-7005.

Social Security considers all calls confidential. We also want to ensure that you receive accurate and courteous service. That is why we may have a second Social Security representative listen to some calls.

**Figure G.1b Estimating Social Security Benefits (cont.)**

### Request for Earnings and Benefit Estimate Statement

---

**Request for earnings and benefit estimate statement**

1.   Name shown on your Social Security card:

_____
First                              Middle Initial                              Last

2. Your Social Security number as shown on your card:

| | | | | - | | | - | | | | |

3. Your date of birth:

_____
Month          Day          Year

4. Other Social Security numbers you have used:

| | | | - | | | - | | | | |

| | | |    | | | |    | | | | |

5. Your Sex:                              ☐ Male  ☐ Female

6. Other names you have used (including a maiden name):

_____
First                              Middle Initial                              Last

7.   Show your actual earnings for last year and your estimated earnings for this year. Include only wages and/or net self-employment income covered by Social Security.

8.

       A. Last year's actual earnings:

          $ | | | |    | | | |    | | |
          Dollars only

       B. This year's estimated earnings:

          $ | | | |    | | | |    | | |
          Dollars only

8. Show the age at which you plan to retire:    | | |

                                   (Show only one age)

9.   Below, show the average yearly amount that you think that you will earn between now and when you plan to retire. Your estimate of future earnings will be added to those earnings already on our records to give you the best possible estimate.

Enter a yearly average, not your total future lifetime earnings. Only show earnings covered by Social Security. Do not add cost-of-living, performance or scheduled pay increases or bonuses. The reason for this is that we estimate retirement benefits in today's dollars, but adjust them to account for average wage growth in the national economy.

However, if you expect to earn significantly more or less in the future due to promotions, job changes, part-time work, or an absence from the work force, enter the amount in today's dollars that most closely reflects your future average yearly earnings.

Most people should enter the same amount that they are earning now (the amount shown in 7B).

Your future average yearly earnings:

          $ | | | | , | | | | . | | |
          Dollars only

---

**Figure G.2a. Request for Social Security Estimate**

10. Address where you want us to send the statement:

Name

Street Address (Include apt. No., P.O. Box, or Rural Route)

| City | State | Zip Code |
| --- | --- | --- |

I am asking for information about my own Social Security record or the record of a person I am authorized to represent. I understand that if I deliberately request information under false pretenses I may be guilty of a federal crime and could be fined and/or imprisoned. I authorize you to send the statement of earnings and benefit estimates to the person named in item 10 through a contractor.

Please sign your name (Do not print)

Date                                                            (Area Code) Daytime Telephone No.

ABOUT THE PRIVACY ACT
Social Security is allowed to collect the facts on this form under Section 205 of the Social Security Act. We need them to quickly identify our record and prepare the earnings statement you asked us for. Giving us these facts is voluntary. However, without them we may not be able to give you an earnings and benefit estimate statement. Neither the Social Security Administration nor its contractor will use the information for any other purpose.

**Figure G.2b. Request for Social Security Estimate (cont.)**

# Glossary

# Glossary

**Accumulated value:** The value of all amounts accumulated under the contract prior to the annuity date.

**Accumulation unit:** A measure of your ownership interest in the contract prior to the annuity date.

**Administrative fee:** An annual fee, usually 0.15% or less of the daily subaccount asset value, charged to reimburse administrative expenses.

**Advisor:** One who gives investment advice in return for compensation.

**Aggressive growth:** High-risk/high-reward investments, funds, or securities classes.

**Analysis:** Process of evaluating individual financial instruments (often stock) to determine whether they are appropriate purchases.

**Analysts:** Those on Wall Street who study and recommend securities.

**Annual insurance company expenses:** Annuity contracts include charges for the insurance companies' annual expenses. In addition to the asset management fees, there are three other annual charges: annual policy fee, mortality and expense risk, and administrative.

**Annual interest income:** The annual dollar income for a bond or saving account is calculated by multiplying the coupon rate of the bond by its face value.

**Annual policy fee (maintenance fee):** An annual fee, usually $50 or less, charged for the maintenance of annuity records. The fee pays accounting, customer reporting, and other general expenses associated with financial recordkeeping requirements.

**Annualized return:** The total return on an investment or portfolio over a period of time other than one year, restated as an equivalent return for a one-year period.

**Annuitant:** The person whose life is used to determine the duration of any annuity payments and upon whose death, prior to the annuity date, benefits under the contract are paid; usually, but not always, the contract owner.

**Annuitant's beneficiary:** The person(s) to whom any benefits are due upon the annuitant's death prior to the annuity date.

**Annuity:** An annuity is a contract between an insurer and recipient (annuitant) whereby the insurer guarantees to pay the recipient a stream of income in exchange for premium payment(s).

**Annuity date:** The date on which annuity payments begin. The annuity date is always the first day of the month you specify.

**Annuity payment:** One of a series of payments made under an annuity payment option.

**Annuity payment option:** One of several ways in which withdrawals from the contract may be made. Under a fixed annuity option, the dollar amount of each annuity payment does not change over time. Under a variable annuity option, the dollar amount of each annuity payment may change over time, depending upon the investment experience of the portfolio or portfolios you choose. Annuity payments are based on the accumulated value of the contract as of 10 business days prior to the annuity date.

**Annuity unit value:** The value of each annuity unit which is calculated each valuation period.

**Asset allocation:** The decision as to how a customer should be invested among major asset classes in order to increase expected risk-adjusted return. Asset allocation may be two way (stocks and bonds), three way (stocks, bonds, and cash), or multiple (i.e., value mutual funds, growth mutual funds, small mutual funds, cash, foreign mutual funds, foreign bonds, real estate, and venture capital).

**Asset class:** Assets composed of financial instruments with similar characteristics.

**Asset-class funds:** Funds composed of financial instruments with similar characteristics. Unlike managers of index funds, asset-fund managers actively manage costs when buying and selling for funds.

**Asset-class investing:** The disciplined purchase of groups of securities with similar risk/reward profiles. This strategy is based on valid academic research, and its results are predictable rather than random.

**Asset mix:** Investable asset classes within a portfolio.

**Average daily trading:** The average daily trading is the number of shares of stock traded in the preceding calendar month, multiplied by the current price and divided by 20 trading days.

**Average return:** The measure of price of an asset along with its income or yield on average over a specific time period. The arithmetic mean is the simple average of the returns in a series. The arithmetic mean is the appropriate measure of typical performance for a single period.

**Back-end load:** A fee charged at redemption by a mutual fund or a variable annuity to a buyer of shares.

**Bailout rate:** Feature offered on some annuities that allows the customer to surrender the annuity with no penalty if the interest rate falls below a certain floor.

**Balanced index:** A market index that serves as a basis of comparison for balanced portfolios. The balanced index used in the Monitor is comprised of a 60% weighting of the S&P 500 Index and a 40% weighting of the SLH government/corporate bond index. The balanced index relates unmanaged market returns to a balanced portfolio more precisely than either a stock or a bond index would alone.

**Balanced mutual fund:** This term can be applied to any kind of portfolio that uses fixed income (bonds) as well as equity securities to reach goals. Many "boutique" investment managers are balanced managers, because it permits them to tailor the securities in a portfolio to the specific clients' cash flow needs and objectives. Balanced portfolios are often used by major mutual funds. They provide great flexibility.

**Basis point:** One basis point is 1/100 of a percentage point, or 0.01%. Basis points are often used to express changes or differences in yields, returns, or interest rates. Thus, if a portfolio has a total return of 10% vs. 7% for the S&P 500, the portfolio is said to have outperformed the S&P 500 by 300 basis points.

**Bear market:** A prolonged period of falling stock prices. There is no consensus on what constitutes a bear market or bear leg. SEI, one of the most widely used performance measurement services, normally defines a bear market or leg as a drop of at least 15% over two back-to-back quarters.

**Beginning value:** The market value of a portfolio at the inception of the period being measured by the customer statement.

**Benchmark:** A standard by which investment performance or trading execution can be judged. The most widely used performance benchmark is the total return of the S&P 500.

**Beneficiary:** Similar to the beneficiary of a life insurance policy, the annuity contract beneficiary receives a death benefit when another party to the annuity contract dies prior to the date upon which the annuity begins paying out benefits.

**Beta:** Beta is the linear relationship between the return on the security and the return on the market. By definition, the market usually measured by the S&P 500 index has a beta of 1.00. Any stock or portfolio with a higher beta is generally more volatile than the market, while any with a lower beta is generally less volatile than the market.

**Bond rating:** Method of evaluating the possibility of default by a bond issuer. Standard & Poor's, Moody's Investors Service, and Fitch's Investors Service analyze the financial strength of each bond's issuer, whether a corporation or a government body. Their ratings range from AAA (highly unlikely to default) to D (in default). Bonds rated B or below are not investment grade — in other words, institutions that invest other people's money may not under most state laws buy them.

**Bonds (long-term, short-term, and high-yield):** Debt instruments that pay lenders a regular return. Short-term bonds are 5 years or less. High-yield bonds pay lenders a higher rate of return because of greater perceived risk.

**Book-to-market ratio:** Size of company's book (net) value relative to the market price of the company.

**Broker:** An individual with a Series 7 license entitled to buy and sell securities, especially stock, on behalf of clients and charge for that service.

**Broker dealer:** A firm employing brokers among other financial professionals.

**Bull market:** A prolonged period of rising stock prices. SEI, one of the most widely used performance measurement services, normally defines a bull market or leg as a rise of at least 15% over two back-to-back quarters.

**Business day:** A day when the New York Stock Exchange is open for trading.

**Call option:** Gives the investor the right, but not an obligation, to buy a security at a pre-set price within a specified time (a put gives the investor the right to sell a security at a pre-set price within a specified time). Calls and puts are therefore essentially bets on whether the underlying security will rise or fall in price. The option holders gain or lose in proportion to changes in the values of the new indexes, which in turn reflect the net asset value performances of the funds that comprise the indexes.

**Cap (small-cap, large-cap):** The stock market worth of an individual equity. Large-cap stocks can be found on the New York Stock Exchange. Small-cap stocks are often listed on the NASDAQ.

**Capital appreciation or depreciation:** Increase or decrease in the value of a mutual fund or stock due to a change in the market price of the fund. For example, a stock that rises from $50 to $55 has capital appreciation of 10%. Dividends are not included in appreciation. If the price of the stock fell to $45, it would have depreciation of 10%.

**Capital preservation:** Investing in a conservative manner so as not to put capital at risk.

**Cash:** Investment in any instrument (often short-term) that is easily liquidated.

**Commission:** A transaction fee commonly levied by brokers and other financial middlemen.

**Compound annual return:** Another term for geometric mean, which is more appropriate when one is comparing the growth rate for an investment that is continually compounding.

**Compounding:** Reinvestment of dividends and/or interest and capital gains. This means that over time dividends, interest, and capital gains grow exponentially. For example, $100 earning compound interest at 10% a year would accumulate to $110 at the end of the first year and $121 at the end of the second year, etc., based on the formula: compound sum = principal × (1 + interest rate) × number of periods.

**Conservative:** Characteristic relating to a mutual fund, a stock, or an investment style. There is no precise definition of the term. Generally, the term is used when the mutual fund manager's emphasis is on the below-market betas.

**Contrarian:** An investment approach characterized by buying securities that are out of favor.

**Contract anniversary:** Any anniversary of the contract date.

**Contract date:** The date of issue of this contract.

**Contract owner:** The person or persons designated as the contract owner in the contract. The term also includes any person named as joint owner who shares ownership in all respects with the contract owner. Prior to the annuity date, the contract owner has the right to assign ownership, designate beneficiaries, and make permitted withdrawals and exchanges among sub-accounts and guaranteed rate options.

**Core savings strategy:** Having a base of safe dollars that provides overall financial security and is a long-term commitment of savings not to be touched except in an emergency.

**Correction:** A reversal in the price of a stock, or the stock market as a whole, within a larger trend. While corrections are most often thought of as declines within an overall market rise, a correction can also be a temporary rise in the midst of a longer-term decline.

**Coupon:** This is defined as the periodic interest payment on a bond. When expressed as an annual percentage, it is called the coupon rate. When multiplied by the face value of the bond, the coupon rate gives the annual interest income.

**Correlation:** A statistical measure of the degree to which the movement of two variables is related.

**CPI:** Consumer Price Index, which is maintained by the Bureau of Labor Statistics and measures changes in the cost of a specified group of consumer products relative to a base period. Because it represents the rate of inflation, the CPI can be used as a general benchmark for gauging the maintenance of purchasing power.

**Currency:** A nation's paper notes, once redeemable but not now.

**Currency risk:** Possibility that foreign currency one holds may fall in value relative to investor's home currency, thus devaluing overseas investments.

**Current return on equity (ROE):** A ratio that measures profitability as the return on common stockholders' equity. It is calculated by dividing the reported earnings per share for the latest 12-month period by the book value per share.

**Current yield:** This is a bond's annual interest payment as a percentage of its current market price. The current yield is calculated by dividing the annual coupon interest for a bond by the current market price. The coupon rate and the current yield on a bond are equal when the bond is selling at par. Thus, a $1000 bond with a coupon of 10% that is currently selling at $1000 will have a current yield of 10%. However, if the bond's price drops to $800, the current yield becomes 12.5%.

**Death benefit:** The greater of the contract's accumulated value on the date the company receives proof of death of the annuitant or the adjusted death benefit. If any portion of the contract's accumulated value on the date proof is received of the annuitant's death is derived from the multi-year guaranteed rate option, that portion of the accumulated value will be adjusted by a positive market value adjustment factor, if applicable.

**Deferred annuity:** Annuity whose contract provides that payments to the annuitant be postponed until a number of periods have elapsed (for example, when the annuitant attains a certain age).

**Deviation:** Movement of instrument or asset class away from expected direction. In investment terminology, it is most often associated with asset-class analysis.

**Dissimilar price movement:** The process whereby different asset classes and markets move in different directions.

**Diversification:** In broad terms, an investor might diversify his or her investments among mutual funds, real estate, international investments, and money market instruments. A mutual fund might diversify by investing in many companies in many different industry groups. Diversification also can refer to the way large sponsors reduce risk by using multiple mutual fund styles.

**Dividend:** Payment from a company's earning normally paid on common shares and declared by a company's board of directors to be distributed *pro rata* among the shares outstanding.

**Dollar cost averaging:** A system of buying stock or mutual funds at regular intervals with a fixed dollar amount. Under this system, an investor buys according to dollar amounts rather than number of shares.

**Dow Jones Industrial Average (DJIA):** A price-weighted average of 30 leading blue-chip industrial stocks, calculated by adding the prices of the 30 stocks and adjusting by a divisor, which reflects any stock dividends or splits. The Dow Jones Industrial Average is the most widely quoted index of the stock market, but it is not widely used as a benchmark for evaluating performance. The S&P 500 index, which is more representative of the market, is the benchmark most widely used by performance measurement services.

**Efficiency:** The process of generating maximum reward from funds invested across a spectrum of asset classes.

**Efficient frontier:** The point where the maximum amount of risk an investor is willing to tolerate intersects with the maximum amount of reward that can potentially be generated.

**Emerging growth mutual fund:** A mutual fund manager is looking for industries and companies whose growth rates are likely to be both rapid and independent of the overall stock market. Emerging, of course, means new. This implies such companies may be relatively small in size with the potential to grow much larger. Such stocks are generally much more volatile than the stock market in general and require constant, close, attention to developments.

**Emerging markets:** Countries beginning to build financial marketplaces with appropriate safeguards.

**EPS (earnings per share) growth:** Annualized rate of growth in reported earnings per share of stock.

**Equities:** Shorthand for stocks, bonds, and mutual funds. Equity mutual funds are made up of many individual stocks (a stock is a right of ownership in a corporation).

**Excellent/unexcellent companies:** Companies with either high (excellent) or low (unexcellent) stock market performances.

**Exchange:** One exchange will be deemed to occur with each voluntary transfer from any sub-account or general account guaranteed option.

**Exchange privilege:** Shareholder's right to switch from one mutual fund to another within one fund family, often done at no additional charge. This enables investors to put their money in an aggressive growth stock fund, for example, when they expect the market to turn up strongly, then switch to a money market fund when they anticipate a downturn.

**Execution price:** The negotiated price at which a security is purchased or sold.

**Expected return:** A tax term that means the expected amount to be received under an annuity contract, based on the periodic payment and the annuitant's life expectancy when the benefits begin. Calculated as the weighted average of possible returns, where the weights are the corresponding probability for each return.

**Expenses:** Cost of maintaining an invested portfolio.

**Fee-based:** A manager, advisor, or broker whose charges are based on a set amount rather than transaction charges.

**Fee-only:** A manager, advisor, or broker who charges an investor a pre-set amount for services.

**Financial advisor/planner:** One who helps investors with a wide variety of financial and investing issues, including retirement, estate planning , etc. Often licensed and working for a larger financial entity.

**Fixed annuities:** The fixed annuity offers security in that the rate of return is certain. Typically, with a fixed annuity the insurance company declares a current interest rate and sets the interest rate.

**Fixed-income mutual funds:** Mutual funds that invest in corporate bonds or government-insured mortgages, Treasury bills, or Treasury bonds; if the funds own any stocks at all, they are usually preferred shares.

**Forecasts:** Predictions of analysts usually associated with stock picking and active money management.

**401(k):** In its most simple terms, a 401(k) plan is a before-tax employee saving plan.

**Free look:** Most annuity contracts provide a 10- to 15-day period after contract delivery during which the owner can return the annuity and receive a full refund of the premium.

**Front-end load:** A fee charged when an investor buys a mutual fund or a variable annuity.

**Fund ratings:** Evaluation of the performance of invested money pools, often mutual funds, by such entities as Chicago-based Morningstar.

**Fund shares:** Shares in a mutual fund.

**Fundamentals:** Financial statistics that traditional analysts and many valuation models use. Fundamental data include stock, earnings, dividends, assets and liabilities, inventories, debt, etc. Fundamental data are in contrast to items used in technical analysis — such as price momentum, volume trends, and short sales statistics.

**General account:** The account which contains all of our assets other than those held in our separate accounts.

**Global diversification:** Investing funds around the world in regions and markets with dissimilar price movements.

**Guaranteed interest rate:** In a fixed annuity, the minimum interest rate that is guaranteed by the insurance company to be credited each year to the cash value.

**Guaranteed rate options:** The one-year guaranteed rate option and the multi-year guaranteed rate option.

**Hot tip:** Slang for an individual investment, often a stock, that is apparently poised to rise (but may not).

**Income growth mutual fund:** The primary purpose in security selection here is to achieve a current yield significantly higher than the S&P 500. The stability of the dividend and the rate of growth of the dividends are also of concern to the income buyer. These portfolios may own more utilities and less high-tech and may own convertible preferreds and convertible bonds.

**Index fund:** An index mutual fund is a passively managed portfolio designed and computer controlled to track the performance of a certain index, such as the S&P 500. In general, such mutual funds have performance within a few basis points of the target index. The most popular index mutual funds are those that track the S&P 500, but special index funds, such as those based on the Russell 1000 or the Wilshire 5000, are also available.

**Interest:** The rate a borrower pays a lender.

**Interest-rate guarantee:** Guarantee that the renewal rate will never fall below a particular level; typical policies today have a 4 to 5% guarantee.

**Indexing:** Disciplined investing in a specific group (asset class) of securities so as to benefit from its aggregate performance.

**Individual investor:** Buyer or seller of securities for personal portfolio.

**Inflation:** A monetary phenomenon generated by an overexpansion of credit which drives up prices of assets while diminishing the worth of paper currency.

**Institutional investor:** Corporation or fund with market presence.

**Intrinsic value:** This means the theoretical valuation or price for a stock. The valuation is determined using a valuation theory or model. The resulting value is compared with the current market price. If the intrinsic value is greater than the market price, the stock is considered to be undervalued.

**Investing**: Disciplined process of placing money in financial instruments so as to gain a return. Given the emergence of valid academic research regarding asset-class investment methods, an individual who depends primarily on active management and stock-picking may come to be considered a speculator rather than an investor.

**Investment discipline:** A specific money strategy one adopts.

**Investment guru:** A money manager or analyst, often employed by Wall Street and commonly looked on as having special insight into the market. *See* noise.

**Investment objective:** Money goals one wishes to reach.

**Investment philosophy:** Strategy justifying short- or long-term buying and selling of securities.

**Investment policy:** An investment policy statement forces the investor to confront risk tolerance, return objectives, time horizon, liquidity needs, the amount of funds available for investment, and the investment methodology to be followed.

**Investment policy statement:** Embodies the essence of the financial planning process. It encompasses (1) assessing where you are now, (2) detailing where you want to go, and (3) developing a strategy to get there.

**Investment wisdom:** Process of understanding valid academic research concerning asset allocation.

**Investor discomfort:** Realization that, in a given portfolio, the risk is not appropriate and rewards are not predictable.

**IPOs:** Initial public offerings; the sale of stock in a company going public for the first time.

**Joint owner:** The person or persons designated as the contract owner in an annuity contract. A joint owner shares ownership in all respects with the contract owner.

**Liquidity:** Ability to generate cash on demand when necessary.

**Load funds:** A mutual fund that is sold for a sales charge (load) by a brokerage firm or other sales representative. Such funds may be stock, bond, or commodity funds, with conservative or aggressive objectives. The stated advantage of a load fund is that the salesperson will explain the fund to the customer and advise him or her when it is appropriate to sell as well as when to buy more shares.

**Lump-sum distribution:** Single payment to a beneficiary covering the entire amount of an agreement. Participants in individual retirement accounts, pension plans, profit-sharing plans, and executive stock option plans generally can opt for a lump-sum distribution if the taxes are not too burdensome when they become eligible.

**Management fee:** Charge against investor assets for managing the portfolio of an open- or closed-end mutual fund as well as for such services as shareholder relations or administration. The fee, as disclosed in the prospectus, is a fixed percentage of the fund's asset value, typically 1% or less per year.

**Margin:** A loan often offered to investors by broker-dealers for the purpose of allowing the investor to purchase additional securities. In a down market, margin loans can be called and portfolios liquidated when the value of the loan threatens to exceed the value of the portfolio.

**Market:** In investing terms, a place where securities are traded. Formerly meant a physical location but now may refer to an electronic one as well.

**Market bottom:** The date that the bear leg of a market cycle reaches its low, not identified until some time after the fact. In the peak-to-peak cycle ended September 30, 1987, the market bottom came on August 12, 1982, when the S&P 500 closed at 102.42, down 27.1% from its previous bull market peak. The most recent bear leg ended on December 4, 1987, when the S&P 500 closed at 223.9. Market bottoms can also be defined as the month- or quarter-end closest to the actual bottom date.

**Market capitalization:** Current value of a company determined by multiplying the latest available number of outstanding common shares by the current market price of a share. For example, on December 29, 1989, IBM had about 590 million shares outstanding and the stock closed at $94.13. Thus, its market capitalization was $55 billion. Market cap is also an indication of the trading liquidity of a particular issue.

**Market timing:** This is defined as the attempt to base investment decisions on the expected direction of the market. If stocks are expected to decline, the timer may elect to hold a portion of the portfolio in cash equivalents or bonds. Timers may base their decisions on fundamentals (e.g., selling stocks when the market's price/book ratio reaches a certain level), on technical considerations (such as declining momentum or excessive investor optimism), or a combination of both.

**Market value:** Market or liquidation value of a given security or an entire pool of assets.

**Matrix pricing:** As an example of this technique, consider an asset-class fund that is limited to securities with maturities of 2 years or less. The manager will extend maturities when there is a reward for doing so (when the yield curve is steep), and will hold short maturities when longer maturities do not provide additional expected return (when the yield curve is flat or inverted).

**Maturities:** Applies to bonds, the date at which a borrower must redeem the capital portion of his loan.

**Model portfolio:** A theoretical construct of an investment or series of investment.

**Modern Portfolio Theory:** In 1950, Harry Markowitz started to build an investment strategy that took more than 30 years to develop and be recognized as the Modern Portfolio Theory; he won the Nobel Prize for his work in 1990.

**Money market fund:** Money market fund managers invest in short-term fixed instruments and cash equivalents. These instruments make up the portfolio and their objective is to maximize principal protection. Even though these accounts have short-term (one-day) liquidity, they typically pay more like 90- to 180-day CDs vs. passbook or one-week CDs.

**Municipal bonds:** Fixed-income securities issued by governmental agencies.

**Mutual fund:** A pool of managed money, regulated by the Securities and Exchange Commission, in which investors can purchase shares. Funds are not managed individually as they might be by a private money manager.

**Mutual fund families:** A mutual fund sponsor or company usually offers a number of funds with different investment objectives within its family of funds. For example, a mutual fund family may include a money market fund, a government bond fund, a corporate bond fund, a blue-chip stock fund, and a more speculative stock fund. If an investor buys a fund in the family, he or she is allowed to exchange that fund for another in the same family. This is usually done with no additional sales charge.

**National Association of Securities Dealers (NASD):** The principal association of over-the-counter (OTC) brokers and dealers that establishes legal and ethical standards of conduct for its members. NASD was established in 1939 to regulate the OTC market in much the same manner as organized exchanges monitor actions of their members.

**Net asset value (NAV):** Market value of each share of a mutual fund. This figure is derived by taking a fund's total assets (securities, cash, and receivables), subtracting liabilities, and then dividing that total by the number of shares outstanding.

**Net trade:** Generally, this is an over-the-counter trade involving no explicit commission. The investment advisor's compensation is in the spread between the cost of the security and the price paid by the customer. Also, a trade in which shares are exchanged directly with the issuer.

**Noise:** Information about investing that is not supported by valid academic research.

**No-load funds:** Mutual fund offered by an open-end investment company that imposes no sales charge (load) on its shareholders. Investors buy shares in no-load funds directly from the fund companies, rather than through a broker, as is done in load funds. Because no broker is used, no advice is given on when to buy or sell.

**Nominal return:** The actual current dollar growth in an asset's value over a given period. *See* total return and real return.

**Nonqualified contract:** An annuity which is not used as part of or in connection with a qualified retirement plan.

**Operating expenses:** Cost associated with running a fund or portfolio.

**Optimization:** A process whereby a portfolio, invested using valid academic theory in various asset classes, is analyzed to ensure that risk/reward parameters have not drifted from stated goals.

**Outperform:** Any given market that exceeds expectations or historical performance.

**Over-the-counter:** A market between securities dealers who act either as principals or brokers for their clients. This is the principal market for U.S. government and municipal bonds.

**Owner's designated beneficiary:** The person to whom ownership of an annuity contract passes upon the contract owner's death, unless the contract owner was also the annuitant — in which case the annuitant's beneficiary is entitled to the death benefit. (Note that this transfer of ownership to the owner's designated beneficiary will generally not be subject to probate but will be subject to estate and inheritance taxes. Consult with your tax and estate advisor to be sure of which rules will apply to you.)

**Packaged products:** Specific types of products underwritten and packaged by manufacturing companies that can be bought and sold directly through those companies. Packaged products are not required to go through a clearing process. Packaged products include mutual funds, unit investment trusts (UITs), limited partnership interests, and annuities.

**Partial liquidity:** Most annuities allow policy holders to withdraw up to 10% a year of their account value without a penalty or surrender charge.

**Payee:** The contract owner, annuitant, annuitant's beneficiary, or any other person, estate, or legal entity to whom benefits are to be paid.

**Percentage points:** Used to describe the difference between two percentages. For example, if a portfolio's performance was 18.2% vs. the S&P 500's 14.65, it outperformed the S&P by 3.6 percentage points.

**Portfolio turnover:** Removing funds from one financial instrument to place them in another. This process can be costly.

**Price/earnings ratio (P/E):** The current price divided by reported earnings per share of a stock for the latest 12-month period. For example, a stock with earnings per share during the trailing year of $5 and currently selling at $50 per share has a price/earnings ratio of 10.

**Principal:** The original dollar amount invested.

**Prospectus:** The document required by the Securities and Exchange Commission that accompanies the sale of a mutual fund or annuity outlining risks associated with certain types of funds or securities, fees, and management. At the core of the prospectus is a description of the fund's investment objectives and the portfolio manager's philosophy.

**Put:** A put gives the investor the right to sell a security at a pre-set price within a specified time.

**Qualified contract:** If an annuity contract is part of an employee benefit plan and has met certain requirements, it is "qualified" under the Internal Revenue Code. The contributions made into a qualified contract are income tax deductible to the employer.

**Quality growth mutual fund:** This term implies long-term investment in high-quality growth stocks, some of which might be for larger, emerging companies while others might be for long-established household names. Such a portfolio might have volatility equal to or above that of the overall market but less than that of an emerging growth portfolio.

**Quartile:** Ranking of comparative portfolio performance. The top 25% of mutual fund managers are in the first quartile; those ranking from 26 to 50%, in the second quartile; from 51 to 75%, in the third quartile; and the lowest 25%, in the fourth quartile.

**Rate of return:** The profits earned by a security as measured as a percentage of earned interest, dividends, or appreciation.

**Ratings:** Performance and credit-worthiness measurement of funds and corporations generated by Lipper, Moody's, Morningstar, and others. These ratings, when used to evaluate active fund managers, may be misleading, as past performance is no guarantee of future success.

**Real return:** Inflation-adjusted return on an asset. Inflation-adjusted returns are calculated by subtracting the rate of inflation from an asset's apparent, or nominal, return. For example, if common stocks earn a total return of 10.3% over a period of time, but inflation during that period is 3.1%, the real return is the difference, or 7.2%.

**Rebalancing:** A process whereby funds are shifted within asset classes and between asset classes to ensure efficiency. *See* optimization.

**Reinvested dividends:** Refers to dividends paid by a particular mutual fund that are reinvested in that same mutual fund. Some mutual funds offer automatic dividend reinvestment programs. In the complex equation theoretically used to determine the performance of the S&P 500, each company's dividend is reinvested in the stock of that company.

**REITs (real estate investment trusts):** Bundled, securitized real estate assets often trading on the New York Stock Exchange.

**Relative return:** The return of a stock or a mutual fund portfolio compared with some index, usually the S&P 500. For example, in 1989, American Brands had a total return of 12.2% in *absolute* terms. In isolation, that sounds good. After all, the historical annualized return on common stocks has been 10.3%. But, because the S&P 500 had a return of 31.7% in 1989, American Brands underperformed the index in *relative* terms by 19.5 percentage points. Thus, its relative return was –19.5 percentage points.

**Renewal rate history:** Banks should be able to supply you with records of their renewal rates, to see how their rates have held after the initial rate guarantee periods.

**Risk:** Risk is nothing more than the uncertainty of future rates of return, which includes the possibility of loss. This variability or uncertainty causes "rational" investors to expect higher returns on investments where the actual timing or amount of payoffs is not guaranteed. A mutual fund portfolio has a type of risk called market risk, which captures the amount of portfolio variability caused by events that have an impact on the market as a whole.

**Risk-free rate of return:** The return on an asset that is considered virtually without risk. Treasury bills are typically used as the risk-free asset because of their short time horizon and the low probability of default.

**Risk, systematic:** Potential for predictable, quantifiable loss of funds through the application of valid academic research to the process of disciplined asset-class investing.

**Risk tolerance:** Investors' innate ability to deal with the potential of losing money without abandoning investment process.

**Risk, unsystematic:** Associated with investment in an undiversified portfolio of individual instruments through active management.

**ROI (return on investment):** Amount of money generated over time by placement of funds in specific financial instruments.

**Rule of 72:** By dividing the number 72 by the compound interest rate you have chosen. you will find the number of years it will take your money to double.

**S&P common stock rankings:** Measurement of the historical growth and stability of earnings and dividends. The system includes these rankings:

A+, A, and A-, above average; B+, average; B, B–, and C, below average; NR, insufficient historical data or not amenable to the ranking process. As a matter of policy, S&P does not rank the stocks of foreign companies, investment companies, and certain finance-oriented companies.

**S&P 500:** The performance benchmark most widely used by sponsors, managers, and performance measurement services. This index includes 400 industrial stocks, 20 transportation stocks, 40 financial stocks, and 40 public utilities. Performance is measured on a capitalization-weighted basis. The index is maintained by Standard & Poor's Corp., a subsidiary of McGraw-Hill, Inc.

**Securities:** Tradable financial instruments.

**Securities and Exchange Commission (SEC):** The keystone law in the regulation of securities markets. It governs exchanges, over-the-counter markets, broker-dealers, the conduct of secondary markets, extension of credit in securities transactions, the conduct of corporate insiders, and principally the prohibition of fraud and manipulation in securities transactions. It also outlines the powers of the Securities and Exchange Commission to interpret, supervise, and enforce the securities laws of the United States.

**Securities Investor Protection Corporation (SIPC):** This is a government-sponsored organization created in 1970 to ensure investor accounts at brokerage firms in the event of the brokerage firm's insolvency and liquidation. The maximum insurance of $500,000, including a maximum of $100,000 in cash assets per account, covers customer losses due to brokerage house insolvency, not customer losses caused by security price fluctuations. SIPC coverage is conceptually similar to Federal Deposit Insurance Corporation coverage of customer accounts at commercial banks.

**Security selection:** Process of picking securities, especially stocks, for investment purposes.

**Separate account:** Independent of the general assets of a company; the separate account invests in the portfolios.

**Shares:** Specific portions of tradable equity, a share of stock. It generally refers to common or preferred stocks.

**Single-premium deferred annuity:** An annuity purchased with a lump-sum premium payment which earns interest for a period of years before the payout period begins.

**Speculator:** One who uses an active management style to invest.

**Standard deviation:** Volatility can be statistically measured using standard deviation, which describes how far from the mean historic performance has been, either higher or lower. Mean is simply the middle point between the two historic extremes of the performance of the investment being examined. The standard deviation measurement helps explain what the distribution of returns likely will be. The greater the range of returns, the greater the risk. Generally, the current price of a security reflects the expected total return of its investment and its perceived risk. The lower the risk, the lower the return expected.

**Stock:** A contract signifying ownership of a portion of a public or private company.

**Stock picker:** Someone who is actively trying to select companies whose equity may rise in the short or long term. Valid academic research shows this process is unworkable and results are no better than random.

**Strategic asset allocation:** Determines an appropriate asset mix for a customer based on long-term capital market conditions, expected returns, and risks.

**Sub-account:** That portion of the variable annuities separate account that invests in shares of the funds' portfolios. Each sub-account will only invest in a single portfolio.

**Surrender charge:** A charge made for a withdrawal (in excess of 10% per year) from or surrender of an annuity contract before the annuity starting date; often scales down over time.

**Surrender value:** Accumulated value (adjusted to reflect any applicable market value adjustment for amounts allocated to the multi-year guaranteed rate option) less any early withdrawal charges for amounts allocated to the one-year guaranteed rate option, less any amount allocated to the guaranteed equity option, and less any premium taxes incurred but not yet deducted.

**Systemic withdrawal plan:** A program in which shareholders receive payments from their mutual fund investments at regular intervals. Typically, these payments are drawn first from the fund's dividends and capital gains distribution, if any, and then from principal as needed.

**Tactical allocation:** Investment strategy allocating assets according to investor expectations of directions of regional markets and asset classes.

**Tax-efficient fund:** Money pool which makes no taxable distributions to investors.

**Technical analysis:** Any investment approach that judges the attractiveness of particular stocks or the market as a whole based on market data, such as price patterns, volume, momentum, or investor sentiment, as opposed to fundamental financial data, such as earnings dividends.

**Time horizon:** The amount of time someone can wait to generate or take profits from an investment.

**Time-weighted rate of return:** The rate at which a dollar invested at the beginning of a period would grow if no additional capital were invested and no cash withdrawals were made. It provides an indication of value added by the investment manager and allows comparisons to the performance of other investment managers and market indexes.

**Total return:** A standard measure of performance or return including both capital appreciation (or depreciation) and dividends or other income received. For example, Stock A is priced at $60 at the start of a year and pays an annual dividend of $4. If the stock moves up to $70 in price, the appreciation component is 16.7%, the yield component is 6.7%, and the total return is 23.4%. This oversimplification does not take into account any earnings on the reinvested dividends.

**Trading costs:** Fees or commissions paid to move money from one financial instrument to another.

**Transaction costs:** Also known as execution costs, total transaction costs (or the cost of buying and selling stocks) have three components: (1) the actual dollars paid to the in commissions, (2) the market impact (i.e., the impact a manager's trade has on the market price for the stock, which varies with the size of the trade and the skill of the trader), and (3) the opportunity cost of the return (positive or negative) given up by not executing the trade instantaneously.

**Treasury bills:** A U.S. financial security issued by Federal Reserve banks for the Treasury as a means of borrowing money for short periods of time. They are sold at a discount from their maturity value, pay no coupons, and have maturities of up to one year. Because they are a direct obligation of the federal government, they are free of default risk. Most Treasury bills are purchased by commercial banks and held as part of their secondary reserves. Treasury bills regulate the liquidity base of the banking system in order to control the money supply. For example, if the authorities wish to expand the money supply, they can buy Treasury bills, which increases the reserves of the banking system and induces a multiple expansion of bank deposits.

**Turnover:** Turnover is the volume or percentage of buying or selling activity within a mutual fund portfolio relative to the mutual fund portfolio's size.

**12b-1 mutual fund:** Mutual fund that assesses shareholders for some of its promotion expenses. These funds are usually no-load, so no brokers are involved in the sale to the public. Instead, the funds normally rely on advertising and public relations to build their assets. The charge usually amounts to about 1% or less of a fund's assets. A 12b-1 fund must be specifically registered as such with the Securities and Exchange Commission, and the fact that such charges are levied must be disclosed.

**Underperform:** Securities or markets that do not meet expectations.

**Value added:** These are returns over and above those of the stock market.

**Value mutual fund:** In this instance, the mutual fund manager uses various tests to determine an intrinsic value for a given security and tries to purchase the security substantially below that value. The goal and hope are that the stock price in the fund will ultimately rise to the stock's fair value or above. Price to earnings, price to sales, price to cash flow, price to book value, and price to break-up value (or true net asset value) are some of the ratios examined in such an approach.

**Value stocks:** Stocks with high book-to-market valuations (i.e., companies doing poorly in the market that may have the potential to do better).

**Variable annuities:** Insurance-based investment products, which like other forms of annuities allow for growth of invested premiums to be free from taxation until withdrawals are made from the contract. Unique to variable annuities are several forms of investment alternatives that vary in both their potential for reward and risk. Variable annuity choices are broad enough that an investor can employ either an aggressive or conservative approach, or a combination of both, while enjoying the benefits of tax-deferred growth. Guarantee of principal from loss upon death of the owner is covered by a death benefit provision.

**Variable annuity accumulation and distribution phases:** There are two phases of the life of an annuity. The initial phase is the accumulation phase, which is the period in which contributions are made, either as a lump-sum or in systematic payments. The contributions are invested in either a fixed or variable annuity. The assets compound tax-deferred until the contract owner makes the decision to distribute the assets (distribution phase), either in a lump sum or systematically.

**Volatility:** The extent to which market values and investment returns are uncertain or fluctuate. Another word for risk, volatility is gauged using such measures as beta, mean absolute deviation, and standard deviation.

**Weighting:** A term usually associated with proportions of assets invested in a particular region or securities index to generate a specific risk/reward profile.

**Yield (current yield):** For stocks, yield is the percentage return paid in dividends on a common or preferred stock, calculated by dividing the indicated annual dividend by the market price of the stock. For example, if a stock sells for $40 and pays a dividend of $2 per share, it has a yield of 5% ($2 divided by $40). For bonds, the coupon rate of interest divided by the market price is called current yield. For example, a bond selling for $1000 with a 10% coupon offers a 10% current yield. If the same bond were selling for $500, it would offer a 20% yield to an investor who bought it for $500. (As a bond's price falls, its yield rises, and vice versa.)

**Yield curve:** A chart or graph showing the price of securities (usually fixed income) through time. A flat or inverted yield curve of fixed income instruments is thought by many to be an indicator of recession. This is because those who borrow at the far end of the curve usually pay more for their money than those who borrow for only a little while. When the yield curve is flat or inverted, this means there is little demand for long-term money, which can be interpreted as a signal that there is little demand in the economy for the products that long-term borrowing would generate.

**Yield to maturity:** The discount rate that equates the present value of the bond's cash flows with the market price. The yield to maturity will actually be earned if (1) the investor holds the bond to maturity, and (2) the investor is able to reinvest all coupon payments at a rate equal to the yield to maturity. When a bond is selling at par, the yield to maturity and the coupon rate are equal.

# Index

# Index